The distinctive sound of Dave, Duane, and Neil, enhanced by their lives of integrity, have made them a favorite for five decades. The words of their carefully chosen songs, many written by Neil, has struck a chord in people's hearts the world over.

Don Argue, Ed. D, Commissioner
United States Commission on International
Religious Freedom

Integrity, excellence, steadfastness defines the lives of Dave, Duane and Neil, the Original Couriers. Heaven's book contains the stories of the impact of their ministry and it is a powerful record for sure!

Rev. Gary Dembow, President
Central Bible College
Springfield, Missouri

God took three young men, Dave, Duane, and Neil, and gave them a rare, uncommon music ministry called the Couriers. We're proud to call them "Our Boys."

Dr. George O. Wood, General Superintendent
The Assemblies of God
Springfield, Missouri

It is very important for young men to have mentors. God blessed us with many, yet none greater than the Couriers. Their music inspires our musical style. Their friendship is a blast!! Their relationship with Christ is contagious. Though they may not have known of their impression on us, we are forever grateful that God allowed the Booth Brothers to be mentored by the Couriers.

The Booth Brothers
Nashville, Tennessee

The Couriers: great songs, unique harmonies, unusual arrangements, great vocal talent, unlimited variety of musical choice, all with a positive way of life found in following Jesus Christ. These three men did more to establish gospel music in the northeast than any other gospel group. May God bless this book! May God continue to bless the Couriers!

Duane Allen
The Oak Ridge Boys
Nashville, Tennessee

In an industry where the shelf life of an artist is sometimes measured in minutes, you are truly the exception. For over fifty years the Couriers have stayed on key with the timeless gospel message through anointed song and testimony. Thanks for your faithfulness. Your love for God, family, missions, and ministry supersedes your great musical talent. As you enter your final quarter we look forward to another fifty. I love you guys.

Larry Kerychuk, Exec. Director, Athletes International
Phoenix, Arizona

The Couriers have always been about "heartfelt music" and "life-lived integrity." I count it the highest honor to be counted as one of their friends. In the early days, they were innovators. Today they represent a "life-time of honor" to the power of the Gospel through music.

Lawrey Berteig, Music Pastor
Westminster Chapel
Bellevue, Washington

When I think of the Couriers, I think of integrity, longevity, first-class people, and the very best in gospel music. Their ministry of music has touched many lives around the world.

Rev. Ken Gaub, World Evangelist

Dave, Duane, and Neil have a long history of effective ministry. Their music is the vehicle they use to communicate the reality of Jesus that they live out on a daily basis. Their character and integrity is matched only by the excellence of their presentation.

Rev. Stephen R. Tourville, District Superintendent
Penn Del Ministry Network

Dave, Duane, and Neil represent what is best in our Assemblies of God Fellowship when it comes to family, friends, music and ministry. They have been some of the greatest ambassadors the Assemblies of God have ever had. It was our great pleasure to honor them during the 2007 General Council with the General Superintendent's Medal of Honor.

Rev. James Bridges, General Treasurer
General Council Assemblies of God

Our Final Quarter

The Inspiring Stories of

DAVE, DUANE & NEIL
{ THE ORIGINAL COURIERS }

Celebrating More Than 50 Years in Gospel Music

Dave Kyllonen | *Duane Nicholson* | *Neil Enloe*

DD&N
publishing

Our Final Quarter

Published by DD&N Publishing

© 2008 by Dave Kyllonen, Duane Nicholson, and Neil Enloe
International Standard Book Number: 978-0-615-24721-2

Cover design by Lookout Design, Inc.

Printed in the United States of America

For information: DD&N Publishing
                  45 Tannery Road
                  Dillsburg, PA 17019
                  www.daveduaneandneil.com

This book is dedicated to
Ted and Marietta Terry,
without whose persistence,
encouragement,
and selfless support
this entire project would
not have been possible.
Thank you, dear
and precious friends.

Our Silent Partners
in Ministry

Most men are only as good as their wives challenge them to be. We find noble and inspired motivation in their loyal support and trust.

Our wives have kept the home fires burning while we have literally circled the globe, chasing our godly calling. They have raised our children, maintained order, and played the part of both mother and father while we were away. Their ceaseless prayers have sustained us through crises and traumas that they could never imagine without being with us on the road.

When heaven's rewards are handed out it will be our life partners and soul mates who will be rewarded beyond ourselves. Their unwavering inner strength and faithfulness over these long years of ministry have made it possible for us to continue without catastrophic consequences in our very homes.

Judy Kyllonen, Jean Ann Nicholson, and Ruth Enloe are our queens enthroned in the deep of our hearts. They are living examples of the "virtuous woman" from Proverbs 31, whose "heart of her husband doth safely trust in her" and whose "children arise up, and call her blessed."

Contents

Foreword: 9

Introduction: 13

Section One:
It's a Lot More Than a Game — *Dave Kyllonen*

    Introduction 21

    1. Here's the Plan 23

    2. The Fourth and Final Quarter 27

    3. Making the Right Choices 30

    4. The Best Day of the Year 2000 37

    5. You Don't Understand Football? 40

    6. Our Children's Children 44

    7. Surprise, Surprise, Surprise 60

    8. Great Front Lines 64

    9. We Need Cheerleaders Too 70

    10. Time for Missions Again 80

    11. How to Reach an Incredible Maturity 89

    12. Who Likes Gospel Music? 104

    13. Three Great Sons-in-Law 107

    14. A Final Quarter Inspiration 113

    15. Exceeding My Dreams 115

Section Two:
Nothing I Could Have Predicted — *Duane Nicholson*

    Introduction 121

    1. One More Time, With Feeling 122

    2. Days of Preparation 133

    3. On to Bible School 140

    4. The Couriers Call 147

5. Decision Time 158

6. Early Trials 164

7. Growing Pains 177

8. Moving Up 187

9. Life-Changing Call 204

10. The Days of Dave, Duane, and Neil 222

11. Trouble Ahead 229

Section Three:
How it REALLY Happened — *Neil Enloe*

Introduction 262

1. Humble Beginnings 265

2. Parent Trap 270

3. Young and Restless 278

4. I Sing the Mighty Power of God 287

5. We Can't Hear You 294

6. I Don't Think I Can Handle It 298

7. Psalmist of Sorts 306

8. Former Members 316

9. Like Brothers 322

10. Beyond the Sunset 326

11. It's Not My Job 334

12. When You Least Expect It 341

13. But if I Fail 353

14. A Final Word 358

15. I'm Outa' Here 366

Foreword

The year was 1964 and the town was Vermilion, Ohio, then a tiny fishing village tucked along the north shore of Lake Erie. My wife and I were pioneering a church there. We had rented a school building, but the entire structure was being painted during the summer months, and we had to leave that venue until the fall.

A leaky old tent was our only alternative. On the Sunday night in question, the place was packed—maybe 150 people max. They had come to hear the famous Couriers Gospel Quartet. Our church hardly had enough money to keep the lights on, but those wonderful singers came anyway, asking only for a freewill offering to cover their expenses. They sang for us that night as if they were performing in a packed football stadium. They gave that small group of happy people everything they had. Only their best!

But then, those were the same Couriers I've known as college chums since the mid-50s, when they set out to seek God's will rather than their own fortunes. In all those years they have never given God less than their best. They have offered Him the "fine linen" of their ultimate service, not the unraveled dishrags of mediocrity. Every concert has been a "command performance for the King."

Over the decades it has also been my joy to host them countless times, as recently as February of 2008. On that night they asked me to sing a few songs with them. From the platform I said that we four should be called the "300 Club," because our combined ages came so close to that.

See, I can remember those days in Bible college so clearly. I recall a number of young guys and gals who openly proclaimed that they were going to serve God with all their hearts and all their abilities for all their days. But many of them have long since left the frontlines for other pursuits. Still others, among them Dave, Duane, and Neil, have done exactly what they set out to do to the absolute best of their abilities. For all these many years the Couriers have sung about Christ himself, and they have lived what they sang.

Many times we have ministered together, played golf together, and just sat around drinking coffee and remembering the past. I cannot think of one inconsistency, one failure, one misstep that the Couriers have taken in all these years. They blazed new territory for Southern Gospel Music in the northeast United States. They sang the Gospel in nations all over the world. They were among the first to champion the Gospel on regular television. And they have done so with unfailing dignity and class.

One day, in eternity, they will sing in a "nobler, sweeter tongue . . . the power of God to save." By the grace of God, I plan to be singing with them.

—Dan Betzer
Fort Meyers, Florida

Introduction

I was fourteen years old when I heard the unique sounds of the Couriers for the very first time, sitting in the front of my dad's church in a small Pennsylvania town. By that age I had already developed an appreciation for Gospel Music. I owned all the recordings of the Blackwood Brothers and Statesmen quartets. But something was very different about the Couriers—a very practical and incontestable difference.

As a teenage boy I wanted to be like these guys. Four years later I enrolled at Central Bible College in Springfield, Missouri, where every member of the Couriers had attended. I joined a group, the Crusaders Trio, and traveled the country for an entire summer.

Fifty years have now come and gone since that first encounter with the original Couriers. My wife, Marietta, and I still remain among their most faithful admirers, because these guys are for real all the way down to their toes. In recent years I have even had the privilege of booking concerts in Southern California, the Pacific Northwest, and a most memorable trip to Alaska for a full week of concerts.

But beyond all that, I became a Christian at a very early age and thought I knew my own Bible fairly well. Even so, not long ago one of my friends told me something I didn't know about one of the most familiar stories from the New Testament.

"When Jesus was talking about turning the other cheek," he said, "He was using a Hebrew idiom that doesn't translate very well into English. What He meant at a deeper level was that we Christians should live our lives so that—regardless of what "direction" people see us from—the views will be identical. When we 'turn the other cheek' we should still show the same face to the world, so others will want to live the same kind of consistent, God-centered lives."

I thought immediately of my three beloved friends, Dave Kyllonen, Duane Nicholson, and Neil Enloe. For more than five decades I don't think I've ever met anyone who could "turn the other cheek," and still be quite as consistently the same people no matter when or where.

To me, that simple truth says it all. With Dave, Duane, and Neil, what you see and hear when they're on the platform is what you get when you catch them at their most unguarded. In fact, I don't think the term *unguarded* even applies—for fifty years now these guys have lived their lives for one single purpose: to tell others of their wonderful Savior, Jesus Christ. And yes, they've used music as their main medium, but they've also done it through the personal testimonies of their own lives, lived out in public under the kind of scrutiny most of us cannot even imagine. On the other hand, when you're simply being "who you are" and aren't doing any pretending at all, scrutiny is not a problem!

The only thing I might add is this: When I think about what I've just said, it seems pretty easy to identify the single most important ability each member of The Couriers had to have to occupy his spot on the team for all those years:

The Ability to Blend.

After all, though the members all had outstanding voices, they had to sing with just one, and they had to maintain that single, unified sound through thousands and thousands of songs. In musical terms, no matter how far they might roam or how much they might embellish the main thread, they had to return to it and "fit back in" almost every single time.

But not anymore! This book still includes a certain amount of "blending," because their stories do overlap and reinforce each other at many points. But even so, this book might still be the biggest "non-blender" that Dave, Duane, and Neil have ever put out there. And in its own way it might be the most fascinating, too, because now you get to hear the three original Couriers as the "unique voices" each one of them has always been.

And if you pay attention you'll soon begin to recognize which was which. I'm not going to spoil all the fun—and besides, all I really have is my own opinion anyway. But I'm betting that you'll be absolutely captivated by what you'll find in the following pages. Each of the original Couriers takes his own section to tell his own story, but they don't all do it in the same way or the same style. For once they're not "blending in" at all, and suddenly you'll see three entirely different personalities, each one emerging "in his own write," to quote an overused pun from the 60s and 70s. Think about it. How many of us remember precisely what we were doing in the 1950s, assuming we were even *here* then? These guys do a remarkable job, and through their shared remembrances they offer you a remarkable story.

In the larger picture, God's "call" on each of our lives is different, and none of us is wise enough to come up with a "better way" on our own. However, many of us try to do exactly that, as though our human intelligence and our earthly inclinations might be just as good as His divine plans. These three fellows did exactly the opposite, and they stayed utterly true to their original decisions made more than a half-century ago, to follow Him wherever He might lead.

Aren't those the lyrics from a well-known Gospel song? What better way to segue into the story of Dave, Duane, and Neil, as laid out for us in the following pages by the only three guys who were there through it all. My hope is that you will enjoy the book as much as I've enjoyed knowing the authors.

Take it from me—Dave, Duane, and Neil are truly unique in the way they've been used by God through all these years. They are disciples and ministers, husbands and fathers, above all else. That they are also among the most popular, highly respected Gospel Music groups of all time is a huge fact that will make itself readily apparent as you read their inspiring stories.

It's not what you *do*, it's who you *are*. These men are truly servants of God.

— *Ted H. Terry*
Issaquah, Washington

Our Final Quarter
by Charlotte Findlay Bahr

It's been a long, hard game.
So many things we've overcome –
Sacks and fumbles,
Hard hits and penalties, too.
And now we're in the fourth quarter,
Depending, Lord, on You.

You've never failed us.
Your Holy Spirit blocked and tackled the foe,
While we protected the ball—
Our precious faith, to attain the goal.

Now we're fourth and goal,
The saints are cheering us on,
And our eyes are on the game beyond.

It's a Lot More Than a Game

by Dave Kyllonen

INTRODUCTION

I would have to say that my Gospel goose bumps peak whenever I hear the Couriers sing "The Statue of Liberty" or "I Sing the Mighty Power of God." I am thrilled that they are still singing and hope that they will be singing many years from now, even if all three have to be brought out in wheelchairs.

Not long ago I played golf with Dave and Duane, in Dillsburg, Pennsylvania. Prior to our round, Dave mentioned that these are some of the sweetest years of his ministry. Instead of taking his ease in Zion, he is helping his daughter, Connie, and her husband, Mike, pioneer a brand-new church in Dillsburg. He is 100% energized by the process.

Duane also talked with great fondness of the missions trips he has been on in which he helped build churches all across our country. One of them is in Wisconsin, just one hour from my house. He is also trying to fit in another missions trip next year.

Meanwhile, I am reading a book entitled, *Want More?* by Tim Enloe, Neil's son. Tim writes that "Without our godly parents' influence, Rochelle and I would never have known the person and power of the Holy Spirit."

Two nights ago, I was in the home of Mike and Connie. Five of Dave and Judy's granddaughters were there. One of them sat down at the piano and soon all five were gathered around, singing songs of praise. Here comes another generation ready to sing "The Mighty Power of God."

All of this brings me to what I consider the most important thing about the Couriers. Through the years I have loved being in the crowd and hearing three of my favorite singers sing unique, inspired, and original songs. But over those same years I have been most impressed by how Dave, Duane, and Neil live their lives, in ways that continually bring praise and glory to the Father.

—Rick Olson
Dallas, Minnesota

- 1 -

Here's the Plan

In football, the fourth quarter is often the most amazing fifteen minutes of the game. Is there enough time for another touchdown? Will a field goal be enough?

The final quarter is the time to look at the score. If we are ahead, it's time to keep the defense going at top efficiency. If we are behind, it's time to talk to the offense. Who has the momentum? Which team is more tired? Time-outs suddenly become very important, and first downs take on added significance too.

In preparing to write my portion of this book, I decided to look at my life like a football game.

My first quarter..................birth to 21 years.

My second quarter............22 to 40 years.

My third quarter...............41 to 65 years.

My fourth quarter.............66 to... ?

I am now living in my fourth quarter and finding it more exciting than I ever expected. I am living in some awesome days I think I'm winning the game. However, before I get into that, let me give you an "instant replay" covering the first three quarters of my life.

I was born on April 28, 1935, in Monessen, Pennsylvania, to godly parents who taught me how to live for God. They taught me to pray for God's will for my life, and then to follow His plan.

When I was nineteen years old I felt God was leading me into ministry. I didn't know what phase of ministry, or even if I could respond effectively to such a high calling, for I was a shy, quiet-natured young man and felt quite frightened about venturing into ministry. However, I was determined to follow God's will, so I left home to study at Central Bible College in Springfield, Missouri. Thus began four incredible, delightful, happy years that led me into my second quarter.

At that point I found myself anxiously waiting for the coach to say, "Kyllonen, it's time to get into the game." Where would I fit? What position would I play? Could I score a touchdown, kick a field goal, or would I be a blocker and tackler?

Fortunately, during my training at Central Bible College I met some other players who joined the team, and together we are still playing the game in our fourth quarter. I was invited to sing with the Couriers along with Duane Nicholson and Neil Enloe. At that moment my life changed forever, and I found precisely where I would fit.

In fact, I not only found my life's work in the second quarter but I found the love of my life at the very same time.

Judy Robbins was also a student at Central Bible College. She was also finding God's will and wondering where she would fit in His plan.

She joined the team when we were married on November 28, 1958. We then moved to Harrisburg, Pennsylvania, and began our first twenty-five years together. We became a family of five when our three girls were born. What a wonderful experience that turned out to be! I can't wait to tell you about my fourth quarter with my girls—Kristie, Robin, and Connie.

Never a Dull Moment

During that same time my ministry with the Couriers kept me extremely busy. For twenty-five years we traveled mile after mile after mile, ministering in all fifty states and eighty countries. The years went by very quickly; truly, it would take ten books to tell all the stories of our ministry together.

And then along the way God suddenly made some profound changes in His plan for me. He asked me to make a very tough decision and resign from the Couriers.

Judy and I and our three daughters then began our family ministry together, during which we traveled for two more years from one end of our country to the other. We were then invited to hold a crusade in Barbados, West Indies. Two weeks turned into three years. We loved our missionary years. Nothing could have been more rewarding.

Then came the call from Davenport, Iowa. "Dave, would you be interested in becoming our pastor?" Seven more years went by very quickly. I had always longed to be a pastor, and

God allowed me to fill the pulpit at Westside Assembly of God. It is one of the great churches in our country.

But even more changes were in store. One day I couldn't believe my ears when I found myself saying to my wife and girls and their husbands that I was prepared to leave Davenport, give up my pastor's position, and go on the road again in a family ministry called "Homefire." I insisted on just one condition, and that was that everybody had to be willing to go.

Surprise! They all said yes and we did it for thirteen years. If you ask us today, we'll tell you it was a miracle brought about by God.

At the beginning of our thirteenth year I stopped one day and said to myself, "Hey, Dave, you're turning 69 this year and you're already four years into your fourth quarter. Will this be the best quarter of your life?"

That's what most of this book is all about.

-2-
The Fourth and Final Quarter

The clock is winding down toward the end of the game.
How are we doing? The scoreboard says that we're winning.
The momentum is with us. We're turning third downs into
first-and-tens. Every play, whether a pass or a run,
is gaining good yardage. Touchdowns and extra points
are coming easy . . .

B efore I go any farther, let me tell you a little bit about Judy and me.

Here in the "final quarter" we are celebrating more than fifty years together. We are finding ourselves in the pathway of blessing. Year after year we are seeing our goals and dreams come true. Psalm 5 has been such a comfort. Verse 11 says,

"But let all who take refuge in you be glad; let them ever sing for joy. Spread your protection over them that those who love your name may rejoice in you." (Psalm 5:11 NIV)

However, our journey through life hasn't always been without tackles or fumbles. We have experienced joy, sorrow, challenge, and change.

A few days after our wedding in Fresno, California, we arrived back in Pennsylvania to begin our life together. That evening, while we were opening our wedding gifts, the furnace in our mobile home exploded, and in about twenty minutes everything that we owned was burned up. What we thought would be a big touchdown turned into a terrible fumble. Not such a good start for the second quarter.

Judy and I just stood there in the middle of the road, watching fire trucks, yelling firemen, snow and ice, neighbors and friends. I held Judy in my arms and we cried together until there were no tears left.

With not much money left we had to sleep that first night with friends. I remember staring into the darkness, asking God about the future. I knew immediately that it was time to trust God completely. It was time to dig in and watch God take my life in a good direction. And since then our life has been unbelievable, fantastic, beyond description . . . and absolutely full of adventure.

For example, in 1992 we were traveling in Homefire Family Ministry. Judy and I, our three daughters and their husbands, and all eight of our grandchildren were starting the first of thirteen years of traveling, holding special family seminars. With our caravan of RVs we were destined to live out our lives in the parking lot of every church.

This new ministry was so expensive to start up that we had to sell everything we owned just to get started. We had to buy 5th wheel campers and pickup trucks to pull them. We had to buy a PA system, make music background tapes and CDs, print posters and publicity material, and many more things I've already forgotten about. We probably would have said, "No, we can't do this!" if we had known all the unknowns before we started.

In our first year we were invited to Charlotte, North Carolina, where Sam Johnson was the pastor. He immediately felt that we needed a headquarters city and a home to live in during our down times. So, the church rented us a house big enough for all of us to live in. However, we were soon so busy traveling all over the nation that we rarely got back to live in the house. As a result we moved out after only one year and lived on the road for the next twelve.

- 3 -

Making the Right Choices

by David Whitcomb

NOTE FROM DAVE KYLLONEN: *While in Charlotte we met the Whitcomb family—David, Laura, and their daughter, Kristin. After our service in their church they told us they wanted to help. They immediately asked us what we needed most in our ministry. In the end they answered their own question, which is what this chapter is all about. I think you'll enjoy David Whitcomb's version of what happened.*

Choice. What a powerful word. It can be defined in many ways, but at its most basic it's the process of making a decision when you're faced with two or more possibilities.

We make choices every day, from the minute we get up until we go back to bed. Think about some of the choices you made today. Were they right or wrong? If you had chosen differently, what might the outcomes have been?

In this book, Dave Kyllonen has been talking about football. What do you think happens after a game? I'll bet every player and every coach sits down and breaks apart every aspect of what they did, to see if the right plays were called, the right blocks were thrown, and the right protection was given to the quarterback.

But life is not always as structured as a football game, and many times we just take it for granted. We go through each day without ever recognizing whether we made the right choices.

I was taught to listen for the voice of God. Not necessarily in audible terms, but in the inner sanctum of my soul. I was also taught many other important things by my parents, at a young age, and I quickly caught on to the concept of learning from others. That's a great way to figure out what to do and what not to do—most of the more valuable lessons of my life came from obeying the "what not to do" understandings that God presses upon us if we listen.

The most important lesson I ever learned was that if God calls upon you to do something—*just do it.* If it comes from Him it cannot ever be wrong.

That brings up my Couriers connection. My wife and I and our daughter lived for many years in Charlotte, North Carolina. It was very much an up-and-coming area, and we had really settled in and were making plans to retire there. We built our dream house, we owned property on a lake north of town, the winters were perfect, the people were great, and we were all very comfortable.

We thought it was all settled until our family got to know Dave Kyllonen, his family, and Homefire Family Ministries.

Let me give you a little more background so you'll understand.

I grew up as a preacher's kid, so I knew from a very young age what the ministry was all about—the good, the bad, the hurts, and the hours that had to be invested. My father and mother were very committed people, and for the first eighteen years of my life, all I knew was that they lived the way they preached. That was the norm.

But things changed a lot, shortly after my eighteenth birthday, when I suddenly came face-to-face with a different reality following the death of my father. He and five other people were killed because of a mechanical failure on an aircraft he was piloting.

What ensued in the following years was an even greater tragedy for me. Because of my parents' connections and my ready access to the "ministry world," I had a front-row seat. I won't go into detail, but it didn't take me long to realize that not everyone in the ministry shared the same views or lived their lives as my parents had.

Now, fast forward twenty years to my first encounters with Dave Kyllonen. It became apparent in a very short time that this man and his family were right on. His heart, his motives, and the way he preached and lived struck a cord with me and my family. We spent hours getting to know Dave, his wife, and his kids, enjoying every minute together.

We loved everything that Homefire Family Ministries stood for. We loved what they were trying to do to help reverse the ever-increasing trend toward divorce and other problems within the Christian home. I mean, these people *really worked* at keeping husbands and wives, dads and moms together, and at straightening out issues between kids and their parents. We actually got involved in the ministry to the point of overseeing the donations and recording, depositing, and sending out statements to the contributors. And we loved reading all the testimonials that came in from those whose lives were changed.

Both my wife, Laura, and I flew with Piedmont Airlines when we first met Dave. We would often give up our house on days when we were out of town, so that one of the Homefire gang could have a night out of their fifth-wheel trailers. Can you imagine four couples, some with kids, living out of two trailers that had only one bathroom in each? For most of us this would be impossible. Plus, Dave and Judy Kyllonen had sold everything they owned to start their ministry, and this struck another cord within our family.

And, of course, these things resonated with me even more because I had kept my "pastor's heart." Growing up in a pastor's home had made me very sensitive to what Dave and his family faced. I knew there would be major disappointments and discouragements along the way, and someone needed to be there to support them and validate their dream on a "human" level, to keep them focused on what God had chosen them to do.

All of this brings me back to the point I made earlier about making the right choices and how monumental those choices can become. God laid on our hearts the future of Dave and Judy, their family, and their ministry. We needed to be the encouragers and dream sustainers, and this meant relocating to an area that would be a good base for their operations.

We had a *choice* to make, but once we told Dave what we were about to do he shared it with his family and the fun began. The journey we would all make together in the next ten years would fill several volumes . . . if I just had time to write them!

Much of the vision and commitment of Dave and his family, through Homefire Ministries, was fueled and focused by our shared choices to listen, obey, and react to what God laid on our hearts. The pieces of the puzzle began coming together with the rapid sale of my business, the eighth-day sale of our house at a price above what it appraised for, and the sale of our property on the lake. It all happened so fast that we had to move into an apartment in Charlotte until we could figure out where to go next. Even so, it was the greatest feeling in the world to know that we were in the will of God while we watched Him work out the details.

We started by looking up in Pennsylvania, near where Dave and his family had once lived. We made a few trips by airplane and fell in love with the area. Soon we found a great church with a great pastor with a big heart. We left Charlotte in 1995, moved to Harrisburg, Pennsylvania, and—wow! Did all of this ever fall into place!

In every way possible we attempted to figure out how we would buy land and then build three homes on the money that Laura and I made. Granted, we made a good living, but not one that could support this kind of a dream. There were a few people and churches that caught the vision and helped us financially, but more than once I had to refocus and remind myself that this was something God had laid on *our* hearts, not theirs.

Meanwhile, Laura and I went to a builders' show in Harrisburg after we moved into the area, looking for ideas for the house we would eventually build. I came across a gentleman in one of the booths who was a distributor for irrigation supplies. I was really interested in what he had to say, because part of the business I had owned in Charlotte dealt with irrigation parts. As we continued to talk, he introduced himself as Tim Watson and said, "You look familiar." It turned out that we went to the same church.

He told me Harrisburg was in need of an irrigation contractor who really knew the business, and he would help me get started if I was interested. Wow! Maybe this was how God intended to make this land and building thing happen. So, we started a business that same year and it took off like a rocket ship.

We eventually found fifty acres of land in Dillsburg, Pennsylvania, and developed it into thirteen lots. Within a short time, combining the profits from the sale of the lots, my contracting business, and our airline jobs, we were able to build three homes for Homefire—thus completing, after twelve years, the mission that was placed on our hearts.

In the intervening years the members of Homefire have gone on to other ministries. Homefire served its purpose, and I knew that once the homes were built it would only be a matter of time before everyone would move on. But what an exodus!

The Hammers pioneered a church in Dillsburg, Pennsylvania, called Celebration Community Church—and they are thriving.

The Eschbachs started their own business in counseling and have been very successful.

The Hollises pastor a new church, called "The Power Place," in Kennett Square, Pennsylvania.

Dave joined up with Duane and Neil to form "Dave, Duane, and Neil" (clever name, eh?), all original members of the Couriers. And they are still having the time of their lives.

To return again to my original point, all this came to be as direct results of *choices*. I cannot imagine how different things would be had those God-inspired choices not been made. My guess is that you wouldn't be reading this book.

Always do what God tells you is right. Make the tough choices, even though you might have to get out of your comfort zone and do something others consider crazy or on the edge. Ultimately, the only one you should please is God.

And even at that, He gives you a choice.

—Dave and Laura Whitcomb
Dillsburg, Pennsylvania

- 4 -

The Best Day of the Year 2000

We moved into our new house—as introduced by David Whitcomb in the previous chapter—on April 20, 2000. I had my sixty-fifth birthday eight days later. What a way to start the fourth quarter. Really! I wish you could have been there.

We had been away from Pennsylvania for almost four months. The excitement to see our house for the first time was incredible. We slowly pulled up to our new address and turned into our thousand-foot lane. All eyes were on the house. Then came the tears. But soon we were all talking and shouting at the same time.

As we ran from room to room, all I could say was, "It's better than we ever thought it would be." I sat down on the floor and marveled at God's blessing. He provided a brand-new, never-lived-in house—free. It was time to thank Him for this great gift.

Seven years later, we look back to see how much living we have done in our home. It's been a God house for sure. Many friends, who are evangelists and travel in RVs, have parked in our RV corner. It's a great place to get away from it all and find peace and quiet for a few days. We've had as many as a half-dozen RVs at the same time.

On September 10, 2006, a new church was started in our little town of Dillsburg. The pastors are Mike and Connie Hammer. Mike is our son-in-law and married our youngest daughter, Connie. They invited me to be a part of the staff. They call me the Legacy Pastor. The fourth quarter is looking better all the time. I still sing with Duane and Neil most weekends but get to Celebration Community Church when I can.

We've rented the Grand Ballroom at the Range End golf course for our Sunday services. Our house, along with several others, has handled a huge number of events. Judy and I have enjoyed all the things that happen at our house, including:

- Ladies Bible study on Tuesday evening
- Adult Bible study on Wednesday evening
- Home cell groups on Sunday evening
- Christmas Eve candlelight service

I remember when I went to our basement for the first time. It was so big that I said there was room there for a small church. I wanted to start right away to finish it and make it one big room.

Then reality set in, and with all the other things I had to do I didn't get back to the basement for two or three years. Again I got all excited about finishing it but soon realized that I was a singing preacher and not a carpenter. At that point I found a professional named Ron Sadler and put him to work instead.

During his hours of work, Ron and I talked and talked and quickly became good friends. When the basement was finished, Ron and his wife, Pat, started coming to the house for Bible studies. What good times we had encouraging each other in the things of the Lord. Friendships like this never end.

- 5 -

You Don't Understand Football?

Judy wasn't all that interested in football for the first twenty-five years of our marriage. Then one day I discovered that she didn't really understand the game. So, for the next few years Judy would watch the games with me and I would explain the rules. Now for the last twenty years she has enjoyed football very much.

In the Homefire days we staged a contest each week to see who could pick the most winners. At the end of the year, guess who won! The funny thing was, before she really knew football Judy would pick the team with the uniforms she liked best. It was amazing how she could pick the winners without knowing anything about the team. Ask her now and she is up to speed with which ones are good and which ones aren't.

We have stayed up many times past midnight biting our nails until the final seconds.

When writing this book became a real option, I was talking a lot about football and comparing it to our lives. I asked Judy where she thought all that would fit. She thought about it for a few days and then came back. As she read to me, tears filled my eyes. Only a wife who loves you could come up with this kind of an answer.

Thanks, Judy—I thought our readers would enjoy what you had to say!

MVP = Most Valuable Player

People who watch football games look for outstanding players. These are the ones who makes their teams "jell," who have the ability to make good plays and show a great attitude. These things can result in big honors for a football player.

Well, in this game of life, I have watched closely for the person who most deserves this really big honor, to be chosen the Most Valuable Player, and it is Dave Kyllonen. Dave and I are celebrating fifty years of marriage in 2008. So when I say I have watched closely—I have watched closely! Here is what I have seen.

M = Most

This word can be defined as "greatest in quantity, extent, or degree; superlative in many ways." Needless to say, there have been many, many times when I have pinned the "most" award on Dave's lapel.

For example, one time our car desperately needed tires, and we carefully saved for them because we weren't making very much money. They hadn't been on the car very long when Dad and Mom Kyllonen came for a visit.

I looked out the window one morning while they were here to see Dave taking our brand-new tires off our car and putting them on Dad's car. I couldn't believe my eyes! When I got Dave to the bedroom, I said, "What are you doing with our tires?" His response was, "Judy, Dad needs them more than we do."

Now, that is a true definition of the word *most*—the "most giving" to the highest possible degree.

V = VALUABLE

The dictionary defines this word as "highly important; esteemed."

Someone once asked J. P. Morgan what the best collateral for a loan would be, and he replied, "Character." It has also been said that "Life is built on character, but character is built on decisions." The decisions you make, small or great, do to your life what the sculptor's chisel does to a block of marble. You are shaping your life by your thoughts, attitudes, and actions and becoming either more or less like Jesus Christ.

In August, 2007, we attended the General Council of the Assemblies of God. The Couriers were honored by receiving the highest award, "The Superintendent's Medal of Honor." I was so proud of Dave, Duane, and Neil as Rev. Thomas Trask placed the medals around each of their necks.

Sitting there on the front row and hearing the applause, I asked myself, "How did this come to be?"

I began to reflect back through the years and thought of the many times when a major decision needed to be made that would affect the future of the Couriers. Always, that decision was made based on their commitment and dedication to Jesus Christ. Strong character does matter.

We must set the example of God's standard in a world that desperately needs to see character in action.

P = PLAYER

A player is defined as "one who plays a specified game." Well, the game is still being played. True, we're in the final quarter, but it's not over yet!

The phone still rings. Pastors and promoters are still requesting dates for the Couriers to appear in their churches or concerts. After fifty years of being married to a "player," I still hear those famous words: "Judy, the Van is here. I've got to go."

Always, my response is, "Okay, honey; be safe, and God be with you. I love you!"

— *Judy*

- 6 -

Our Children's Children

The final quarter of your life is a great adventure that has to include your grandchildren. All eight of ours are bringing us such blessings and comfort. And two of them were married in 2008.

Isaiah Hollis
and Brittany Grandizio

All I can say is, "Wow!" Today I take the time to think about what I celebrate: Family, friends, my Jeep, health, but most important, God. I thank God for the many blessings He has laid on my family and how He has molded and shaped me into the man of God I am today.

One of the biggest influences in my life has been my Pappy. He is my cheerleader. I was always told that one of the most important decisions in life is who you choose to be with for the rest of your life and how you choose to get there. Pappy truly taught me how to love and respect women. Lesson 1—Choose to fall "in like" before you fall "in love."

I lived for years on the road, traveling with my family in ministry, being criticized for my standards: "You are an idiot, it will never happen. There is no possible way you can do it." Let me tell you, I did it. I prayed from a very young age for the Lord to send a God-fearing woman into my life. Little did I know that she was out there praying the same prayer.

Her name is Brittany Grandizio. We met at Trinity Assembly of God Church, on the platform, after church. It was a moment never to be forgotten.

In 2004, my family and I planted a church in Kennett Square, Pennsylvania. She was there the first Sunday and she came in looking for the person who owned the Jeep outside that was for sale.

It just happened to be me. A common interest in Jeeps led to the best friendship I ever had. We were best friends for a year, and that it got to a point at which I didn't like other guys looking at my "best friend." I even bought a new Jeep and it was purple (her favorite color), so something had to happen.

My parents made a rule: "As for me and our house we will not date until age 16." Once I got to that age I followed my brother and his promise to God not to date until 18. I wanted to do the same. I wanted to be mature in God. So I did it! I did it! Did you hear me, guys? You don't have to date every girl in the world.

I went in for the kill on Valentine's Day, 2005. I placed a pink rose on the seat of my new Jeep. We were going, as friends, to dinner and to a young adult's meeting all the way into New Jersey, an hour's drive. Then came the actual moment. We were on our way home, but my body was in convulsions, my speech was slurred, and I was a mess.

I waited until one minute before midnight and then I let her have it. I asked the stupidest question I could have come up with: "What are your feelings for me?" Stupid, stupid, stupid! I became very close to the Lord after that one, praying, "Please, Lord, if she says no, come back NOW." But I then told her how I felt, and she felt the same.

I would not turn 18 until February 26, so when that day came I took her out. Now, if you have not met my family, you have to realize that they're a little strange. They are awesome, but strange. So, yup, the whole family huddled around us and prayed for us and our relationship. And, let me tell you, it was awesome.

Parents, if you have never prayed for your kids like that, do it. It will change their lives.

Brittany and I had both promised God we would save saying "I love you" for our engagement day. "I like you, Britt," was what I got used to saying. People didn't get it, but it was my biggest testimony. "Wait—it's worth it," I told every boy I came in contact with. Two and a half years later it was time to say the word—"love."

The planning started. I took her to the beach in Ocean City, New Jersey. I had placed candles in the sand, forming an aisle that ended in a large heart. There were rose petals everywhere. The sunset was beautiful, the music was perfect. We walked hand in hand down that candle lit aisle, and I told her everything in my heart. Then I told her, "I love you." What a moment. I had never felt like that in my life. Our families were hiding and videotaping from the dunes. It was the most precious day ever.

Now, saying "I love you" to each other has become sacred and precious. It was sometimes difficult, when we really wanted to say it, but now that moment is priceless to us. We would not have changed it for anything. If your day has not yet come, I hope you have the same amazing feelings—and *love*! To this day, that is still the most meaningful word in our relationship.

I'm so thankful for the influence my Pappy had on me at such a young age. He and Granny were mine and Brittany's inspiration to want to fall madly "in like" before we fell "in love" and to save that precious, amazing moment. There is nothing like having influence in your life. To this day I still love to just simply watch Pappy and glean every bit of wisdom from him.

Along with my amazing family, Pappy believed in me and has always cheered me on. I am so proud of my family, and so thankful that he took time to totally pour all that he is into my life.

Pappy . . . you rock and I love you!

—*Isaiah*

Elijah Hollis
and Ashlee Kreiling

Once upon a time there was a boy of seven and a little girl of five who became friends and hung out together once a year. The little boy visited the little girl's church in Kansas City while he traveled with his family, telling the world about Jesus. As the years passed, the two became good friends until the boy's family felt called by God to stop traveling and plant a church in Pennsylvania. The girl stayed where she grew up, to minister at her home church in Kansas City.

One day the little girl received an email about the little boy's church and what he was doing as the youth pastor. They started writing back and forth and talked on the phone for almost two months until, one day, she decided to go visit him and his family and see what they were up to after all this time. That's where our story begins.

Elijah . . .

As I drove to the airport to pick her up, I couldn't stop thinking to myself, *Could she be the one?* Somehow, in the midst of all of our emails and phone conversations, I had already begun to have feelings for this girl. After all the years we spent just hanging out as friends, I couldn't believe that this one time could change everything.

Ashlee . . .

I waited patiently in line to board the plane at 6 AM. It was the only plane ride that I didn't sleep through, even though I was very tired, because I couldn't stop thinking that in a few hours I would be seeing the most amazing guy I knew. Through all of our conversations, I had learned so much about him.

We finally landed in Philadelphia. I picked up the phone to let him know I was there, and as I dialed the number I felt excited, nervous, and jittery all at the same time—even though we had talked so many times before.

Elijah . . .

I remember hearing the phone ring. My hands were shaking as I answered it. I cleared my throat and tried to sound manly as I spoke. I got her flight information, told her I'd see her at baggage claim, parked the car, and went to meet the girl who would completely change my life. I remember walking through the doors, searching through the crowd, and finally finding her. She was radiant, more beautiful than I ever imagined. The first thing I noticed as I walked toward her was her eyes. They were breathtaking. As I tried to regain my composure I blurted out, "Hey!" while thinking inside, *Don't look stupid!* I finally hugged her and it seemed too good to be true.

Ashlee . . .

I was so excited to finally be with him. I knew I liked him, but I had tried to push everything else aside and just think of him as a friend. But as he gave me that hug my feelings for him increased.

As we got my luggage, I remember thinking two things: *Wow, he's so handsome, and such a gentleman.* We got both bags, got in the car, and headed out to see the family. The moment we had both looked forward to had blown away all our expectations. From the first moment, there weren't any times of awkwardness—just pure romance.

ELIJAH . . .

I never enjoyed anyone as much as I did Ashlee. We talked about everything, from chitchat about rocks to deep conversations about our passions and dreams for the future. Everything was so amazing in a God-ordained way, and I was so happy. I remember being in bed late one night a couple days before Ashlee got in, and I just stayed awake, praying and seeking God on the matter of dating this girl.

I had dated before and it was anything but special, so I decided in my mind that I was not going to have "just another relationship." It would have to be for a reason. So I prayed, "God, if Ashlee is the one, please make it clear to me." I had prayed for the girl of my dreams since I was a little boy—that God would lead her and raise her up and bring her to me. All those thoughts, prayers, and dreams had been part of my life, but now they were changing to prayers for guidance to make the right decision. The answer didn't come until Ashlee was there, but when it did come I was ready.

ASHLEE . . .

As a little girl, I loved princesses and always dreamed of becoming one. But as we all know, every princess needs a dashing prince. So, when I was little I prayed for and dreamed of the guy who would be my prince. I made a list of everything I wanted in a prince and prayed over that list every day in my devotions. I knew that God had the perfect guy out there for me, and I refused to settle for anything else.

A few years after I made my list I started a prayer box full of prayers for the man of God I would someday be with. As I got to know Elijah, it was amazing to see how God was answering my prayers for him even before we were together.

Elijah . . .

It was a rainy Wednesday night after youth group, and we had just finished doing a bunch of donuts in the Giant parking lot with my car. We pulled up to the house and, while still in the car, I asked her if we could talk.

Ashlee . . .

When he asked me that, there were a million things going through my mind. I thought we had been having so much fun the past few days; why was he going to end it now? I never could have guessed what was coming next.

Elijah . . .

As I looked across the car, I could see Ashley anticipating what I was about to say. After stammering awhile, I finally got to the sentence, "I have had so much fun getting to know you and I would like to take this relationship to the next level and begin a courtship with you." She said yes, and we were both the happiest we had ever been.

Though we'd been long distance for our entire relationship, the phone calls, conversations, and monthly visits that followed turned our "Like" for each other to Love. In trying to make long-distance fun, we decided to spend the next nine months surprising each other with books we had made, scavenger hunts, and long dream dates in the park. Finally, after all the long-distance romance, on August 7, 2007, I set up a big "surprise day" in Indianapolis.

I picked Ashlee up in a convertible sports car and we drove around the city to the zoo. We ate lunch by a fountain in the park, and finally, I led her to our ultimate destination.

We pulled up to the church which, from the outside, looked just like another building. Then we walked inside. The sanctuary was filled with 500 candles and hundreds of rose petals sprinkled over the floor leading up to the stage. I walked her up the aisle, shaking as I went, and sat her down to make sure the glass slippers I had gotten for her would fit. After all, she is my princess. After slipping on the glass slipper, I walked her to the piano, which was covered with roses and candles. We sat down and I sang her the song I had been writing for her for six months. After telling her I loved her for the first time in the song, I popped the question in the last line. In the midst of shaky hands and teary eyes, I got down on one knee and gave her the ring.

Since family is so important to both of us, I had arranged for all of our families to be hiding around the church to share this important moment with us. After the song they all came out from hiding and we spent the night hanging out and having fun. Our story is nothing more than pure romance. A little boy and a little girl who waited on and trusted God to bring them together as prince and princess.

—Lige and Ash

My Other Six Grandchildren, All Girls

Madison Hammer — 11 years old

Hi, my name is Madison. My Pappy's book is called *Our Final Quarter*. He says his part has something to do with football. I don't know a lot about football but I do know that four quarters equal one dollar.

My favorite day comes when my Pappy takes me out for "Pappy Day." Every "Pappy Day" is different. On one of these days we had school-supplies day.

There were many more. We had jean day, sneaker day, bowling day, flip-flop day, and history day. History day was all about where Pappy grew up.

We never know when Pappy is going to call us for "Pappy Day," but we know it's going to be fun.

Pappy, I love you soo much!

— Maddy

Ellie Eschbach — 13 years old

What I love about my Pappy is his voice. It is so low that it vibrates the floor. I also love how tall he is. His height makes him Pappy. I love him.

Pappy has a really neat train set down in his basement. It's a tiny world with houses, trees, cars, and little people.

I enjoy how happy he always is. He is so lovable. He is like a really skinny teddy bear. Of course, you could never forget his smile. It makes you happy whenever you think about it. My Pappy is the best on this earth. I love him!

—Ellie Be-lell-ie

TIFFANY HAMMER — 13 YEARS OLD

My name is Tiffany. My Pappy is the best in the world. I don't know what I would do without him. He is very inspirational to me and my family. He is always there when we need him. My Pappy has a great sense of humor and is very loving. I wouldn't trade him for the world.

My Pappy loves to paint pictures. He recently joined an art class. He has been an evangelist and ministered in many countries. He also was a pastor and a missionary. Now he travels with the Couriers and sings so low I can feel the floor vibrating. I hope someday I could grow up to be like my Pappy.

I love sports such as field hockey, gymnastics, and much more. Whenever I am playing in the field, I love seeing my Pappy standing on the sidelines.

I also enjoy singing. I help out by singing with our Wednesday night youth program. I often help with the worship team at my church, Celebration Community Church. I am very active in my church and love to be in the church dramas. All I can say is that I love Jesus and He is my Savior. I couldn't live without Him. He is my best friend.

Thanks for everything, Pappy. I love you!

—Tiffers

Erica Eschbach — 15 years old

I do not want to brag, but I think I have the best grandpa. What can I say? He is amazing! He has always encouraged me to trust in God. He has been such a huge influence in my life. Not only do his words honor God, but his actions do, too.

I am so proud to be able to say that Dave Kyllonen is my grandpa. I know that I can always count on him for good advice. I have become a better person because of his willingness to pour into my life.

I went on a missions trip to Trinidad this last summer, and through the whole experience I remembered little things he told me. It truly made my missions trip the best it could be.

Pappy is one of my biggest role models. To eventually become like him would be an honor and a privilege.

—E J

Victoria Hammer — 15 years old

Hey, my name is Tori! I love my Pappy so much. What I love about him is his spirit of adventure. My goal, before I die, is to go to as many countries as my Pappy has been to. I think it's about sixty. Whenever there's a door open to go anywhere or do anything, he is the first to say, "I'll go."

I recently went on a missions trip to the Dominican Republic. While I was there, the thing that impressed me the most was when this little girl of about four or five years old came and hugged me. She didn't even know who I was, but she still showed me love and kindness. I gave her a little plastic ring and her face looked like Christmas morning with tons of presents. She really showed me how ungrateful I can be. She just got a little plastic ring and was so excited.

I loved being in the Dominican; I loved what it taught me. I can't wait to start my next adventure of going somewhere and telling people about Jesus!

So, you better watch out, Paps, I'm catching up! I love my Pappy and want to be just like him. I am so blessed to have a great Pappy.

— *Tori*

ALEXSONDRA HOLLIS — 16 YEARS OLD

I am the eldest of the Kyllonen's six granddaughters. Growing up in an all-Christian family has been the biggest blessing of my life. My family and I planted a church in Chester County three and a half years ago. It is called The Power Place. There have been blessings after blessings, and God has been the center of everything.

I have been put in the greatest, most fantabulous family. *Ever!* There are some families these days that don't even like to be in one another's lives. But in my case, that is the total opposite. I honestly believe that I have the most incredible family and grandparents.

Every single day my life gets poured into by not only my family that surrounds me but also my Granny and Pappy and my aunts and uncles. The heroes in my life are my parents, my brothers, and my Granny and Pappy. I have been taught from a very young age that, "As for me and my house, we will serve the Lord."

And that line has been passed down from generation to generation. It hasn't mattered to me at all what others think because of what my family has instilled in me. I am the way I am because of Pappy and Granny. They raised my mother as she has now raised me, and I wouldn't want it any other way. My mom and dad have taken everything that has been taught to them from their parents and have put all of that influence into my life.

The choices they made have influenced everything that I am. Ever since I was born I have been a God-fearing grand-daughter, and I always will be. I watch all the choices that my family makes, and they push me more and more to continue my relationship with God.

My whole life I sang with my family, doing ministry in a different church every week. I traveled in an RV until I was twelve. I have been pushed out of my comfort zone from a very young age, and that has made me a much better and stronger person. Every week I had to get up on a stage and sing in front of hundreds of people I had never met before.

Talk about freaky! I had to make choices in those days, to say, "Am I going to let being scared keep me from doing what I love to do, or am I going to go up on that stage and sing my heart out and push myself to the point where I won't fear anymore?" It took me a lot of time to feel comfortable in front of people, but I never gave up trying to not be afraid. And I got that far only because of the big push from my family.

My parents gave me solos, and I wasn't happy at the time to sing them, but they knew what they were doing and because of that I now sing every week on the worship team at my church. Without getting that encouragement from my family I would never be the outgoing person I am today, and also outgoing for God in my church. Now I am not afraid to get up on the stage and sing in my youth group, *High Voltage*. Sometimes I even do something as simple as getting up in front of the kids and running something like a game that night, or just saying something. Because of my choice to get out of my comfort zone I have been able to influence a lot more people and tell them the amazing things God has done for me, and the awesome things He can do for their lives.

Without that constant push from Granny and Pappy and my parents, I know that I would still be that shy little girl. Now, every week, I can't wait to go to my church and really be involved, to let God totally use my life in any way that is according to His plan.

One of my favorite quotes is, "When God is for me, who can be against me?" That line speaks total truth, because if you have God on your side, who could ever go against you? He is bigger than absolutely anything.

Another very important thing that has been taught to me is that hiding God's word in my heart will make the most special relationship with Him. Every morning my dad takes me to school and we memorize scriptures. Even to this day, everything we have studied is in my heart and I can quote certain scriptures because my dad has taken the time to put that "want" in my life.

Everything that has come from my parents and grand-parents has only made me a better person. I love the Lord with all my life and I love my family and I would not change a thing for anything in the world. Thanks, Pappy and Granny—you rock my world!

—Ali

- 7 -

Surprise, Surprise, Surprise

T o be singing with Duane and Neil again is the biggest surprise of my final quarter. It never entered my mind that this could even be possible.

I heard that Duane and Neil were retiring from the Couriers and I wanted to attend their last concert, which was in Toronto, Canada, on December 31, 2000. I never made it to the concert but I knew they deserved to retire after all the years of traveling all over the world.

My ministry with my family was coming to a close. By 2003, we were doing just a few dates a month. I was asked to fill in and preach for a Christian Missionary Alliance Church, in Lewisburg, Pennsylvania. This was perfect. I love to preach and this fit me to a T.

On Friday a board member of the church called to make sure I was coming that Sunday. Then he said, "There are two guys who want to sing with you before you preach. Could you sing a couple of songs?" I said, "Sure, I'll come early so we can practice." Then he said, "Their names are Duane and Neil."

The next Sunday morning I got to the church early, and sure enough, Duane and Neil were there. It had been twenty-three years since I had resigned from the Couriers, in April of 1980. When they called us to come to the platform, no one knew what was going to happen. Neil went to the piano and started to play an old song. What happened next was incredible. The music poured out of us. Instead of two songs, Neil just kept playing one song after another.

Nine songs later we knew that something wonderful was happening. It was like old times. Our voices fell into place just as they had twenty-five years earlier. After the service, everyone—including our wives and close friends—said, "You guys sound the same as you always did. You need to sing again."

I remember driving home and quietly talking to the Lord. I said that I was willing if it could all be worked out. Two days later the three of us had breakfast together and talked about our future. I felt blessed to hear them say they would be happy to try it again. We agreed that maybe once a month would be a good way to start.

After a couple of months, the news got out that Dave, Duane, and Neil were back. The phone began to ring. Calls came from all over the country, and even Canada. We were booking two or three weekends a month. In late 2007 we sang for twenty weekends in a row. Wow! What fun we are having in our final quarter together.

TRANSPORTATION SOLUTION

We were using Duane's van to get us to all our dates, putting thousands of miles on his personal vehicle. One day we got a call from Michigan. The man on the other end of the line said, "Dave, my name is Paul Corrin from the little town of Morenci, Michigan. My family hasn't heard anything about the Couriers for years, but we are interested to know if you are still singing together."

"Paul, it's funny you should ask," I said. "We just reorganized a few months ago. We are enjoying it more than ever."

"What are you traveling in?"

"Duane's personal van," I said.

Then he told me his story. His father-in-law had passed away that year and his mother-in-law, Pat Sepeers, was left with a 1999 motor home that she didn't want anymore. The family came together to help her sell it. Pat said that she and her husband had decided, before he died, that she should give it to a ministry team.

When the family discussed who, they remembered the Couriers coming to their town many years ago. They all said, "Let's try to find them and see if they could use it."

"What timing," we said. "Yes, yes, yes!"

A few days later we drove up to Michigan to get it. We pulled up in the driveway and took our first look. It was beautiful, and we found ourselves saying a prayer of thanks. God knows what we need.

We met Paul and his wife, Leana. Pat was there, too. They were as happy as we were. We had a special prayer and hugged each of them. Then Pat handed us the keys and we were on the road, heading home. Surprise, surprise! Only God could have done that. And I looked at the scoreboard of my life and saw another touchdown. It was so good to be on the winning side.

A few months later we got a call from Pat, wanting to know how we liked the motor home. But more than that, she wanted to know how our ministry was going. I was so glad to give her the good news. We had put thousands of miles on the coach. We were singing better than ever, and the phone was ringing every day, booking our ministry. I can tell you, if you do things for the Lord, the phone will always ring.

- 8 -

Great Front Lines

Any ministry team, to be successful, must hear the phone ring. Many times I have answered my phone and been rewarded with some of the most surprising people on the other end.

When there is a great game going, the quarterback must give credit to the offensive linemen. They're very important. They give time to the quarterback to throw the ball for a touchdown. We've had a Super Bowl talented team who helped us win in the game of life.

I ALWAYS LOVE TO HEAR DAN BETZER'S VOICE ON THE PHONE . . . .

We were classmates together in the fifties at Central Bible College. Our paths have crossed many times since. Dan is a great communicator, a great preacher, and a great singer. He pastors a great church in Fort Meyers, Florida. He calls and wants a date every February.

When Dan sings with us, things happen. Last year we sang five or six songs and ended with "How Great Thou Art." Let me tell you, *it doesn't get any better than that*. Dan is one of the most generous pastors we work with. He serves the best food, puts us in the finest hotels, and blesses us with the biggest offerings. What a way to go.

I always love it when the Terry brothers call . . . .

We met the Terry family in the 50s. Brother and Sister Terry invited us to their church for a concert. They had seven children—six boys and one girl. The brothers have stayed in touch with us all these years.

A few of years ago, Harold Terry called and said their mother was getting up in years, and would we sing and preach at her funeral service when she passed away? I said that would be special and we would love to be a part of her funeral celebration. This year, 2007, we went to the funeral and sang our songs, and I preached my message.

I still have fond memories of that service. What I preached has truly come to pass. I talked about the sunshine during the day, but in the night the moon and stars bring an indescribable afterglow that blesses us and brings great comfort. When our loved ones are gone, there is an afterglow that is often very rewarding.

Harold calls often. Many times it's to book us in a church near him. What welcomed phone calls his have been. Sometimes he just wants to talk. His wife, Shirley, gets in on the conversation. Harold and Shirley were married on the same date as Judy and me. We often eat our anniversary dinner together at the Outback Steakhouse.

HERE IS A NOTE FROM HAROLD TERRY . . . .

Dave, Duane, and Neil have lived in and around our lives for the past fifty years. We watched the first man land on the moon together right after hearing them blend their voices in praise and worship at a local Williamsport, Pennsylvania, church. Before and after that evening we had the privilege of sharing over forty venues with them in different churches, parks, and auditoriums in central Pennsylvania.

Many spiritual and lasting relationships have been planted, nurtured, and blossomed from these three dedicated servants of God. It has been our gain to call them friends and brothers in Christ, and we love them dearly, along with their precious families. May God continue to bless them and use their voices and lives to touch many needy people.

TED TERRY ALWAYS MAKES A CREATIVE PHONE CALL . . . .

I remember when Ted called to ask us if we would let him book the Couriers in Southern California. What great memories we have of those dates. Then he called again and asked if we would sing in the Northwest. We love that part of the world, and Seattle has some wonderful churches. Way to go, Ted!

In 2007 Ted called and said, "How about Alaska?" We couldn't agree fast enough. Everyone wants to go to Alaska. In the summer it's the hot spot for tourism.

When the call for 2008 came Ted said, "Let's travel to Montana." It's going to be exciting. Ten days in the Wild West! Judy lived in Great Falls for a while. My classmate Dean Conklin, with whom I sang in a quartet before I met the Couriers, lives in Montana. I haven't seen Dean in many years. We will sing together at the concert in his town.

The final quarter of life has some great moments, and this tour will be a big touchdown in the game of life. "Thanks for the memories, Ted. Keep calling. I've got the world map open on my desk."

The phone rang again and it was my neighbor Chuck Fichtner . . . .

Chuck grew up on Long Island, New York. We went to his church in Smithtown when he was just a teenager. He always came early to help carry in the PA system and tapes. He would sit on the front row and take it all in. We enjoyed having Chuck around.

Chuck finished school, got married, and now has a lovely family. I met Chuck again one day, and what he said to me was overwhelming. He was so thankful for the friendship between us and wanted to give to our ministry. Chuck and his family have supported all my ministries.

Chuck and Vicky heard that there was a lot open next to Judy and me in our housing development. They immediately bought it and have built a lovely home next to us. There isn't anything they wouldn't do for us. Getting a call from them is always incredible. Thanks a million!

Hello, Dave, this is Gerry Hindy calling. . . .

Gerry and his wife, Carolyn, came into my life during the third quarter. God has great timing. I was traveling with my entire family, serving under the name *Homefire*. It was really tough going from the very beginning. But when we couldn't keep up with all the bills and travel expenses and it began to look like we could not continue, a phone call from the Hindys changed all that. Gerry decided that we should pay off one of our pickup trucks. "Get rid of some of the debt load," he said.

In a few days, to our surprise he sent a letter of encouragement and a check to pay off our entire truck bill. In football, that's what you call moving the ball the whole hundred yards in one play. Our family ministry was never the same. God used Gerry and Carolyn to continue supporting Homefire for thirteen years. What a touchdown!

THANKS FOR THE MEMORIES, FROM GERRY, CAROLINE, AND FAMILY....

Dave Kyllonen and his family warmed our hearts through Homefire. But more than that, through their own lives and ministry they were constant reminders of how God intended the family to function. Stretching the limits while believing in a passionate cause—what a way to fight so effectively to help keep families together.

IS DAVE THERE? IT'S GLENN PYLES CALLING....

Glenn Pyles joins those who have contributed many thousands of dollars to our ministry. Glenn and his wife, Margaret, are in the trucking business. They live and work out of the little town of Goodfield, Illinois. They once got a burden for Panama and began to support pastors all over that country.

God has blessed their business, and through the years they have sent thousands of dollars. They now support missionaries in Poland, Peru, and Panama in addition to the Couriers. We just wouldn't be here without Glenn's help every month for many years.

My memories of going to Panama with Glenn are comforting and happy experiences. Visiting twenty-four churches that he and Margaret have cared for, and preaching through an interpreter, was an awesome experience and filled me with a sense of well-being. Thank you, Glenn, for everything.

Hey Couriers — It's Glenn and Margaret. How about letting us get a word in here?

Thinking of the many times we shared together, my mind goes back to the first time I heard them sing. Here was a group that instantly stood out above all the others. Beyond their singing there was something about their message, their appearance, and the way they presented themselves. We soon became good friends from that point on—how could it be any other way?

-9-

We Need
Cheerleaders Too

*Cheerleading is encouragement. It's a glad, excited shout
that urges you to carry on. A rallying cry of joy and glad-
ness. People in the ministry sometimes need cheerleaders desperately, and to always love them dearly—which often makes
a special kind of "sense" when they're good friends and
family members. What comes next is especially precious to us,
because our three daughters have always been among our
most devoted cheerleaders.*

OUR THREE DAUGHTERS

KRISTIE HOLLIS — THE FIRST ONE . . .

Today is Christmas Day and I am flying to Wichita to spend
the holidays with Greg's family. However, there is one very
major problem. I hate to fly.

But life is full of choices. We make them every day, all day long. I made a choice today to get on the plane. Every step closer was tougher to take, and yet Grandma's was just three hours away. I knew she longed to see her son and beloved grandkids. My choice to get on the plane . . . priceless.

In the Kyllonen home, making choices for ourselves started at a very young age. Daddy and Mom taught us girls how to make choices with purpose. Daddy would say, "Every choice has an ending. You have to live with the result of whatever choice you make." Even when I cried and begged them to "Take my choice back!" they held fast to that simple rule.

And they were absolutely right. After a few bad choices, I started taking every single one very seriously. Now I am no longer a little girl. In fact, I have a girl of my own who is sixteen years old.

Along the way I made a lot of choices and took a lot of turns—some easy, some as tough as nails, and some I didn't even want to make. But I knew that if I didn't take each one I would regret it forever. Looking back (always a thriller, eh?), I shudder to think where we would be if I hadn't chosen the right turns.

Is it an easy way to live? I wish! Do I have a lot more choices to make? Every day! Will Daddy's voice continue to ring in my ear? All the time! Because making choices that count will make you a strong leader. People want to follow someone who makes choices with a purpose.

I can still hear Daddy say, "Who is following you? Where are you taking them? What does the end result look like?" And most important of all, "Is Jesus in the center?"

Today, Greg and I pastor a church in Kennett Square, Pennsylvania. We started it from scratch in 2004. I am excited as we are leading others down a road that will someday lead to eternity with Jesus. Has it been fun? You bet! Has it been hard? Oh my, yes! Has it been rewarding? The smile on my face every night as I climb into bed says it all.

Thank you, Daddy, for watching me make all my choices. I know it must have killed you to watch me make some of them, but you held my hand and led the way. Now, today, I am holding the hands of many others, helping them do the same thing I was taught. Making choices with a purpose. Providing such leadership that God looks down, smiles, and says, "Good choice, Kristie."

I love life and I love you, Daddy—my hero!

—Kristie

ROBIN ESCHBACH — THE SECOND ONE . . .

Big things rarely start off big. My dad didn't begin singing in huge auditoriums and making recordings in fancy studios. But over many years he worked hard and created for himself—the good life!

I like the way God cares for the righteous. The Bible says that Phinehas's zeal for the Lord "was credited to him as righteousness for endless generations to come" (Psalm 106:31 NIV). That includes me. My children, their children, and their children. That's a lot of family with the opportunity for the good life.

Dad paved the way with his ability to dream, to think big—to think beyond right now. Dad also taught me that my reputation, character, trustworthiness, and integrity must be above reproach.

Dad accomplished most of his dreams because of the generosity of friends and ministry opportunities. In return, he himself proved to be generous as well. He gets such a kick out of obedience to God. That makes me smile.

I think Psalm 112:1 sums it up. "Blessed is the man who fears the Lord and finds great delight in his commands" (NIV). I'm so glad I'm a part of the Kyllonen family heritage. I desire the good life. Dad has proven it can be done.

—Robin

Connie Hammer — the third one . . .

A cheerleader is someone who stands on the sidelines and cheers like crazy for their team, sometimes yelling, sometimes dancing, sometimes jumping for joy, and sometimes encouraging those around them to join in.

But ultimately, cheerleading is about making sure the players know they are loved and appreciated for all their efforts. That's me! I applaud your life, Dad, and the way you've lived it so far.

Of course, I learned this from the best cheerleader in my life . . . you. You supported me in each and every dream I presented. Wow! One year I wanted to be on the radio, so you let me get on the air and try it out. Another year I wanted to be a singer, so you let me sing in public standing right next to you. Another year I wanted to be a missionary, so you helped me set up an overseas ministry. Thank you for continuing that even today.

Not long ago I got to sit on the front row of one of your concerts. My head swirled with memories of people, events, places, and songs. I bowed my head in thankfulness that God allowed me to see your heart, embracing the heart of God and following His direction for your life.

It inspires me. It also humbles me, to think that God's plan is so beyond what we could have asked for. His plan is big.

To hear the stories of your missionary journeys, to see how you wrap your arms around every church denomination, to understand the sacrifice you consistently make in letting people use their gifts and talents in your services, giving them a chance to serve—it's all just plain cool.

I also love that all your stories aren't in the past, but they are current. You are still traveling and singing. You are a pastor at Celebration Community Church. You teach a weekly Bible study in your home. You meet and mentor young people every week. You spend time with your grandkids, do missions, and so much more.

I love you, Dad. I cheer you on!

—*Connie*

Other Cheerleaders and Friends

Grace Davis

When I hear the word *Courier* I think of three men in a church service, singing with all their hearts the best music this side of heaven. Dave, Duane, and Neil are men I have known since 1960. For twelve years they were on TV every Sunday morning. When they taped the program, I would take a full coffee pot to them so they could take a break and have coffee, along with my specialty, Brown Bobbies (greaseless donuts), to help them sing their songs.

So many stories could be told about the Couriers. We are thankful to have had the privilege of knowing their wives and children. The Couriers and their families continue to show the way to be what God wants us to be until He comes.

Thank you, Couriers. I love you!

— Gracie

Shirley Terry

When I consider the "Fourth Quarter" of a football game I naturally tend to think that, by this time, one team will be in the lead and likely to win, and one team will be trailing and likely to lose. Both teams will be reviewing their strategies, and each member will have a job to do. Quite probably, the fans of each team will also be extremely attentive.

Yet another distinctive group comes to mind: the cheer-leaders. Intermediate between the team and the fans are the faithful, determined men and women whose major role is encouragement. By doing their jobs well, cheerleaders can influence the momentum of both the fans and their team. I would even say that these encouragers have influenced the outcome of many games by helping to maintain the momentum of a winner or helping reverse the momentum of a team on the verge of losing.

For years, along with many others we have cheered for the Couriers, because we believed in the ministry of Dave, Duane, and Neil. We heard the love of Jesus in their songs. We always looked forward to hearing their anointed preaching at the end of each service, and often encouraged non-Christians or those needing spiritual revival to come and receive the Couriers' ministry.

They understood that their call was to go into all the world, preaching the Gospel and making disciples. We have also seen them serve as loving husbands and fathers, further evidence of their dedication to the Lord.

The best cheerleaders somehow find the energy to go into the fourth quarter still fighting the good fight. Likewise, the Couriers have staying power and have spent their lives introducing Christ as "the way, the truth, and the life." Cheerleaders in the body of Christ are all about winning eternal glory in worship of the King himself. During the fourth quarter, will you cheer with me and the Couriers as we look forward to the words of our King: "Well done, good and faithful servant" (Matthew 25:21 NIV).

—Shirley A. Terry

June Graham

I was living in Toronto, Canada. Several members of my family, including me, were vacationing in Allentown, Pennsylvania. We attended Green Lane Camp Meeting, met the Couriers, and were quite astonished by their music and ministry. Their harmony and delivery were professional, yet they were lauding the Lord and proclaiming their love for Him.

Our family set up dates for them to come to Toronto Evangelistic Centre. They were fresh out of Bible college with a testimony that rang true, and to cheer them on to also minister in Canada would be a plus for us.

The Couriers invited me to be their secretary in Mechanicsburg, Pennsylvania. When I awakened from my dream I discovered that the invitation was real, and so I prepared to move from Canada. I arrived on a Sunday evening and reported for work on Monday.

It immediately became obvious that this was far different from any kind of "city office" I was familiar with. Duane was in the corner, counting money. Neil came in with another fellow, discussing the sound. Dave had the calendar in his hand and was making phone calls to verify the Couriers schedule for that week.

My mind was flying with thoughts about keeping this together. Had I known, at that moment, the future events and schedules and where God had already planned for their ministry to happen, it would have had me fasting and praying for days. I was in my glory because there were so many opportunities to promote the group and cheer them on.

And best of all, I felt relaxed and could be myself.

I had attended Bible college in Providence, Rhode Island, but that was not Pennsylvania. This part of the United States had a personality all its own. Many times people didn't understand me, even as I tried my best to comprehend what they were saying as well. However, I loved their food except for the difficulty I had with the mincemeat pie at Mom and Pop Davis's house.

Also, I had the personality of a sergeant. If it is going to be done, it had to be done right now. Well, most often this approach was not desirable. I was very emphatic, and no one wants to be told what to do. The necessary change in my personality probably required almost all the years I worked for the Couriers.

When expansion came also, I saw how the Couriers took their time in making decisions, because they were setting up for the Gospel to be preached and that was far more important than advancing their singing careers. I saw how flexible they were—they took everything in stride and served the people.

Meanwhile, other expansions were also taking place via the Courier families. Some births were not planned to suit the schedule, so several times the Couriers became fathers while they were thousands of miles from home.

Many spiritual lessons were also taught to me. These were the first ten years of the Couriers' ministry. "Pioneering" best describes those years, but how can you be equipped to know the road?

My passage was Proverbs 3:5–6: "Trust in the Lord with all your heart and lean not on your own understanding.

In all your ways acknowledge Him and He will direct your paths" (NKJV). This proved successful because so often, just in the nick of time, God made a way.

RESULTS OF CHEERING

It was not difficult to cheer the Couriers on because so many good results came from their ministry. Many non-Christians converted, and many lonely people found that they had new friends and were filled with hope again.

I am always proud of what God has done through the lives of Dave, Duane, and Neil. I am also elated that I had a part in the ministry from my "window in the office." The Lord did this good thing for me. God bless you!

—June Graham
Toronto, Ontario, Canada

-10-
Time for Missions Again

Doug Hollis is a missionary who has given his life to the people of Indonesia. Doug is the brother of Greg Hollis, who married our oldest daughter, Kristie. While on furlough in 2007, he came to spend a few days with Judy and me.

One afternoon I said to Doug, "I have never been in one of your services and I know very little about Indonesia. Maybe you could give a presentation to me, eh?" He agreed, and in a few minutes, with his Power Point and pictures, he dropped the whole load on me. When he was finished I was stunned. After a minute or two I found myself saying, "Doug, what can I do to help you?"

He said, "I need a good film of my work in Indonesia." My thought for the moment was, *Could I do that? Do I have the time to go to Indonesia? Do I have the money? Is it safe to visit? What would Judy think?*

At the end of our afternoon session, I finally said to Doug, "You can count on me. I'll come at the end of the year." After Doug left, I said to Judy, "We better get our missions fund going." And little by little the fund started growing.

But life was so busy I soon forgot all about Indonesia. The end of the year came and went. Then one day I was stopped in my tracks by the news that Greg had heard from Doug. All of a sudden I realized that I had forgotten my commitment. I looked at my schedule and I found ten days in which I could fit a trip. I asked Judy if she had saved enough money, and she surprised me with more than enough.

I looked around to see if anyone wanted to go with me, including Elijah, my oldest grandson. Boy, did that ever turn him on. When he agreed, everything about the trip changed. I was going to travel halfway around the world with my grandson. What could be better than that?

A few weeks later the Fichtners' son, Hans, came to talk to me. He said he had heard about my trip and about Elijah going with me. Then he said, "Mr. Kyllonen, is there enough room for me to go with you?" Without hesitation I said, "Yes, I would be honored to take two young guys with me. Surely God has something important for us to do."

Off to Indonesia

It took us forty hours to get from Philadelphia to Indonesia. On the way, our flight made a stop in Seoul, Korea, where we had a ten-hour layover. I remembered that the world's largest church is in Seoul. Maybe we could take a taxi and visit it.

I went to the information desk and found out that we were an hour from the church. We were discouraged because the taxi fare was way too much. But after sitting around for another hour, I decided to take a walk and ended up talking to a taxi driver about a trip to the church and back. He told me he would take us for forty-two dollars.

We thought about it for another hour and finally said to each other, "We are only here one time in our life. It would be terrible to miss seeing the world's largest church." We found the cabbie and were soon on our way. The traffic was horrendous, but we finally pulled up in front of the church.

Meanwhile, we had a lot of trouble talking to the cabbie, who didn't speak English. We told him, by hand motions, that we would be just a few minutes. We only wanted to take a few pictures and we would be right back so we could hurry back to the airport and catch our flight.

All three of us ran to the church door. Three or four people immediately came running up to see who was coming to the church at this hour. None of them spoke English, so we tried to tell them that all we wanted was to take a picture of the main sanctuary.

We were in such a rush that they thought we needed to use the bathroom. They took us down a long hallway and opened a door, and when we hurried inside we were in a men's rest room. After a big laugh we made more hand motions and climbed three sets of stairs to the main sanctuary. We took our pictures but wished we could be there on Sunday, when seven services took place.

We never met the pastor, just four maintenance people. But we got on the platform in the world's largest church, where they have seven hundred fifty thousand members. We thanked them and even gave them a hug, then ran for the taxi.

We breathed a sigh of relief to find the taxi still there. But the driver wouldn't move until we paid another forty-two dollars. We had no other way to the airport so we had to pay another forty-two dollars. In football this is known as a fumble, and every fumble will cost you.

Doug met us at the airport in Indonesia. We were tired but happy as could be. On the way to Doug's home, he gave us a report on his work and what he had planned for us for the next ten days. I couldn't believe the schedule, but I was ready for the challenge and decided that Elijah and Hans, being younger, would be a big help in carrying out our duties.

We were here to make a film of Doug's work. However, Indonesia is a big country. Two times we had to fly to other islands. His car also got a huge workout, because we were going to visit some forty-five "outstations" and churches. Some days we traveled eight hours to get to the churches for filming.

We usually visited four or five a day. Our car wasn't the biggest, and there were always several other team members who wanted to go along. Talk about a big load! We had to put all our stuff on top. Getting everything up and into the car rack, then back down again, was quite a job. Plus, every time we stopped for something to eat we were served rice. Three times a day was soon more than I could handle.

So Where's My Passport?

One morning we were driving through the city of Bali, looking at the sights, when suddenly I saw a sign that read Krispy-Kreme Donuts. "Stop!" I yelled. "I'll buy donuts for everyone!" Well, there wasn't anywhere to park, so they pulled over to let me out. They would go around the block and come back.

The city was crowded with people. People were going in every direction as I made my way into the mall to find the donuts. Sure enough, the place was just like a Krispy Kreme at home. I had had enough rice for a year. It was time to splurge.

After what seemed an eternity I got my donuts and made my way through the crowd to find the gang. We had ourselves a fine time, eating donuts and thanking the Lord that I had seen the sign. But an hour or so later I reached for my wallet and passport and I couldn't find either one.

At that point we all got out and searched every inch of the car several times. Nothing showed up. I knew I had lost it when I got the donuts. I was absolutely sick. A thousand things went through my mind. How could I be so dumb? I have traveled all my life. I know the importance of a passport. Plus, all my money was in my wallet—more than five hundred dollars. I didn't know what to do.

We finally decided to go back to where I got out of the car and start from there. Can you imagine what it was like to be eating a donut, "happy as a pig in mud" one minute, and the next minute being overwhelmed by frightening feelings that you've never felt before?

I stood on the street in the middle of the crowd and prayed, "Oh, God, I've got a big problem. Please help me." I felt so hopeless. No passport and no money. I was in Indonesia, a country that was extremely foreign to me. What could be worse?

When we got back to the mall I went inside and made my way to the donut shop. I never saw anything on the floor and, believe me, I looked everywhere. Then I walked to the counter to ask the big question. Just then someone behind the counter yelled, "There he is! The tall white American!"

All the clerks ran from everywhere to see me. Then they said, "You're the one who dropped your passport on the floor. We found it and told each other, 'Give him time. He needs it and he'll return.' We know you have been devastated and sick over this, but now you can breathe again. We all are so happy to give your passport back to you. Here it is."

I don't think I've ever been more relieved than I was in that moment. I began to hug all of the people behind the counter. I begged them to let me give them a gift or buy them all lunch, but they would have none of it. "Your smile of relief was worth everything," they said. Finally, I took a picture, picked up my wallet and passport, and walked away. I waved both arms toward them all the way out of the mall, yelling, "Thank you, thank you. I'll never forget you."

After I was out of sight I looked inside my wallet, in the secret compartment, and all my money was there, untouched.

I don't know what you would call that in football. Was it a fumble? I called it a God moment. I never let that wallet out of my sight the rest of the trip. I was so grateful for how it turned out. Some things you can't describe. One thing for sure, I got a fantastic opinion of the wonderful people of Indonesia.

In a House Built for Two . . .

One day Doug said we were going to meet some teenagers. What happened next moved me, emotionally, to a place I have rarely been. Doug pulled up to a little house, and before we could get out of the car the door of the house opened and about sixteen teenagers came running toward our car. They were so happy to meet us. They shook our hands and were talking a mile a minute. Bringing two handsome boys with me was sure paying off. Then we went inside and heard their story.

In their country, if you live outside the city limits you can only attend school until the seventh grade. Many students want to finish school but can't because they live in the country. So Doug searched until he found a family inside the city that was willing to open their home and let students live with them so the young people could finish their education.

Here they were living together in a house that was way too small for eighteen people. Bedrooms were too small for one person, let alone four or five. The kitchen was very little and they had only one bathroom. I sat down and looked at the couple who had opened their home. What dedication. What love and what sacrifice.

Finally I said to myself, "There has to be a better way." Sixteen young people plus two parents all living together in a house built for two. At that point Doug told us the rest of the story.

He had found a piece of property and had bought it. Plans were being drawn up for a beautiful home that would include everything needed to house twenty teenagers and their house parents. In this way he set out his dream and waited for the Lord to provide someone to build the house.

I was thrilled to hear him tell about our church, Christian Life Assembly of God, Camp Hill, Pennsylvania. They had brought a team of workers to get things started, so we drove over to see what progress they had made. When we got there we literally jumped out of the car and ran inside. The side walls were up, but as yet they had no roof. We could see the big bedrooms, bathrooms, and kitchen. We stood in the middle of the living room, on a dirt floor, and thought about the future of the teenagers who would someday live in these accommodations.

However, Doug told us there wasn't enough money to finish the house and that nothing had been done for the last six months. If there was ever a day when I wished I was a millionaire, it was that day. However, our schedule was still full and we had to keep moving, so we traveled on to other outstations and new churches. Even so, I couldn't get the half-done house off my mind. Later that night, as we were heading home, I asked Doug if we were anywhere near that first home where all the teenagers were living. I wanted to buy some ice cream and stop for a surprise party with the kids.

We found a gas station that had a little grocery market. All they had were ice cream bars in a little freezer, all of which we bought. On the way to the house I had a meeting in the backseat with Elijah and Hans. I asked them if we could gather enough money between us to give every kid five dollars. They said yes, and in few minutes we were ready for our visit.

We drove up to the house expecting that everyone would be in bed. We had already made up our minds to barge in and wake everyone up, right or wrong. But wow! The lights were all on. They were still up doing homework. What a great time for a break. We knocked on the door and waited for the excitement to start.

When they saw us they screamed with joy. After hugging everyone we passed out the ice cream bars and talked about everything we could think of. Then Elijah, Hans, and I started passing out our money. I think that was the happiest offering I ever gave. Sometimes the little things of life bring the biggest blessings.

After coming back home I heard that the New Hope Church in Des Moines, Iowa, sent Doug a twenty-five thousand dollars offering to finish the house. Was that great news or what!

I can't tell you the blessings of my trip to Indonesia. I hope you get to see the film we made. Maybe you would like to build a church with a small donation of $2,500. Doug has a goal of two hundred new churches and has built forty-five to date. You will never regret putting your name on a church you built with your finances. You could be responsible for number forty-six. Just $2,500. Think about it.

-11-

How to Reach an Incredible Maturity

I am terrible about exercising. Duane and I try to play golf once a week, but that only works in the summer. At Christmas this year, Robin asked each member of our family to commit to walking fifty miles this year. I hope to do more than fifty miles.

This past summer our church sponsored a bike tour on a Saturday—a twelve-mile ride. I haven't been on a bike for an extended time for fifty years. Believe me, I was glad when we got to the six-mile post. A sandwich and a cold drink helped me make it back. I was proud of myself.

Visiting our home that day was a young college student from Zambia, Africa. His name was Mukluli Katampi, but we called him Moon. He hadn't been on a bike in a long time but he was excited to go with us. However, Moon didn't totally understand what the ride was all about. He didn't realize we were stopping for lunch at the six-mile post.

Actually, he thought it was a race and the trail was a big circle, and if he went fast he would be back at the starting point before anyone else. Moon passed up everybody and was soon out of sight. He was young and energetic. He was having the time of his life and winning the race, he thought.

What Moon didn't realize was that the trail went straight south for more than thirty miles. There was no circle. When we got to the lunch stop, Moon was nowhere in sight. We didn't know what to do at first but finally we split up, with half of our group going back and half staying to look for Moon.

Eventually we found out what happened. At mile post twenty-three he stopped for a rest and began to realize that maybe something was wrong. At that point someone told him he had to turn around and go back, because it was the only way home. By the time he arrived back at the starting point it was almost nine o'clock, and he had been biking for forty-six miles. There he was—smiling, tired, thirsty, hungry, and with no money.

The moral of the story is, if somebody comes to your house and you decide to do something with them, make sure they understand the plan. Needless to say, I never went on another bike ride.

FIND A NEW CHALLENGE

I always wanted to paint pictures, but my artistic abilities leave much to be desired. So this year Judy surprised me by arranging a series of art lessons. Before I started, the art teacher told me that if I was working on a picture, I should bring it along. Talk about a challenge. I was so embarrassed to take in my picture that I hid it the best I could. I didn't want anyone to see it.

I was ushered into a room with six other artists, some of whom had been taking lessons for more than ten years. I looked around and peeked at some of their pictures. They all were great. All I could say was, "Wow! That's beautiful!"

Jean Moyer, my teacher, came to greet me and made me feel at ease. Before the session was over she had helped me with every part of my picture. She didn't say it, but I knew my painting was all wrong and I needed to start over.

I was a long way from being an artist. But I was encouraged to take all my lessons in the next few weeks. And I was enjoying myself. Now I love Thursday. It's art lesson day.

You're never too old to start something new . . . and I'm finally fulfilling a lifelong dream.

RETAIN YOUR SELF-CONFIDENCE

We all have four deep, undeniable emotional needs in common.

We all need to be loved.

We all need to feel forgiven.

We all need to experience security.

We all need to have adequate hope for the future.

All our other needs for confidence, acceptance, self-esteem, affirmation, freedom, and purpose flow from these four. When these are in place, life doesn't get any better. It's easy to relax when these are cared for.

"For it is God who works in you, both to will and to do for His good pleasure." (Philippians 2:13 NKJV)

BE A MENTOR

Mentoring gives us older people a significant purpose in the fourth quarter. It adds satisfaction to our lives and allows us to teach naturally from experience, and this is what so many younger people desperately need and want. It's a great time to give hope, wisdom, vision, and encouragement.

Poor is the man who goes through life without a mentor. I want to mentor at least twelve people in my lifetime, and I'm well on my way. Sometimes we are mentoring and don't even know it. For example, here is part of a letter I recently received from Sue Duffield:

As a young, aspiring singer in the 70s I attended concerts of well-known Christian artists and would come home disillusioned and disappointed with their live performances. Musically it might have been good, but what they said or didn't say between the songs really bothered me. Rarely would you hear a coherent grunt, let alone a passionate testimony or personal reflection from the stage. Often the audience would give a little advice: "Just sing—don't talk—that's what we paid to hear."

As the quartet circuit rose in popularity, it was better sometimes if the emcee or designated spokesperson for the group didn't talk between their songs. Announcing, "This next song is from our latest album," or repeating some over-used joke bored me to tears.

In 1968 I heard the original Couriers for the first time. Most of us Christian kids were sneaking around listening to the Beatles, Herman's Hermits, or the Rolling Stones on our little transistor radios, and I was convinced I wouldn't be impressed. But much to my surprise I was quite moved. These guys were good and I knew it even at thirteen years of age.

In time, my husband, Jeff, and I both agreed that there is no better tenor than Duane, and no better singer/song-writer than Neil. Our favorite "on the road" game is to rem-inisce about the details of Courier lore. Jeff can tell you what songs are on any given album, who produced them, and who the musicians were. But my earliest memory consists of what Dave said, how Dave told a story, and how he brought it all to meaningful closure at the end of the service. I also remember crying the day Duane got married, but that's another story.

Yes, that's right. Dave got my attention. No one has been more instrumental in giving me a clear vision and pure example of what putting a program together should look and sound like. I still see the children of South Africa; I still smell the streets of foreign cities—and I've never physically been to these places. But I have been there through the amazing word pictures that Dave painted.

One of my favorite Courier songs is "The Vision" from the *Sweet and Shoutin' Spirituals* LP. Neil's vocal in the open-ing verse sets the stage for what's to come and literally blows me away. But my feelings have more to do with Dave's mono-logue than with anything else. This, indeed, is a work of art.

What Dave does in their services, and even on Courier albums, is what I call *framing*. Here's a definitive comparison

between the accrual art of picture framing and "framing—
Dave Kyllonen style."

1. FRAMING A WORK OF ART CAN BE A SIGNIFICANT EXPENSE.

Sometimes the frame can be nearly as costly as the artwork
itself. The Couriers' music portrays Jesus as the artwork, but
Dave has survived at the "expense" of going against the typical "grain" of Gospel Music as it's often presented. He actually says something substantial between songs. And this is not
merely a side dish—it's part of the main course.

2. DON'T FRAME THE ART TO MATCH A ROOM IN YOUR HOUSE.

Avoid framing that overwhelms the artwork. Remember,
the artwork is the star—the matting and framing are just supporting players. Dave has learned the art of self-sacrifice in
his speaking. He portrays Proverbs 25:11 perfectly: "A word
aptly spoken is like apples of gold in settings of silver" (NIV).
He's not nearly as enamored with his own voice as he is with
the voice of the Holy Spirit. And if it were about his own
agenda, he would never introduce Duane or Neil the way he
does, with such endearing admiration.

3. CONSULT THE ARTIST.

Understand what the artist is portraying and do not take
away from his concept. This requires "consultation time." I
don't doubt that Dave has spent quality time with the ultimate
Artist. A great communicator knows the power of persuasion,
but never abuses or interferes with the real message.

4. FRAMING GUARDS ITS VALUE.

Be sure to secure your painting for preservation. It's no
wonder that Dave, Duane, and Neil have new life, even in

their later years. They have guarded and protected their true value. They're still doing what they've always done—building their lives around the Holy One.

I will leave you with this. I don't think I impressed Dave in my early years of speaking. It seems funny now to look back, but I felt he barely tolerated my female frivolity on stage. He never said much to me but I had lots to learn. Even the late Rev. Thomas Zimmerman told a congregation once, "Sue reminds me of the Little General."

Now, was he referring to the silent movie or Napoleon himself? Either way, I decided to smooth out my rough edges, for which I needed to spend some time with a framer. So I became a hardworking student. I watched, listened, and took notes. I wanted to speak so that others would be inspired and encouraged. I wasn't content to just sing—I wanted to say something with substance, too.

Eventually, things started to change. To quote from a private journal entry, Michael Sykes (producer of the Gaither Vocal Band) recently said: "Sue knows how to not only stay out of the way of a lyric, but how to convey it with passion."

Thanks, Michael, but you have no idea how I got there. It didn't come overnight. Getting out of the way but still conveying the lyrics with passion should be the goal of every speaker or musician. It takes diligence and a teachable spirit. Dave set the standard for me.

As I shared this across a dinner table with Dave and Judy recently, I could feel my heart beat fast. I could hardly get the words out. "Can we somehow, someway teach this to every singer and musician? You know—to our aspiring worship leaders and artists? In our prepackaged, finely tuned, orchestrated worship services, can somebody p-l-e-a-s-e show spontaneity and anointing while still knowing what to say?"

At that moment Dave leaned across the table, grabbed my hand, and said, "Write that. Put that in our book!" Dave's message still resonates in my heart.

Jesus said, "Go ye into all the world, and preach the Gospel to every creature" (Mark 16:15). This command is not obsolete. It's still vital. It bears eternal rewards. Will you, even now, ask God for a new vision?

—Sue Duffield
Singer/speaker/songwriter

Correct Your Errors

Douglas MacArthur once said:

You are as young as your faith, as old as your doubt; as young as your self-confidence, as old as your fear; as young as your hope as old as your despair. In the central place of every heart there is a recording chamber. So long as it receives messages of beauty, hope, cheer and courage, so long are you young. When your heart is covered with the snows of pessimism and the ice of cynicism, then, and then only, are you grown old. And then, indeed as the ballad says, you just fade away.

When are we old? When we think we are. The question is often asked, "When are you going to sing your last song?" As long as we think we can sing, most of us won't quit. Somebody might have to tell us it's time to give it up, but until then our hearts still go on singing.

Spend Time With Your Spouse.

Judy and I are having a great time in our fourth quarter. We have scored many touchdowns together, and according to the scoreboard we are winning the game. Our family got together and planned a boat cruise for our fiftieth anniversary. All eighteen of us are on for the trip of a lifetime. I love the adventure of it all!

Pass the Baton to the Next Generation

After football, the sport I like next is track. I always wanted to run the relays. Passing the baton was always of interest. Now in my final quarter, I'm looking back to remember who passed the baton to me.

Otis Keener, my pastor when I was a teenager, passed me his baton. I took hold of it and ran as fast as I could. I wanted to be in the ministry no matter how many times I had to run around the track with that baton.

Later on, a missionary named Maynard Ketchum came to our church and passed me the baton of missions. His stories of life in Africa stirred me deeply. After ministering in sixty countries, I'm still carrying that baton.

But, now I'm looking for the young man who waits at the end of my run, to take the baton another leg of the race. Actually, we are all running the race and getting ready to pass the baton to the next runner. The Bible is very clear—the Gospel must be preached to the next generation.

> Therefore, since we are surrounded by such a huge crowd of witnesses to the life of faith, let us strip off every weight that slows us down, especially the sin that so easily hinders our progress. And let us run with endurance the race that God has set before us. (Hebrews 12:1 NLT)

Hold firmly to the word of life; then, on the day of Christ's return, I will be proud that I did not run the race in vain and that my work was not useless. (Philippians 2:16 NLT)

Do you not know that in a race all the runners run, but only one gets the prize? Run in such a way as to get the prize. (2 Timothy 4:7 NIV)

I have fought a good fight, I have finished the race and I have remained faithful. (2 Timothy 4:7 NLT)

STAYING IRRESISTIBLE

The big question in my mind is: What makes a husband irresistible? I don't have all the answers but let me offer a few suggestions.

Always be a gentleman. Keep opening the car door for your wife. Never stop chasing the bus.

Men who are irresistible are full of kindness. Kindness is attractive in a man.

Men who know how to control their spirit are irresistible. Wives want their husbands to control their tempers. When you blow your cool you become a loser. In fifty years of marriage I have yet to raise my voice to my wife or children.

Husbands need to recognize their wives' gifts. For a long time our life centered on me. It seemed like everything we did concerned the Couriers. Judy soon got involved with the youth of our church and for twenty years she cared for the youth department. During our Homefire years she was on the platform every night, singing and giving her testimony. She is the most important person in my life.

Establish a good reputation.

Be honest.

Ladies, what makes you irresistible?

Poise is attractive in a woman. Any lady who can walk into a room of twenty other ladies and feel comfortable with herself, by the way she dresses, the way she combs her hair, and the way she talks and carries herself, has poise.

She must know how to give her husband praise and admiration.

She must be grateful.

Her behavior must be above reproach.

Life Is About Finishing Strong

Jesus gives us a desire to work. Then He gives us the confidence to get started. Strength always follows. Grace is always abounding. The working of inner principles and moral vision result from what Christ does for us. The final quarter really becomes exciting when you understand this concept.

We were asked to sing for a senior's banquet at the Red Mountain Church in Phoenix, Arizona. We were sitting at our table before our concert started. Pastor Jeff Peterson asked if we had room for one more. The fellow in question then introduced himself as Joe Jackson. We all perked up instantly. The famous Joe Jackson, as in football? He was, and that started a conversation that could have lasted all night. Joe took off his Super Bowl ring and let us put it on our fingers. He was quite a man with a great story—and here it is.

It was a typical December Sunday afternoon in Bloomington, Minnesota. Fifty thousand fans crammed into the old Metropolitan Stadium to cheer the Purple People Eaters to victory. The temperatures had plummeted to ten degrees below zero. Our coach, Bud Grant, was old school. He would not allow his players the luxury of gloves or heaters. We were twenty-four points down to San Francisco going into the final quarter. Our Hall of Fame quarterback, Fran Tarkenton, had sustained a broken leg. The 49ers were not our only opponent. The clock was against us too. It didn't look good. Our loyal fans began to boo. Did I mention that it was cold?

Into the game entered a rookie quarterback named Tommy Kramer. You're right. What's a Tommy Kramer? That question was answered with two strikes to a wide open receiver, Ahmad Rashad. The Viking scored two more touchdowns and the Purple People Eaters' defense shut out the 49er's offense. We won the game 28 to 27 on December 4, 1977. It was the greatest deficit that the Minnesota Vikings have ever overcome.

Many years have passed since that memorable afternoon, but I've taken a number of lessons from that game. One lesson is to never allow circumstances to shut down your dream, purpose, and destiny. Stay focused on the game and not the scoreboard. After all, the scoreboard only tells who has the most points. The Vikings went to four Super Bowls and lost them all. And yet, over time we learned to focus on what we did accomplish, not our losses.

No matter where you are in your journey, I believe that life is about finishing strong, it your best even though your best might not be enough. As a former NFL player I'm constantly looking back at my nine-year career. What could I have done that would have elevated me to the Hall of Fame or extended my career another year or two? Did I give it my best shot? Had I known that 1981 would be my final quarter, what would I have done differently?

In 1984 the Lord called me into full-time evangelism. He prepared me for this work from the foundations of the world. When the final whistle blows I do not want to look back with regret. I want to hear, "Well done, good and faithful servant."

Recently I attended a Gospel concert that featured a well-known trio, the Couriers. The Couriers have been together since the mid-50s, but this was the first time I had heard them live. Their voices were strong, their pitch and harmonies were succinct and angelic. Their gifts speak for themselves. However, what was most impressive was their passion for each other and their love for the Lord. They were one voice and one heart—a servant's heart.

In their fifty-plus years of ministry, the Couriers have established themselves as one of the industry's best. Countless awards and nominations have set them apart. Fifty years ago they began a journey. While others did not finish the race, the Couriers have now entered into what some may describe as their final quarter. Yet they still have work to do. Until the clock runs out and the whistle blows, the game is not over. We are called to finish strong. Run the race. Fight the good fight. Fulfill the Great Commission.

—*Joe Jackson*
Evangelistic Ministries

KEEP ALL RELATIONSHIPS INTACT

We have been friends with the Oak Ridge Boys for more than fifty years. Their letter below, filled with memories of shared concerts, brought comfort and love to us. I just have to let you read it.

Dear Dave, Duane, and Neil:

Very few groups are good enough to capture and hold my attention for a full album. However, when Duane came to a recent concert of ours, he brought with him a complete catalog of Couriers music. I started listening and did not listen to anything else until I finished listening to the entire musical journey of the Couriers. Great songs, unique harmonies, unusual arrangements, great vocal talent, unlimited variety—and the descriptions just go on and on. All with a positive way of life found in following Jesus Christ. You Couriers have always had "your own thing." You have assembled a work that has carried you around the world, as you have sung individually and as a group, adding different group members to the mix.

But the threesome of Dave, Duane, and Neil has been the foundation of that Couriers sound that has improved with time. I consider you friends. I have always respected you as wonderful Christian men, and you are three of the best singers in the business of Gospel Music. You three did more to establish Gospel Music in the northeast than any other Gospel group. Your huge concerts in Pennsylvania were always the highlights of our year.

We loved working those great spectacular events, promoted by the Couriers. I am happy to lend my name to the history of the Couriers.

One of my favorite songs came from the Couriers. Neil wrote, "Oh, the Joy of Knowing Jesus." I get a chill every time I hear that song. No man has ever sung "Christ Returneth" like Duane Nicholson. I will never forget what a great speaker Dave is. He is truly the "Master of Ceremonies."

God bless you guys!

—*Duane Allen - Oak Ridge Boys*
Nashville, Tennessee

-12-

Who Likes Gospel Music?

After thousands of concerts, the last few years of singing have been so rewarding. The sense of satisfaction and well-being has been overwhelming. The love from the audience has been so emotional. Duane, Neil, and I get in our van after each concert and sit with smiles on our faces as hundreds of miles go by.

We always end every trip home with Neil saying, "Enboyed you joys." He has been saying that for all fifty years. Duane and I wait every time we get home to see if he'll forget to say it. When he does we all laugh and repeat the phrase together in three-part harmony. What a way to say "good-bye." Sounds like something we could write on our tombstones.

I love being the emcee of our group. I get to create the program for the evening. I get to be the straight man. Duane and Neil are very easy to work with. Neil fits his sharp wit in between my pauses, and Duane knows all the facts about everything we are discussing at the time. It all works for us and we enjoy being spontaneous.

As I'm writing my portion of this book, Duane and Neil are writing theirs. We do not know what each other is writing, but I know Duane's part will be full of facts that Neil and I have long forgotten. Neil will write his part like he writes a song. Every word will be in its proper place, with great emotion.

In a concert, some of the things we talk about are not planned and haven't been used before. Sometimes I want to write it down so we could use it again. But I forget it, so I say to myself, "Don't worry, we'll have something new to say the next time."

We close every concert with what I sometimes call the two-minute warning. There are two two-minute warnings in every football game. One comes at the end of the first half and the other comes at the end of the last quarter. We love to leave something of eternal value with the crowd. We always pray a blessing on those who spend an evening with us. Many times we give an altar call for people who want to find forgiveness for their sins.

We hear wonderful stories at our concerts. Stories like:

"We have been married for over thirty years and we had our first date at one of your concerts."

"Our dad and mom came to your concert many years ago and bought your records and tapes. We kids went to sleep every night with the songs of the Couriers. Now it's our favorite music."

Grandma Davis, from Salunga, Pennsylvania, told us that when they would be getting ready for church on Sunday mornings her two dogs would hear the Couriers' theme song on channel 8 and come running from the other end of the house to sit in front of the TV until our program was over. She told us at least a hundred times, "And that's the truth." We were on channel 8 for twelve years.

Now, I don't know if doggies go to heaven when they die, but when I get there if I see those Davis doggies, I'm going to say, "Um-hmm—it was all those years of sitting in front of the TV, watching the Couriers."

-13-
Three Great Sons-in-Law

When I began my final quarter I found myself looking back at something that has brought me many smiles and lots of happiness. The three men who married my three daughters have made me very happy. Greg, Mike, and Paul have outdone themselves as husbands and dads. All three give 100% toward helping their families enjoy life.

GREGORY T. HOLLIS, THE SOUND MAN AND THE FIRST SON IN THE DOOR

Some of my fondest memories of Greg came when we were the pastors of the church in Davenport, Iowa. For seven years we took turns preaching the two Sunday services.

Many said, "That will never work." We sure proved them wrong. I knew that if Greg was ever going to become a great preacher he would have to get in the pulpit every week. Listening to me all the time would never make him a preacher. And after seven years I knew he was ready to pastor his own church. Some guys have all the talent. Greg played the trumpet, sang great, and preached up a storm. He became the music pastor and the youth pastor at the same time. Greg had to be the busiest associate pastor ever.

I hope I live long enough to see what all Greg will do for the kingdom of God. I love you, Gregory—thanks for taking Kristie to be your wife!

What Gregory says next brings a smile to everyone's face.

When I met Kristie Kay Kyllonen at Central Bible College in the late 70s I never could have dreamed of the future we would have together. As two lives and family systems came together into one, we soon discovered how the Lord had perfectly matched us for the plans and purposes He had designed us for.

In our twenty-six years of marriage we have been all over the world, ministering side by side and with our children for Jesus. What a thrill it has been. We have had the opportunity to work alongside each of our birth families as well, and the blessings and lessons we have gleaned are too numerous to recount. I praise the Lord for the amazing godly heritage we have received from the Hollis and Kyllonen lineages, which we don't take lightly and are in the process of passing on to the next generation of leaders. Elijah Tyrone, Isaiah Threll, and Alexsondra Kabri are each marching forth with torches in hand to take their generation for God. What more could we ask for? We are wealthy beyond comparison because of all the spiritual treasure that has been handed down to us from our parents and beyond.

When I was in Bible college searching for a wife, I followed my parents' advice and looked not only for a wife but for a ministry partner and a mother for my children. When I found Kristie I found a treasure. Thank you, Dave and Judy, for raising Kristie to be the most wonderful woman of God. She has such incredible insight into the rearing of children and is a ministry partner par excellence.

Mike Hammer Came Next

Mike married Connie. He is from Wisconsin. Everyone from there is a Green Bay Packers fan, but we try not to hold that against him. Mike is right in the middle of the pack. It's been tough on me, because every time the Steelers play the Packers, the Packers win. It sure has brought some great conversations into our family.

When I asked Mike what he thought about our final quarter he immediately knew where he fit. He said, "I think I was the offensive coordinator for our family." You're right, Mike. Here is what he writes:

Every team utilizes an offensive coordinator—someone who is in charge of the offense, who designs and scripts plays and thus allows the head coach to focus on overall (and often more important) issues during the game. He carries the play book and calls the plays, under the direction of the head coach.

During the thirteen years of ministry our families shared, called Homefire, I served as offensive coordinator for many seasons. From calling the plays (preparing the order of service) each time we ministered, to designing an offensive strategy (ministry promotion and marketing), to game management (handling the finances), I was part of a success-ful ministry.

I owe a lot of who I am to my head coach, father-in-law, and terrific friend, Dave Kyllonen, because of the ministry example he modeled before me, the belief he had in my abilities, and the firm yet sensitive tutelage he provided.

I have been able to build upon the firm foundation of leadership established during those years. His confidence in handing the playbook over to me has given me the confidence and inspiration to move on and lead my own team as a head coach.

Now as pastor of a new church I am grateful for the influence of one of the greats, a hall-of-famer for sure. Every day, under the direction of the Holy Spirit, I make important decisions that have the potential to influence people's destinies. Not a single day goes by when I don't refer back, in some way, to those glory days of serving together with Dave Kyllonen.

Thanks, coach—Hammertime!

—Mike Hammer
Dillsburg, Pennsylvania

Paul Eschbach Came Next

Paul Eschbach joined our family when he married our daughter Robin. They were only married a month when our family decided to travel together. Paul brought so many gifts to our ministry. He could play the piano, sing, loved drama, and living in a RV sounded exciting! He always jumped in with both feet to do anything that was needed.

People never understood how we could travel together and keep up an almost impossible pace, but everyone pitched in and the years went by fast. Nowadays, Paul and Robin and their family live so close to me that it's still quite easy to keep tabs on them. I'm proud of what Paul and Robin are doing in their ministry. What a blessing they are to the kingdom of God.

"Hey, Dave, can I say a few words?" Sure, Paul . . .

Every once in a while I hear somebody exclaim, "Bring me back the good old days." I then wonder how far back they would like to go? Before anesthesia? Dentists? Malls?

When Robin and I look back over our lives, we both breathe a grateful, satisfying sigh and then remark about how it has all led to "this," our current place in life: Robin, a stay-at-home mom, a leader at church; Paul, self-employed as a Board Certified Behavior Analyst, working with children on the Autism Spectrum; Erica and Ellie, 15 and 13, living out their teenage dreams in a small town in Pennsylvania.

When Robin and I reminisce we can't help but look back at the markers that helped guide us. Foremost among those are the years we spent with our family in Homefire. Learning how to live in tight quarters led to many laughs and created priceless pictures and videos to watch when we're old.

When most people look back, they can see the earlier sacrifice and energy placed into their marriage, their children, and their work. We're no exception and also enjoy looking back at the precious memories created with Dave, Judy, and family. Never in a million years could we have predicted our current life. Thanks, Dave Kyllonen, for passing on to Robin and me the gift of dreaming and risk taking. We'll do our best to nurture it and pass it on to our girls. God has certainly done an amazing work, above and beyond all that we could have asked.

Paul — the Bachmobile!

- 14 -

A Final Quarter Inspiration

10. Coming together is a beginning, keeping together is progress, and working together is success.

9. As a rule, you will find that those who complain about the way the ball bounces are usually the ones who dropped it.

8. It pays to advertise. There are twenty-six mountains higher than Pikes Peak.

7. Do the right thing and you will please some people and astonish the rest.

6. A contented person is one who enjoys the scenery along the detour.

5. No man finds out what he believes until he begins to instruct his children.

4. If we built bridges instead of fences we could charge tolls.

3. Church members are like autos; they start missing before they quit.

2. You cannot decide when or where you will die, but you can decide how you will live.

1. The six ages of man: spills, drills, bills, ills, pills, and wills.

0. Marriage agreement: When wife stops driving from the backseat and husband quits cooking from the dining room table.

- 15 -

Exceeding My Dreams

Some weekends we are still driving in the fast lane. After Friday and Saturday night concerts and two services on Sunday, the long drive home feels like we are at it full-time again. I sometimes almost think I can hear us saying, "Let's get over in the other lane and slow down."

I'm not sure when that will happen, but retirement isn't yet a part of our regular conversations. We do not feel ineffective in our work for the Lord.

Philippians 2:16–18 (NLT):

Hold firmly to the word of life; then, on the day of Christ's return, I will be proud that I did not run the race in vain and that my work was not useless. But I will rejoice even if I lose my life, pouring it out like a liquid offering to God, just like your faithful service is an offering to God. And I want all of you to share that joy. Yes, you should rejoice, and I will share your joy.

In his great book *Think About It*, our good friend and president of Valley Forge Christian College, Don Meyer, tells about Reverend Kim, the pastor of the Full Gospel New York Church. I liked what he said about life and football:

In life, as in athletics, half time is a time to look back and a time to look ahead. As we look back, we glean from our victories and our defeats, our good times and our bad times. Half time is a time to ponder where we have been and where we are going.

In 1950, anyone who was fifty years old was nearing the latter part of his life. Today, many people are living productive lives at eighty years of age. It is actually not unusual for someone to live to be a hundred years old and, in time, we will probably see that happen more often. With our lives lasting longer, cultivating a "half time" mentality becomes more strategic than ever.

One thing that bothers us about our final quarter is this. In football, every quarterback fears being blindsided. It happens when you can't see the opponent coming. You cock your arm to throw, concentrating only on those in front of you, and *wham!* Your whole body snaps and you're crushed to the ground, wondering, "Where did he come from?"

Usually, after an unusual happening or great concert, we crash and find ourselves reflecting back to what God is doing with us. Or sometimes, during our down times, the devil brings discouragement.

Then I hear the coach say, "Read the blitz, Kyllonen; read the blitz!" I always want to yell, "Easier said than done."

However, over the years I've learned that it's not deficits in our spirituality or our character that dog us. But we have expended so much energy in getting there and delivering our messages that sometimes we don't have much reserve left.

Our ultimate goal in life is heaven. Remember, if you're a quarterback all your passes are completed in heaven. There are no defensive backs up there in heaven—isn't that when we receive our Super Bowl crowns?

I love that old song: "And when the battle's over, we shall wear a crown, we shall wear a crown, we shall wear a crown. And when the GAME is over we shall wear a crown in the New Jerusalem."

Or: "Until then my heart will go on singing. Until then with joy I'll carry on. Until the day my eyes behold that city. Until the day God calls me home."

See you at the rewards ceremony!

Nothing I Could Have Predicted

by Duane Nicholson

INTRODUCTION

When you record an album in a studio, one of the most difficult challenges is getting the right "feeling" for a particular song. In personal appearances you have an audience to feed off and relate to. Not so in the studio, when all you have for inspiration is a microphone, a headset, and an engineer sitting behind a glass partition in another room.

That is why prayer is most important before recording. The listener cannot see the person singing but they can certainly "feel" the heart of the singer. I cannot count the times that an engineer has said to me, "Let's do that song one more time, with 'feeling'!" In other words, get your soul into what you are saying in the song!

When we three Couriers got back together in 2003, the most rewarding comment in the days that lay ahead was, "The sound is still there, but it is more what we feel than what we hear." That, my friend, has to be the Holy Spirit moving through our songs, and if that is the case, Praise God! Our voices may be weaker but our spirits are strong.

I pray that as you read my portion of this book you will "feel" my innermost feelings of gratitude to God, Dave, and Neil and their families, our friends, and most of all to my dear wife, Jean Ann, my daughters, Shannon and Meredith, my two sons-in-law, Fred and Kristian, and my two granddaughters, Aria and Elise. Life would be empty without all of you.

—Duane Nicholson

- 1 -

One More Time, With Feeling

I was born in 1936 in Montezuma, Iowa. My father and mother had been gloriously saved in a tent revival in Montezuma a few years before. By the time I arrived they had already been through some troublesome times with my mother's family.

When Dad and Mom were married, my mother's father, who was a wealthy farmer, gave them farm implements and set them up on eighty acres of land to help them get started. The trouble began when Mom and Dad went to a Pentecostal tent revival. Rev. Morris Plotts was the fiery evangelist. People were being "born again" by the hundreds. Dad and Mom went forward one evening, and that changed their lives.

One day, while Dad was in a cornfield working, God spoke audibly to him and told him to enter the ministry. I don't know what the conversation was like between Mom and Dad, but it must have been quite the scene. Mom knew that her father would be furious.

First of all, she had married a man beneath the standard of living that her family was used to. My father's parents were dirt poor, trying to scrape things together on a small farm. My grandfather Nicholson supplemented his income by hunting, trapping, and fishing along the Skunk River. Fur pelts were worth money back then, and killing small animals and catching fish helped keep the family in food.

My mom and dad were so in love they ignored her parents' objections by traveling to another town and getting married in the living room of the officiating minister. Grandfather Hull did give them that land to live on, but when my parents announced to her parents that they were entering the ministry, that was the final straw. Grandfather Hull immediately disowned them, which lasted until my older brother, Robert, the first grandchild, was born. Only then were the Hulls and the Nicholsons reunited as a family.

Early Ministry Life

When my parents entered the ministry, they went back to Montezuma, Iowa, the place of their conversion, and started a church. That was the scene before I arrived as the second child.

Montezuma proved a hard place to start, so before long we moved to Lynn Grove, Iowa. Thus began a parade of moves before I finally left home for Bible school in 1955. Years later I would take the Couriers to Montezuma to show them exactly where I was born. To my chagrin, the only thing left was the stump of a large tree that had stood in the front yard, and pieces of a foundation where the house had been.

After Lynn Grove we moved to Fort Dodge, Iowa, where my formal education began. I started Kindergarten just a few blocks from our parsonage, next door to the little church with a sawdust floor and a potbellied stove for heat in the winter. I remember that stove very well. One Sunday, while church was in full swing, the vent stuck in the closed position. When the pressure became too strong the stove doors popped open and hot smoke came pouring out into that little auditorium.

Parishioners ran for the doors to escape. I can imagine anyone going by that little "fanatical Pentecostal Church" at that moment, being shocked to see people pouring out the doors at full speed! We were known as "Holy Rollers" but now we were Holy Runners, chased by Holy Smoke!

Fort Dodge was the birthplace of my only sister. My brother and I had requested a sister, and Mom and Dad told us to pray earnestly. Our prayers were answered early one morning when Dad woke Bob and me and took us into the master bedroom to see the bouncing new baby girl. Janet became the delight of our young lives and still is my delight today.

While in Fort Dodge my father was commissioned as an air-raid warden for our section of town. The Second World War was still in progress, and many evenings we heard mock air-raid warnings. When the sirens came it was Dad's job to go around his section of town, on foot, to make sure that everyone had extinguished any outside lights and pulled the window shades so the enemy could not see the lights of town from the air.

Rationing of tires and food staples were facts of life during those dreadful days. Every Monday I was given a small bottle of sugar. That bit of sugar had to last me an entire week. It was a welcome relief when the war was finally over.

After Fort Dodge our family moved to Kirksville, Missouri. Our stay there lasted only six months. The church was a downtown storefront, and the only thing I remember about the town was that the local bar was just a block away from the church. On summer nights we could hear the music from the jukebox. We had no air-conditioning, so the doors of both the church and the bar were open. The most famous song of the day was "Pistol Packin' Mama." I was not more than seven years old but to this day I can still hear that crazy song playing over and over.

We would have starved to death in Kirksville, so we moved to Breckenridge, Missouri, which had a much stronger church. My dad worked at the grocery store as a butcher, and in the late summer he hired out to pick corn. Dad was a tough farm boy, and it became folklore around town that my dad could pick one hundred bushels of corn a day without breaking a sweat. All he needed was a little strap that fit over his hand, with a metal point on one end that snapped the ear away from the stalk, at which point he threw the ear into a wagon following along. Hard work for a minister, but Dad was determined to take care of his family no matter the cost.

Things My Father Taught Me

Preaching was never easy for my father, who quit school after the eighth grade. He never went to Bible school to learn how to preach, so in truth he learned on his knees, by hearing from God what needed to be said. To this day I don't know of a single preacher who prayed as much as my father. Every church he ever led learned very quickly the importance of prayer.

My father never taught me how to play ball, to fish, or to hunt, but the things he taught me about life have sustained me all these years. Later on I learned to fly an airplane, to scuba dive, to play golf, and even to play basketball in college, but those things pale in comparison to what my father taught me—of honesty, loyalty, humility, how to pray, how to maintain a work ethic, and how to have compassion for other people.

Breckenridge was a typical small Missouri town with not much going on. It was a farming community so we never wanted for meat, milk, and eggs. One of my important jobs was to ride my bicycle to a farm at the edge of town and bring home the milk. I had to be careful not to jostle the bottle too much. When I got home, Mom would carefully skim the cream off the top for coffee and cooking.

I do remember one traumatic night in Breckenridge. The house next door to us caught fire when a loud explosion shook the rear. When I looked out our second-floor window, flames were already shooting above the roof next door. I grabbed my clothes and ran, thinking that our house was going up as well. Neighbors from down the street caught hold of me and made sure I was all right.

The only fire truck in town arrived after many agonizing minutes and wet down the side of our home to protect it. Then, just as the firemen finished soaking our house with water, the fire truck quit functioning. I had seen this old relic in local parades and it proudly made the parade route without breaking down, but it was widely known that it broke down many times when it was needed for fires.

We stayed the usual four or five years in Breckenridge, and then Dad got the call to try out in Creston, Iowa. This was a big-time move to a much larger town, and closer to our grand-parents' homes near New Sharon, Iowa.

A Different Kind of Church

The Creston church was quite different from the other smaller churches Dad had led. It was a converted old Methodist Church located in the center of downtown Creston. It also had a large young people's group, and in that church I made my first commitment to Christ—as did Robert and Janet.

I remember the night Janet accepted Christ. She was the only one to respond to the altar call that time and I saw an immediate change in her young life, even at five. Today, my sister is one of the most dedicated Christian ladies I have ever known. She was so much more talented than I could ever be. Unlike me, she chose to stay in the home church after gradu-ation from high school. She had fallen in love with a wonder-ful young man, Wendell Wilson, and has spent her life raising two boys and playing piano and organ in their church in Wood-ward, Oklahoma. She was always busy singing for weddings, funerals, and church functions. Finally, a few years ago she and Wendell moved to Springfield, Missouri, to be near some of their grandchildren and their youngest son.

Rev. Lela Haycook was the evangelist when we all accepted Christ. I had the privilege of seeing Rev. Haycook again in the early 1980s. I was ministering in South Dakota after Dave, Neil, and I had disbanded. I had heard that she was living in semi-retirement in Mobridge, South Dakota, so I drove two hundred miles to meet with her. Now crippled by age, she was still making a meager living by sewing clothes for local people.

She remembered being with us so many times in revival services in many churches in Iowa. I told her what I had been doing. Then I got her to talk about her ministry. She showed me a small black book. That book was filled with the names of people who had received the baptism of the Holy Spirit under her ministry. The book was crammed full of names. I then asked her if she had any account of those who accepted Christ in her meetings. She said that there were just too many to put into a book. Those names are in the Lamb's Book of Life.

When I told her that I traveled by bus with the Couriers, she told me that she also traveled by Greyhound. She had no car. All she carried was a small suitcase and her Bible. She stayed with members of each church, or in the local parsonage with the pastor and his wife. She showed me a record of the offerings she had received. When I saw the great sacrifice this dear lady had made, I wept openly. I owed my spiritual and perhaps physical life to her, for she had presented the Gospel to a preacher's boy who had heard the message repeatedly since birth but had never taken heed.

PAYING JOBS AT LAST

I had my first real job in Creston. When I became old enough I began to spend summers on the farm with my grandfather, learning to drive a tractor and doing all the farming chores.

Those were glorious days for me—I credit my farm days for giving me a solid work ethic. I worked with Grandfather Hull and my uncle, Junior Hull. Uncle Junior had been a bomber pilot with General Chenault in the China theater of World War II. He flew countless missions in the Far East yet came home unscathed, where he decided to raise pigs on the farm.

The smell of pigs was overwhelming, but I labored with my uncle many long hours. When the pigs were born we slept in the hog house to make sure the newborns were not smothered by the sows in their little cubicles. I helped put rings in their noses to keep them from rooting in the dirt of the hog lot and making a mess. I should be deaf from the sound of screaming pigs, since I was the one who held them between my legs as the rings were put in.

I learned to plow with a team of horses and later learned to drive the Allis-Chalmers tractors. The farm taught me about how life begins and what hard work it is to provide food for our consumption. One of my least-favorite jobs was helping to fertilize the fields before planting season. Those who know about farming know that the manure from farm animals is not discarded but is spread on the fields as fertilizer. In those days, things were not as automated as they are today. The manure spreader was pulled by the tractor, but the driver could not start the conveyor belt that pulled the manure back to the revolving blades at the rear of the spreader. Can you guess who sat on a small seat at the front of the spreader and moved a lever to start and stop the conveyor? I lost count of how many times I was hit in the back of the head by a hardened piece of cow manure from an old cow pie.

My first paying job was a newspaper route of my own. Having spending money I earned by myself was such a thrill. I remember one very special day, when the election of a new President of the United States was underway. I was in the back of the newspaper office, getting my papers, which featured that famous headline saying that Thomas Dewey had defeated Harry S. Truman. I had just finished folding my papers when the boss came out and asked us to turn them all back in, because he had just learned that Truman had pulled out a stunning last-minute victory. When the Al Gore Florida vote fight came along in 2000, all I could think of was that Thomas Dewey could have protested and sent the country into confusion and disarray, but for the good of the country he accepted defeat. That was a true statesman.

My First Tornado

In Creston we had our first encounter with a devastating tornado. In those days there were no warning sirens, but I remember looking out the window of our parsonage at the raging storm. I stepped out onto our front porch to watch the large hailstones and the ever-increasing rain and wind. My mother had no idea I was on the porch. As I looked down our street I saw a large tree being lifted out of the ground. I called to my mom when the tree went flying, and she ushered me back into the house because she realized that a tornado had passed by just a few hundred yards away.

The storm subsided as quickly as it came, and then the phone rang. The police said that our church had suffered extensive damage. I remember making my way, with my dad, through debris to the church. To our dismay the entire front roof of the church had been peeled back and was lying over on the other. A large supporting beam had crashed down through the sanctuary and was lying across the pulpit area of the demolished, rain-soaked auditorium. Our sanctuary was ruined.

Fortunately, we were able to use another section of the church, which housed a small auditorium. However, we had been warned to watch for signs of structural failure on this portion of the building. One Sunday morning, during the service, we heard a tremendous crash overhead. It was summertime and the windows were open. My brother was sitting with his buddy by an open window, and they both dove out. I was sitting toward the back and bolted out the back door and down the steep stairs. I did not stop running until I was across the street by a local school.

When I turned around, fully expecting to see the building collapsing, people were still streaming down the stairs at full speed. Once again, anyone driving by that church at that moment would have been in total shock at what they saw. However, the building did not fall down; wet plaster from the ceiling of the Sunday school rooms had fallen onto the floor just above where we were worshiping.

I idolized my older brother, Bob. He was the outgoing one. He kept the bullies at school from picking on me and he was also creative. He built beautiful sailboats almost from scratch. I watched as he carved out holes in the backs of little cars, put little compressed gas cartridges in, and punctured the cartridges with a nail. The little cars would go flying across the yard at breakneck speed.

He also had an erector set and a chemistry set. Somewhere he found directions on how to build little pipe bombs. In those days you could buy a dynamite fuse at the local hardware store. He found bullets somewhere else and opened them up to harvest the gunpowder. He would then cut a small piece of pipe and melt lead to seal off one end. He would put the gunpowder in the middle of the pipe, place the dynamite fuse in the middle of that, and then seal the other end with paper and lead. He now had a small but lethal bomb, and it didn't take us long to figure out how to use it.

Our neighbors were a kindly elderly couple. In their retirement years they kept busy tending a rather large chicken coop, and from time to time they would give us a nice big fryer for our table. However, the dirtiest part of keeping chickens is dealing with all their droppings. When the chicken yard got covered, these folks would rake the droppings into a pile, then someone would come and dispose of them.

Bob and I waited until a fresh pile was formed. Then one evening we made our way next door, stuck the pipe bomb in the middle of the pile, lit the fuse, and ran for our lives. We were stupid to do this but smart enough to use a long fuse. When that bomb went off even the perpetrators were shocked at the loud explosion. We looked in amazement as a mushroom cloud of chicken droppings rose in the air. Neighbors came rushing out and we stood thunderstruck. Fortunately the police were not called, but we felt the sting of our father's belt on our little behinds for days to come.

- 2 -

Days of
Preparation

After another five years it was time to leave once again for a church. This time we made our way to Woodbine in western Iowa, very close to the Nebraska-Iowa border.

I bought my first radio and record player in Woodbine. I also saw my first television programs there. A local store put a set in their display window and placed an audio speaker outside the window. Many a day after school, I would rush downtown to stand and watch this brand-new sensation.

In Woodbine I also started my first business, mowing lawns in the summer and shoveling sidewalks in the winter. And when I was not mowing grass I was once again on the farm, helping our neighbors plant and cultivate corn. I also detasseled corn for seed companies. Plus, we milked several cows each morning by hand. Farming was not easy but I enjoyed it to the fullest.

In my junior year, which turned out to be my last in Iowa, I joined the marching band as a trumpet player. I also got my driver's license—a piece of cake because I had been driving farm equipment since I was ten years old. A car was simple compared to a tractor with a large wagon hitched on behind.

As soon as I got my driver's license I was asked to bring elderly people to church. I also transported Vacation Bible School helpers in the summer. On Saturday evenings in the summer, we rode with Mom and Dad and some of our church members to surrounding towns to hold what were called "Street Meetings." Mom had a portable pump organ, and others brought trumpets, tambourines, and accordions. We would sing and pass out tracts, and then Dad would preach his salvation message.

Lifelong friendships were forged from our years in Woodbine. One such friend is Homer Smith. We hunted squirrels, went fishing for bullheads, and just hung out together. When a storm came up we would run to a haystack in a field on the way to Homer's house and burrow into the side to get away from the rain. In one such storm we would have been pelted by golf ball-sized hailstones. The haystack saved us from serious injury.

Later on Homer moved to Omaha, the nearest large city. He worked for the railroad for years and is now retired. While he and his wife, Elaine, were still quite young they began buying small homes in Omaha, refurbishing them either to rent or sell. Now, in retirement, they are world travelers, quite an accomplishment for a good friend from a rather poor background. Homer and I kept our Christian faith all during those four years in Woodbine, plus all the years since then.

PRANKS GALORE

From time to time, Dad and Mom would have run-ins with board members who wanted to run the church themselves. They did not talk much about it at home, but by the time I became a teenager I knew that board members could sometimes be cantankerous.

The grandson of one of the most outspoken board members in Woodbine was one of my buddies. His parents had divorced and he was living with his grandparents. His name was Dennis. Now, we have all heard of the cartoon character called "Dennis the Menace." No one deserved that title more than my friend.

One time, he and I bought a smoke bomb that attached to one of the spark plugs of a car engine. When the car started, the first thing you heard was an ascending whistle and a loud bang, followed by clouds of harmless white smoke from under the hood.

One Sunday morning, while Sunday school was still on, we attached the smoke bomb to one of his grandfather's spark plugs. When the main service was over, Dennis and I ran to the window nearest the car. Granddad and Grandma got in and turned the key, at which point the smoke bomb worked to perfection.

By the time the noise died down, Grandma and Grandpa were scrambling for the door handles. As they departed the car, white smoke came boiling out from under the hood. We two boys were laughing so hard we fell into a pew. Some people, still in the church, thought we were having some religious experience and came over and started to pray with us.

I recall a rather harsh rebuke from my father, but down deep I think he was laughing too. How sweet our revenge! The last I heard from Dennis, he was the fire chief of a city just outside Kansas City, Kansas. When we were kids he would have been the one suspected of starting fires instead.

That was not the last of my pranks in Woodbine. One of the young ladies of the church was getting married. My father was to officiate the ceremony. Some of the friends of the bride wanted to do something other than put toilet paper and tin cans on the getaway car. I came up with the idea of jacking up the rear of the car and placing enough blocks of wood under the rear axle to keep the drive wheels off the ground. We then put Limburger cheese on the manifold of the car engine.

When the wedding was over the bride and groom made their way through the rice shower and got in the car. They started the car and put it in gear, but of course it wasn't going anywhere. The groom got out and finally figured out what was going on. To make matters worse the groom left the engine running. As he and the bride's father labored to get the blocks out from under the back axle, the cheese began to do its work. Suddenly the bride, in all her white glory, bailed out of the car, holding her nose from the terrible stench made by the cheese. Truly, this was a video moment!

What I didn't know was that there was a reception at the bride's home before the couple went on their honeymoon. For some reason my father and I had to ride with the bride's father. We were in the car with this very irate man who was not a Christian. He was also a very intimidating person who operated large construction equipment and had just returned from helping to build the Alaskan Highway. Thankfully, he had no way of knowing that I was the cause of his anger. My father, also not knowing that I was involved, agreed wholeheartedly with him. I was sitting in the middle and my heart was pounding so hard I thought they would both hear it.

MOVING TO OKLAHOMA

When my junior year was almost over, Dad got a call from a church in Woodward, Oklahoma. I had spent more school years in Woodbine, Iowa, than anywhere else, but now I was asked to move between my junior and senior years. School had not been easy for me. I was not allowed to play sports because of a perceived heart murmur brought on by a bout of rheumatic fever, although my heart was actually just fine. I could not wear gym shorts because of the strict rules of our church, so I had to get special permission to wear jeans for any exercise event. That was embarrassing.

In Iowa, the Pentecostal Movement was perceived as fanatical and weird. Our churches were small and not very nice, and most always on the wrong side of the tracks. I lived with all that during those formative years, which is probably why I felt so relieved when summer came and I could retreat to the world of farming, to see things grow and take care of animals. To this day, when I see a farmer doing his important job, I want to stop and offer my help. It is still locked in my bloodline. But God had other plans for me, and in a few short years I found that out.

My family made plans to move to Oklahoma as soon as Dad was voted in as the new pastor. Meanwhile, I had been informed that my new next-door neighbor had a son who was going to be a senior at Woodward High, and he would help me get adjusted to the new surroundings. Don Holland was such a blessing. His father was an Oklahoma state trooper, and Don was a big bear of a young man with a willingness to help me get a good start in school.

To my surprise, the Pentecostal Church in Woodward was well-respected and I soon discovered that there was no stigma attached. I was now in what is called the "Bible Belt" of our nation, in which churches were all well-respected and well-attended. The people were also very friendly; in fact, this move changed my entire life. I had been beaten down and sometimes ridiculed for being that Pentecostal preacher's kid, but now, all of a sudden, I was asked to be in the prestigious pep band and to have a major seat in the concert band and the marching band. I was asked to sing tenor in the school quartet as well.

I was the most bashful, backwards kid you would ever want to meet and I did not think I had much of a future, but all that changed in the months I spent in Woodward. God had put me in a place where I could flourish, and I did not realize how much it changed me until later in life.

In addition, the new church family was incredible. They encouraged me instead of being critical, and this had a profound effect on me. My senior year went way too fast. Before, I could hardly wait to get out of school, but now I felt sad that I would be leaving so soon. I found myself wishing I had been in Woodward long before I actually arrived there.

Meanwhile, during my junior year I had begun to think about the future in a small way. Now, as I approached the end of my senior year, I had to make some big decisions. I had never had a direct call from God to be a minister. That worried me because I wanted to do something with the voice God had given me. Many hours were spent on my knees in prayer, asking God for an answer, but nothing came.

- 3 -

On to Bible School

During my years in Iowa at Storm Lake Bible Youth Camp, I met Rev. Hilton Griswold. I was amazed that he had left the Blackwood Brothers Quartet as their piano player a few years before, to enter the ministry full time. Living not far from Shenandoah, Iowa, where the Blackwoods were living at the time, afforded me many opportunities to hear James, Doyle, and R. W. Blackwood, along with Bill Lyles, Bill Shaw, and Hilton Griswold. At the time I was unaware of the tremendous impact they were having on my future. On occasion, at youth camp, Hilton even asked me to sing in a makeshift quartet.

In Woodward, several groups from Central Bible Institute and the Assemblies of God Bible school in Texas come by to minister in our church. At least two quartets, also from Bible schools, visited as well.

The King's Choraliers choir, from Central Bible Institute, seemed the most interesting. I was attracted by their new approach to music. The chord structures and the songs were more upbeat and interesting. While they were at our church, the director, Birdie Kovacs, auditioned me. I had expressed an interest in going to Bible school but was not going to be a preacher. After the audition, Birdie assured me that she would place me in her choir immediately if I would come. I found out that they traveled extensively during breaks at school, and that intrigued me all the more. I finally made the decision to go to Central Bible Institute in the fall of 1955.

During that summer I worked at my usual jobs—pumping fuel, selling Firestone tires, and hauling men back and forth from the oil-drilling rigs that dotted the landscape of western Oklahoma. When September came my parents drove me to Springfield, Missouri, to start my new life.

What a shock. I never realized how much of a sheltered life I had lived. When my parents drove away and I realized I was on my own for the first time I thought I would die. I had never experienced homesickness like this. I remember standing at the window of my dorm room on Third Floor East, feeling like I was about to suffocate. What had I done? How could I ever cope with this?

Through a barrage of tears I stumbled out of my room and down the stairs. Yet God surely knew my need, because I had no sooner cleared my eyes and made my way to the sidewalk outside the dorm when I ran into an old friend from Iowa with whom I had gone to youth camp.

No, it was not a boy. It was a girl named Harriet Robinson. My brother had been friends with Harriet's older sister, and Harriet was around my age. Our parents were also great friends. God sent Harriet along at the right time, because I certainly was in trouble in my spirit and my mind. God works in strange ways sometimes. Meeting her, and then seeing others that I had been in contact with over the years of Iowa meetings, made life a little easier. Then I went to see Birdie Kovacs, and slowly but surely began to make new friends, many of whom have supported and helped me in many ways ever since.

LEARNING NEW THINGS

My first year at school was full of new things. I had to learn to get along with people from different cultures. People from the Midwest frowned on makeup, mixed bathing, and movies, but we had people from California who thought nothing of going to movies, using makeup, and going swimming with non-Christians.

I was not a man of the world. I had been completely sheltered and it was a struggle to adjust. I am sure that some at school thought in those early years that I was somewhat of a nerd and not easy to get along with, because I stuck to my own way of life so tenaciously. But little by little I learned to lighten up, to enjoy knowing people of different ideas and mannerisms. The one equalizer was that I could sing with anyone in the choir. They had to respect my abilities no matter how much they might disdain my culture. However, though I didn't realize it at the time, these people were going through the same process, and little by little we came to common ground. Our love of the Lord and our ministries together became the magnets that brought us together.

The choir was my main salvation during that first year. We took two tours off campus, to the Midwest and the East. When I laid my eyes on Pittsburgh for the first time, in 1956, little did I know that within a few years, I would be living in Pennsylvania for the rest of my life.

I was a little distressed when summer came, because I had to go back to Woodward to make more money to return to school the next year. I knew that Woodward held no future for me, but I retreated to family and friends and made the best of it. When September came I returned to Central Bible, hoping this time to hear from God about what I might end up doing with my life after college. I was certainly looking forward to getting back into the King's Choraliers for another year of traveling and singing.

I soon resumed my main job, working in the kitchen for all the meals. My job was to pull the clean dishes and silverware out of the hot washing machine and give them to others to dry and put away. Jim Wilkins, who one day would be the Superintendent of the Nebraska District of the Assemblies of God, was on the other end of the washing machine, putting all the dirty dishes into trays. Behind me was Leland Lebsack. Leland's job was drying all the silverware. Leland became a successful pastor in later years. Our reward for these labors was fifty cents an hour. It wasn't much but it kept us in spending money.

When I really got desperate for cash I would hire out to a local chicken farm. The job required me to go into the long brooder houses early in the morning, when the chickens were roosting, and gather them into large boxes for shipment to the slaughterhouse. I learned how to grab nine chickens at a time—now, that is real talent. The money came in handy, but what a way to get it!

Two weeks went by at college, and I found myself engrossed in learning new songs with the choir. One day a tall, skinny young man, and another fellow that I had not seen much at school, came to talk to me. The tall one was Dave Kyllonen; the other one was Don Baldwin. I had met Dave on the basketball court many times. He was 6'5" and all elbows and legs as he churned up and down the court. I was the recipient of many elbow shots as my 5'11" frame collided with his, trying to snatch a rebound or prevent him from going to the basket.

INVITATION TO JOIN

Don Baldwin, because he was a married student and lived off campus, was not known to me at that time. They told me they were in a quartet called the Couriers and were looking for a lead singer. So in a few days I auditioned with Don Baldwin (baritone), Dave Kyllonen (bass), and Lem Boyles (tenor). They had all heard me sing in various chapel services and around the campus. I think that Dave Kyllonen also heard me sing in the shower, even though he lived on another floor of the men's dorm. That is why, when people ask me how I got in the Couriers, I always tell them it was because of singing in the shower at Central Bible College.

I guess the guys liked what they heard and wanted me to join them. My biggest problem was The King's Choraliers. What would the person responsible for my being at that school,

Birdie Kovacs, think of me if I left the choir? But to my amazement she was very gracious and told me that this was a great
opportunity for ministry every weekend, versus singing with the
choir on limited occasions. With her blessing I made the move
to the Couriers in short order. The only person who tried to
discourage me from joining a Gospel group was my voice
teacher, Mrs. Thompson. She said it would ruin my trained
voice. I overruled her, but now when I think about my long battle after losing my voice in 1978, I suspect she was at least par-
tially right.

Little did I know that this decision would take me on such
an incredible journey. At the time, joining this group did not
seem the answer to my prayers about my life's work. I knew that
the group would break up as people graduated from school,
and when my time came I would still be searching all over
again for what I should do.

I was fortunate to be in such an established group. It had
formed several years before I came on the scene. They had
already spent full summers in ministry across the country, and
sang somewhere within driving range of Springfield almost
every weekend during the school year. We practiced almost
every evening after supper, because I had to get up to speed
and learn the songs right away.

These were exciting times for me, but I still had to get up for
my work shift in the kitchen on Monday mornings, and still
had to make my Monday classes after arriving back on campus
in the wee hours of the morning. We split the offerings and the
profits from the sales of our product, so I was really doing
much better financially. My best buddy, John Brown, who was

struggling financially as well, took my place in the kitchen on many Monday mornings. John would later dedicate his entire life to the mission field of Indonesia, where he had spent his childhood days with his parents. He is still one of my best friends in the ministry—one of the real "Heroes of the Faith" in my book.

At Easter, we made our way to Harrisburg, Pennsylvania, for the largest Assemblies of God youth convention in the nation. The year before I joined, the group had traveled for an entire summer in Pennsylvania, promoting the two youth camps. At summer's end they had logged 30,000 miles. I was looking forward to returning to Pennsylvania in the summer of 1957, as we were about to do the same thing.

On the other hand, even as things were going well in the Couriers, my grades began to suffer. I was consumed and could not wait for each weekend to get out and share the Gospel. By this time I was paying my own school expenses. My parents had been footing the bill, but now, proudly, I was able to stand on my own two feet and pay my bills without being a burden.

- 4 -

The Couriers
Call

There was no such thing as 33 $1/3$ long-playing albums when we started singing. Our only choice was those hard discs called 78s. We recorded four of them with two songs on each. The retail price was one dollar. Later on we recorded a few 45 rpm records as well. Soon the 33 $1/3$ albums did become available, however, at which point we produced our first one, *Beyond the Sunset*, at the Revivaltime Recording studios located on our campus.

Revivaltime was a nationally syndicated radio ministry. Rev. C. M. Ward was the speaker, and the Revivaltime Choir provided the music. Many students, knowing that we were recording, had saved four dollars, and when the album came out they were first to buy. You could hear it being played all over campus.

Some of the students were so kind to help us put together the covers for this album. Two young ladies were the Payne sisters, Georgia and Charlotte. They took a great interest in our ministry and were such a blessing. Charlotte became the wife of missionary Jim Grams and spent years on the mission field. Georgia and her husband, Conrad Cooper, have also spent years in ministry in various positions of authority, the latest being the Convoy of Hope. The sisters' dad, Ernie, was the original bass singer for the famous Haven of Rest Quartet from California.

Rev. Don Argue, who has become one of the Assemblies of God premier educators, was the photographer for the picture of the Couriers and Don Baldwin's '55 Oldsmobile on the back cover of *Beyond the Sunset.* The picture was taken in front of Central Assembly in Springfield, Missouri. These people are in our memory banks as encouragers and supporters, along with a lot of others whose names have faded from memory.

We enjoyed the ministry of two other quartets while at school, the King's Magnifiers and the King's Ambassadors. The King's Magnifiers sang more traditional music, like the Haven of Rest. The King's Ambassadors were mostly southerners and were more southern Gospel in style. The Couriers were somewhere in the middle, and to this day no one can quite put us in any category. I know we can't!

The tenor singer for the King's Ambassadors Quartet was Carl Walker. Years later, Carl and Necy Walker's youngest son, Kristian, attended Central Bible College and met and married my oldest daughter, Shannon. Kristian and Shannon have now been in a music worship ministry for fifteen years.

I have no record of how many dates we sang while in school. All I know is that we will be eternally grateful to those pastors surrounding Central Bible School, who allowed us to come to their churches and literally "practice" our music and message on their congregations.

While we were in school during the spring of 1957, Don Baldwin was busy booking our summer schedule in Pennsylvania. Each week we would pore over the list and make our plans. Records had to be purchased, suits bought, new music learned. It was so exciting for me because, for the first time, I would not be going back to odd jobs in Woodward, Oklahoma. I would miss my parents but I was in the ministry, and we all understood what that meant.

Eddie Reece, our pianist, provided an Oldsmobile for the Couriers to travel in that summer. There were no motel rooms for visiting ministers back then; we stayed in church members' homes. The routine was to make sure we arrived at the local church in time for supper. After the service we split up into groups for overnight. The next morning we would have breakfast with our hosts and try to stay just long enough to be offered lunch before meeting back at the church to head for our next engagement. We had to do this to survive. As we travel nowadays we still meet up with couples—or their children—who remember when we stayed in their homes. Many youngsters gave up their bedrooms for us during these days of ministry.

That first summer brought many exciting times. We even sang for the famous healing evangelist Kathryn Kulhman. She ministered in an early Friday evening healing service in Pittsburgh. She had heard of us and invited us to sing a couple songs for her hour-long service. Kathryn met with us briefly before the service. Several hundred people listened to us sing, and then Kathryn preached and prayed a mass prayer for the sick. She had the people stand for a final prayer. Before she prayed, she turned to us and thanked us for blessing the people. Then she turned to the audience and told them that the Couriers would be standing at the doors with their wonderful 78 rpm albums for one dollar each. She told each person to get out their dollar as they hurried to their buses to go home.

As Kathryn prayed I made a beeline for the back door. In five minutes we sold all four hundred records. Since that time we have sold many more than that at a single concert, but never so quickly. The ironic thing is that we never sang for her again. Soon after that evening she moved her organization to the West Coast, and that was it.

YOUTH CAMPS

Our days at the Assemblies of God youth camps in Pennsylvania—Green Lane and Cherry Tree—were the highlights of our summers. The altar services at the end of those incredible times with the young people were so powerful. Many nights we would stay and pray with the kids for hours. More times than I can count we carried young people back to their cabins, still praying, seeking God, and basking in praise. We prayed, played, ate, sang, and interacted with three hundred young people at each camp. In our travels today we still meet people who were part of those incredible camps.

I will never forget one most precious moment at Green Lane. The Couriers were preparing to leave fairly early the last day, to fulfill a date. We were traveling by motor coach by this time, and we had loaded up and said good-bye to the camp director, Paul

Wislocky. But as we made our way down the long, tree-lined road leading to the highway, we were suddenly surrounded by hundreds of young people. Some laid down in the middle of the road. Others just stood by the roadside waving. The kids were all shouting, "Don't go, don't go!" We all climbed out of the coach and stood in amazement as the kids cheered and shouted at us. Finally, with tears in our eyes we reboarded our coach and made our way slowly on down the lane. It's a sight I can still see in my mind's eye—wonderful young people who were saying thank-you for loving them.

We continued our ministry to the Pennsylvania youth camps until 1974. In those years we were invited to other youth camps across the nation as our ministry continued to grow. However, there comes a time for a changing of the guard, and we were running out of the energy that it took to keep up with the young people. Our ministry took on a new focus, and other younger men and women took our place at the camps. I must admit it was hard to change course, but it was necessary.

Youth camps were not only spiritual blessings but times to have some incredible fun with the campers and fellow counselors. I have to relate one incident to show that the Couriers were fun-loving young men. In fact, my story is not actually about the campers, but about one particular non-fun-loving counselor.

I preface this by telling you that people like the man that I will be talking about were not looked on favorably by the Couriers. This young preacher was overly concerned about the "security" of the campers. Not that we weren't always alert for outsiders coming on the grounds, but this fellow was absolutely paranoid. He was not well liked by the campers because he was always reprimanding them for something. So we decided to play a trick on him.

Our counselor/friend had brought four walkie-talkies for us to use at night when we were patrolling the grounds, making sure the campers stayed in their cabins. In those days, walkie-talkies were a little primitive. To change channels the instrument had to be taken apart and changed manually—a time-consuming job.

In our traveling coach we had a CB radio with many channels. I found the channel that our paranoid friend was using for his four walkie-talkies, then went to our coach in the middle of the night and contacted him. I pretended to be the fire chief of the local fire department in the little town of Green Lane. I identified myself and was more than a little upset that he was on the channel designated for a fire department. I royally reprimanded him for interfering with fire calls and demanded that he change channels.

I then left the coach and went back to the office building that we counselors met in after hours for coffee and fellowship. Our good friend was out somewhere looking for people trying to steal our campers. But in a few minutes he came running into the office, demanding the other three walkie-talkies so he could change the channels. About thirty minutes later he had them all changed and went back out.

Meanwhile, we had asked one of our male campers to help us play another trick. We told this camper to go out into the large field between the main highway and the girls' cabins. He was to hide in the tall grass at the edge of a big dip in the ground in the middle of the field. We would then call our friend and tell him we had spotted someone trying to reach the girls' cabins from the road, and he was to investigate.

Everything worked perfectly. I got on the walkie-talkie, told our friend what we had seen, and asked him to investigate. To make matters better he jumped into his little Ford Pinto to chase this "intruder." He then raced out into that field pell-mell. Our camper friend jumped up from his hiding place and was caught in the headlights of the Pinto. We heard the engine roar as the driver spotted the fleeing camper. Of course our camper dodged into the weeds and disappeared. Meanwhile, the Pinto came to the dip in the ground and disappeared too. All we saw were taillights flying upward, then down, and then a loud *thump* as the Pinto bottomed out.

By this time we were all laughing our heads off. In due time our counselor came back to the office, at which point we told him that it was a false alarm. I don't think he spoke to us the rest of camp. The next morning I inspected his little Pinto for any damage. We were prepared to pay for it, but all I found were clumps of grass under the back bumper and a slightly bent license plate frame.

There were times of legitimate concern about outsiders coming on the grounds. Local groups of young men knew that we had many nice-looking girls at camp, and they did try to make contact. At the Cherry Tree youth camp we had one encounter that I will never forget. One afternoon a report came to the office that there was a carload of young men from town on the grounds, trying to make contact with girls. When I heard about it I got our bus driver, George Smith, and we went to see what was going on.

Now, I got George to help me because I knew he could be tough. He had told me that before he became a Christian he used to fight all the time. George was a tall, intimidating-looking man, and I was not small myself. Sure enough, we found the car with four young men in it. We politely asked them what their business was and they sarcastically told us it was none of *our* business. With that, George took command. He said in no uncertain language that these guys on the count of five had to leave the grounds. Now, I had never seen George in action as a fighter. He counted to five and then the guy in the car started to say, "Yeah, you and who else is going to make us leave?"

The poor guy never got the entire sentence out. With one swift move George opened the door, grabbed the driver by the shoulders, yanked him out, and had him on the ground with his knee on the guy's Adams apple. Then he picked the guy up and threw him back in the car. You never saw such scared guys. I was stunned at how fast big George could move. But it wasn't over yet.

On the last night of camp we loaded up our coach and started home. These same guys were waiting for us down the road, and finally stopped right in front of us on a two-lane road. It was late at night and I guess they thought they could harass us some more. George grabbed a long wooden bar we used to check for soft tires, and I grabbed our fire extinguisher. George went out first, then we sent out six-foot-five Dave Kyllonen, and then I went out. Neil, the smallest, was last. Those four guys, probably fortified by booze, saw us alight from our coach armed to the teeth, dropped their car in gear, and sped off. Nowadays I am sure we would have simply driven around these crazy young guys. But back then we were young and foolish and had Big George on our side.

BACK TO SCHOOL AGAIN

After the summer of 1957 we returned to Springfield to begin another year of studies. It was the senior year for Dave Kyllonen and Don Baldwin. Neil Enloe had joined us as lead singer by this time, and I had moved, under much protest and concern, to the top tenor part. We had tried to get another tenor but it seemed that I could sing higher than anyone we tried out.

Neil Enloe made himself incredibly valuable to our group, via his arranging ability and his piano-playing skills. In the years that followed, Neil was our salvation. His special ability to arrange songs soon won the respect of many Gospel groups across the nation and gave the Couriers our unique sound. Many will agree that Neil is also one of the most underrated lead singers in Gospel Music. Neil refused to showcase his vocal abilities for the simple reason that he did not want to get in the way of the message we were trying to deliver. If he thought his voice was getting in the way, what was the point in singing the song? While so many groups tried to sound like each other, our group tried hard to find our own path. I appreciated this, because I did not have the typical "Southern Gospel" tenor voice. My voice was of a harder-driving type, and Neil learned to wrap our voices around that kind of sound.

As Neil and I entered this seemingly last year of singing with Dave and Don, I was still concerned about my future. I am sure Neil was as well. Neither of us had received a definite call to preach. Nevertheless, I tried to put the whole thing out of my mind and concentrate on my daily studies and weekend singing. Studying was not my strong suit but I struggled on. My heart was just not in my classes. My real joy came when we gathered in the practice room to learn a new song, followed by a sense of excitement and relief when we left the campus for another singing engagement. The early morning returns to campus on Monday mornings were taken in stride, and then it was more classes until the next weekend.

During the school year of 1957–58 a terrible flu epidemic hit Central Bible Institute. I remember getting very sick for one evening, and then overnight getting better. Many others had no such luck. This was not the twenty-four-hour flu but a full-fledged epidemic. Our infirmary was soon overcrowded with students so sick they needed constant care, so I volunteered to help. Some students got so sick from dehydration that we sent them to hospitals. I spent days and nights taking temperatures, feeding soup, and putting damp towels on fevered brows. All school activities came to a halt and many a prayer went up for our student body.

During that long year I spent many moments at the altar of our chapel, and in my dorm room on my knees, asking God for direction in my life. It seemed like the heavens were brass. As in previous years we were again singing each weekend, and from time to time we were asked to provide the music for various executives from our school as they conducted Sunday school conventions and other denominational events.

Another important factor was our close friendships with the siblings of the national executives of the Assemblies of God. At this time most of the executives lived just across the street from campus. I somehow became friends of Bud and Betty Zimmerman. The father, T. F. Zimmerman, became the general superintendent of the Assemblies of God not long after we left school. Mrs. Zimmerman was always inviting some students over for home cooking.

Also living across the street were the parents of John Ashcroft, who later became the governor of Missouri and the attorney general of the United States under George W. Bush. I was good friends with Robert Ashcroft, John's older brother. We were also invited to the Ashcroft home from time to time during school. I played many a hard basketball game against Bob, and he usually won. I also found it extremely sad that because of John Ashcroft's godly stand during his political life he was attacked so many times. Shame on those who tried to use John's commitment to God against him. There are those who cannot stand someone who has high morals and a high opinion of the God he serves.

These people I have mentioned—along with many others—have been such a blessing to the Couriers and our Assemblies of God fellowship. The national executives and district officials have always been there for us. I cannot recall one who ever treated us badly, and for that support we are eternally grateful. A special thanks also to our own Penn-Del District of the Assemblies of God for their constant support through the years of ministry. Our home district was a true launching ground for us.

- 5 -

Decision Time

As the second semester of the 1957–58 school year began, as always, we had to confront the nagging question of what would happen to the Couriers. I knew I was supposed to come back for my final year at CBI, but the prospect of losing the two main members of our group at one time seemed almost beyond comprehension. We had molded together into a singing unit and had such fun together. The thought of breaking up was almost more than I could stand.

My mind is clouded about when I first began to see a possible answer to my prayer for the future. The first hint came when Don Baldwin began to talk about the possibility of going on the road full time. Believe it or not, I was so programmed into thinking that I needed to go one more year and get my degree that I did not really grasp what Don was saying. To disappoint my parents by quitting before getting that all-important degree was almost unthinkable. It had been etched in my mind that I needed that degree to be a success in whatever profession I might choose.

The thing that brought me to my senses was the cold fact that I did not know what my chosen profession would be outside of singing. That finally rang a big bell in my heart, and I began to see the light of God's will right before my eyes.

Discussions began in earnest soon after the initial thought was put forth by Don. We did have the ingredients to make it in Gospel Music. Don was a seasoned man already, from his years of military service before he came to Bible school. Dave was becoming a good preacher and bass singer. Eddie Reece, our piano player, had great experience with Gospel Music, having played for Jim Hamill and Cecil Blackwood in Memphis, his hometown. Neil Enloe was already emerging as a fledgling arranger and a fine singer. And I was holding my own as a tenor.

At Easter break we once again made our way to Pennsylvania to be part of the huge Easter Youth Convention at the Zembo Mosque in Harrisburg, where several thousand young people would come together for fellowship and ministry. We looked forward to the convention because we would again see many of the youths we had ministered to at the camps, and would renew fellowship with all the pastors we had come to know across Pennsylvania. In fact, we felt so at home in Pennsylvania it seemed perfectly natural to make inquiries of district officials about the possibility of setting up headquarters in Pennsylvania, in case we decided to go full-time.

It has always intrigued me to note how God puts people in your life that will be of help somewhere down the road. Rev. Gene Bell, the Secretary Treasurer of the Penn-Del District of the Assemblies of God, had been in the West Central District of the Assemblies when I was growing up in Iowa. He knew my family quite well, and now he was an official in Pennsylvania. Rev. Bell and his wife were of great help to us in deciding whether to move to Pennsylvania.

Another wonderful event happened at the Great Youth Convention in the spring of 1958. On previous trips to Pennsylvania, the Couriers had made friends with the Crone Family from Rohlers Assembly of God Church outside Dover. I had dated the Crones' daughter, Carole, on several occasions. I carried a picture of Carole in my billfold and had shown it to Eddie Reece. I remember his commenting on how pretty she was. My comment to him was that she was even prettier on the inside—always sweet, cheerful, and lots of fun. My relationship with Carole had not progressed to anything serious, and while at CBI, I had been dating another young lady. So when we went to the Easter Convention I told Eddie that I would introduce him to Carole if he was interested—and he was!

It was amazing how God intervened so that Eddie could meet Carole almost immediately. The Couriers pulled up to the Zembo Temple in Harrisburg and jumped out. Eddie and I walked together into the building, and though there were hundreds of young people there we ran into Carole Crone almost immediately. We talked a bit and then I introduced Eddie. The rest of the story is history, because I believe Eddie and Carole were married the very next year.

At this same convention we talked to the Assemblies of God District Officials about moving to Pennsylvania when school was over in the spring of 1958. Our thought processes went like this. Many groups had headquarters in Southern states, especially in the Nashville area. If we went there we would get lost in the shuffle, for we certainly could not compete against the Blackwoods, The Statesmen, The Speer Family, and other famous groups that were already well-established. We were still novices and we needed to go where we could learn at our own pace and could introduce our music to people who had few preconceptions about what a Gospel group should sound like.

It seemed natural to choose Harrisburg, which had already been the scene of many successes at the Easter Convention. It was also the capital of Pennsylvania and was located in a strategic area. It was an economically sound area as well, boasting three major military bases and many state government employees. The Pennsylvania Turnpike was also available, and in later years two major interstate highways made travel even easier.

Within a day's drive of Harrisburg lived one-third of the population of the United States. Easily in reach were Baltimore, Washington, D.C., Philadelphia, Pittsburgh, New York City and its 28 million people, and all of New Jersey and Delaware. Boston, Toronto, Montreal, Buffalo, and many southern cities were within eight hours of us. In fact, if we chose to do so we could spend our entire ministry and never leave the northeastern part of our country. Thousands of churches were available in these markets. Some groups had to travel hundreds of miles just to get to their first stops on a tour. We could travel to many stops and still be home with our families most of the nights.

Thus the final decision was made, and we soon located an apartment in Harrisburg for the four members who were single. Don Baldwin found a spot in a mobile home park for himself and his wife. Meanwhile, we traveled back to Springfield to finish out the school year. I had told my parents of my decision and they were just as excited as I was. They knew what it was to take a step of faith into the unknown, and they were relieved because they knew what a hard time I had gone through to find the will of God. Going to Bible school was not my first choice, but God works in mysterious ways His wonders to perform.

Moving Day

Details of the move are very distant in my mind. Dave Kyllonen had an old Plymouth, and Eddie Reece had his Oldsmobile. Don Baldwin and his wife made their way in their own car. I can't remember whom I rode with.

Words cannot describe the arrangement of Dave, Neil, Eddie, and me in that tiny apartment on Front Street in Harrisburg. Dave Kyllonen's home church had a party for us and gave us some pots and pans, a toaster, and some eating utensils to help us set up housekeeping. Fortunately, we were on the road almost every day in meetings, so most of our meals were not eaten at home.

My main job during that time was to fabricate our only album, *Beyond the Sunset*. We could not afford to have the covers put together commercially, so I did it by hand. I used rubber cement and a roller to smooth out the glue. But a problem arose when the glue hardened from exposure to the air. To thin it out I used a tiny portion of ordinary gasoline.

Unfortunately, when we set up our display of albums and pictures in the lobby of a church, we also got the strong odor of gasoline. More than one person would smell it and begin searching for the source. We never confessed; we simply sold those albums and prayed like mad that the covers would stay intact until the buyers got home. If any reader still has a *Beyond the Sunset* album with a nice cover, be assured that you bought one of the later versions that were fabricated commercially. If you have a ragtag album cover you have an original keepsake. Just don't light a match around it!

Meanwhile, Dave Kyllonen could stand only a few months of life in our bachelor quarters. In November, 1958 he traveled to California to wed his sweetheart, Judy Robbins. The Baldwins drove with Dave all the way to California. Sadly, the other three Couriers could not attend because we did not have traveling money. Those were rough days, but they soon got a lot rougher for the newlyweds.

On the very day when they arrived back in Harrisburg as a married couple, the newly purchased mobile home they were to live in exploded into flames and burned to the ground. Almost everything that Dave and Judy owned was lost. The scene we encountered as Neil, Eddie, and I arrived late that terrible evening to find Dave and Judy standing in shock with their arms wrapped around each other, watching the fireman put out the hot spots, will never erase itself from my memory. The next evening, in a borrowed suit, Dave sang with us like nothing had happened. Somehow Dave and Judy got back on their feet and began life together. Other dramatic things would eventually happen to the Couriers, but none was so devastating . . . at least on the day it happened.

- 6 -

Early Trials

Many of the days, months, and years following our arriving in Harrisburg are still blurry in my memory. A journal certainly could be helpful, but who would have thought that fifty-some years later we would try to remember details? I daresay that none of the Couriers had a vision as long-termed as our partnership turned out to be. We just got up each day and asked the Lord to use us. Beyond that, we formulated our plans day by day, week by week, and month by month. And most of our planning sessions were held while we were traveling somewhere to sing.

The remaining three bachelors finally moved across the Susquehanna River into Camp Hill, Pennsylvania. Most days you could find us hanging out at the Dutch Pantry Restaurant on Market Street. Our apartment was just across the street, and this was where we eventually parked our motor coach. Our bachelor group dwindled down even further when Eddie got married and then left the group.

One of the first things we knew we had to do was to get our music on the radio. Television was around, but radio was still the strong communications vehicle in those days. We finally approached WCMB in LeMoyne, Pennsylvania. When Ed Smith, the station manager, asked us to audition, many employees gathered in the studio to listen. When we finished, we were dismissed and Mr. Smith and the employees had a private meeting.

When Ed returned he said that the station was willing to give us a program. We told him we had no money, but we had done our homework and knew that local radio stations were required by the FCC to keep some times open, free of charge, for local programming. Ed Smith seemed surprised that we knew about this, but he agreed and said we could have 8–8:30 on Sunday mornings. We were elated because this was drive time for people going to church—the perfect time for them to listen.

What started as a one-station, half-hour Gospel program was soon being broadcast on ten stations. We tape-recorded each program and sent copies out to nine other stations in the Central Pennsylvania area. This was incredible exposure for us; it lasted for ten solid years and ceased only when we were given a TV program by a Harrisburg television station. That radio program opened all kinds of doors outside our own denomination, and brought in ministry requests from all over.

We could not go into the studios of WCMB to do our programs live on Sunday mornings, because we were always singing somewhere else. So we began to use our album for the program. We set up two turntables, taped programs onto a recorder, and then sent the tapes to the stations. In the later years I was in charge of preparing the program, which I did in a small room off the newly constructed Baldwin recording studio. One of my tape recorders was an old Wollensack. As I would be duplicating the program, it would overheat from constant use and stop recording. I would put it into a small refrigerator and let it cool down quickly. Then I would start the process all over again until I got all ten tapes finished. It was exasperating but it had to be done.

The Big Black Limo

When we moved to Harrisburg we knew that our transportation problem had to be addressed once and for all. It was not fair for us to continue using personal vehicles; it was time to get a company car. And given Dave's six-foot-five frame, it was important to get something comfortable. We decided to try for a Cadillac Limousine that would give Dave plenty of leg room.

One evening our search brought us to Wampum, Pennsylvania. We had seen an advertisement from a funeral home, wanting to sell their 1953 Cadillac Limo. But when we arrived we could not find anyone in the office. Don had seen a light inside a side door, so we started inside. What we did not know was that in this room the bodies were prepared for burial. Don walked though the door but quickly turned around with a shocked look on his face. The rest of us then looked beyond him and saw a body lying on a slab. As you might expect, the funeral director was as shocked as we were at the intrusion; he was performing an autopsy on a local homeless man and we had walked in unannounced.

A few minutes later, while he was showing us the big black limousine, someone asked him what kind of shape the car's engine was in. We will never forget his answer: "It is in good shape. It will keep up with any funeral procession." That phrase has stuck with us through the years, for we did buy the car and we lived to regret it.

In the short time we owned this monster car we put more than 100,000 miles on it, but we also had to put at least two overhauled engines in it. We stopped more for oil than we did for gas. The problem was that with all our equipment and men it was grossly underpowered, although it did give us more room and was impressive to anyone watching when we drove up.

One event sticks out in my mind. Because of the extra weight we put six-ply tires on it. We found some used six-plies from a mobile home trailer frame and had them put on, but they would barely fit under the fenders. One night as we were tooling along at sixty-five miles an hour on the Pennsylvania Turnpike, the right rear wheel suddenly departed. I was driving, and when the wheel came off the car lurched up in the air and then came crashing down on the right rear side. We screeched to a halt on the berm of the road, with sparks flying everywhere.

When the car finally stopped I yelled at everyone to get out. I was afraid that the gas tank would explode. Upon exiting the car one of the guys saw the wheel and tire still rolling down the ditch—and they were both undamaged. The car did not explode, and we borrowed one lug nut from each of the three remaining tires to put the offending tire back on. However, when we inspected the bottom of the exposed gas tank we did discover a leak. We were about fifty miles from home at the time. One of the guys had some bubble gum, so we chewed it and then placed some in the small pinhole in the tank. With the help of three lug nuts and a wad of bubble gum we made it safely home.

Eventually we'd had enough of that old crate and decided to buy a brand-new 1959 Chrysler Imperial. This was such an impressive vehicle. We drove it for thirteen months and registered more than 113,000 miles. On the other hand, the Chrysler was not without problems, too. One time we were winding down some curvy road in West Virginia, heading north for western Pennsylvania. I was driving this time, too, and I negotiated turn after tight turn, trying to be careful not to throw everyone around in the car. At the end of one vicious turn the car suddenly lurched and the right rear of the car hit the pavement. We skidded about seven hundred feet with no braking power and very little steering. The right rear axle had broken. We sent for a wrecker and called the preacher that we were scheduled to be with that evening. He came and got the guys, and I stayed with the car.

I stayed in a motel in Grafton, West Virginia, and two days later the part we needed came in and I headed home. I was now by myself and was tooling along at quite a fast clip. Suddenly I felt impressed to slow down. I heard no audible voice; just a prompting to slow down. I had no sooner heeded the warning when the axle on the driver's side in the rear broke. This time I got to a telephone, called our dealership in

LeMoyne, Pennsylvania, and told them in no uncertain terms that I was not driving this car another mile and they should come and get it and tow it home. The car had played with my life twice and I was not going to give it another opportunity. Later on we were told that when this particular car was made, the company had bought some bad steel from overseas, and our broken axles were the product of this mistake.

In all the years of travel we had few accidents but many close calls. God certainly had His protective hand upon us on many occasions. On the other hand, we saw hundreds of accidents that we were not involved in, both minor and major. We have driven hundreds of miles in blinding snowstorms, screaming wind, and howling dust storms. We have picked our way through stalled traffic on icy roads. We have been stranded more than once on wintry highways at up to 35 degrees below zero. Passing truck drivers picked us up and took us to heated shelters or we would have frozen to death on the highways of western Canada and Utah.

The most confounding situations came when we struggled for hours, through dangerous conditions, to get to our singing date while the local people, who only had to travel a few miles or less, would not show up because the weather was too bad. We learned very quickly in our ministry that human nature can never quite be explained. Even so, the people who did show up on snowy, rainy, and foggy nights were very special to us because we knew they really wanted to be there. We sang our hearts out to crowds like that, no matter how big or small, because they had made the effort just as we had.

OUR FIRST FULL YEAR

Our first year of full-time ministry was 1959. Here's a birds eye view of what happened that first year, which proved to be a major crossroads for us.

In January we honored twenty-four dates. We were not well known yet, so many of those were in New Jersey, Pennsylvania, and Maryland. Offerings were meager and album sales were slim—we were literally ekeing out a living. There were times when friends from our home church in Harrisburg brought food to the homes of Dave and Don to help feed their wives and children.

In February we traveled to Florida, where we met the famous songwriter Ira Stanphill. Ira and his wife, Gloria, were ministers in West Palm Beach. We spent three wonderful days in their home, basking in sunny Florida for the first time in our lives. We saw Ira for the last time in Alexandria, Indiana, when we all attended a videotaping of *Bill Gaither and Friends*. Ira was featured on one of the videos, and not many months later he passed on to his eternal reward. Ira was one of the first artists we brought to Pennsylvania when we started our first Gospel sings at the Penbrook Community Building in Harrisburg.

Although we did twenty-eight dates in February we were still struggling financially. In March we filled twenty-five dates, which included a five-day trip to West Virginia and Maryland. In turn, that same trip included one of the funniest things that ever happened in Gospel Music.

YOU COULDN'T PLAN THIS

The meeting in question was held in Oakland, Maryland, at a gymnasium. Four hundred people filled the folding chairs set up on the basketball floor. A small portable stage had been erected on one end for the Couriers to stand on. Someone had put a wooden board behind the platform with a large tree painted on it. We sang our first stand of music and then introduced a short intermission to sell albums and take a break.

Just before going back on stage, I went to the rest room located in the boys' locker room. The door to the locker room was about halfway down the auditorium where the people were seated. When I got inside there was no place to hang my suit coat. The floor was too dirty to lay it down, so I left it on when I sat down. However, before doing so I noticed that the toilet seat was quite dirty, so I stripped off a piece of toilet paper and sat on that.

I was just finishing when Don Baldwin stuck his head in the door and told me to hurry because we were going back on stage. I stood up, rearranged my clothes, fastened my belt, and pulled up my zipper as every man does in these situations. I then ran my hands under the faucet and opened the door to the auditorium just in time to fall in step with the others as they made their way back to the platform. As we walked up the steps I heard some snickering but thought nothing of it. Eddie Reece took his place at the piano and we stepped forward to sing our first song of the second half.

On the way to our two microphones, Neil said to me out of the corner of his mouth, "Duane, stand still, you have toilet paper on you." I thought it must be on my foot so I stood still as we began to sing. But Neil was laughing so hard he could barely keep his composure. Meanwhile, Don Baldwin had heard Neil tell me to stand still, but he could not see me because he was facing the other microphone with Dave Kyllonen, who had heard nothing. The song was "Peace Like a River," just before the end of which Dave did a long, drawn-out part that ended on a very low note. When we came to that part the three of us would back up to let Dave do his thing.

When Don backed up he looked over at me and said right out loud, while gesturing with his hands, "Oh, Duane—it's that long!" indicating with his hands how long the paper was. The clean paper I had placed around the toilet lid had stuck to the back of my suit pants when I stood up in the bathroom, and it was dangling out beneath my coat almost to my knees.

With that, Don almost collapsed on the platform, and it was bedlam. I backed over to the piano, reached behind me, ripped the paper out, and tossed it behind the piano. Eddie Reece did not think this was funny at all. We started back to the microphones and began laughing hysterically all over again. Every time we walked to the microphone we laughed again. Finally in desperation Don addressed the audience. He told them that something funny had happened on stage, and that if anyone had noticed it, they should please be assured that it was not a practical joke—it was purely an accident.

Some people had not seen the toilet paper and were literally in shock at what was transpiring. To top it off, Don then said that we were going to sing one more song. Unfortunately, he never thought about what the title of the song would do to us—it was "How Long Has It Been"! That particular song is very serious, but after what had happened we just lost it altogether. The evening was over and Don finally closed in prayer. On the way to the pastor's home for refreshments, we were talking about what had transpired once again. I was again driving and everyone was just killing themselves with laughter. Finally, I pulled the car over to the side of the road, where some of us piled out and literally rolled in the ditch. If a policeman had come along at that moment I think he would have arrested us on suspicion of being stone drunk.

Several years later, Jim Bakker of the PTL television program featured Gospel Music for a whole week. During that week he had various groups perform. On the last day, James Blackwood, Doug Oldham, Don Butler, and Brock Speer were being interviewed and were asked to name their most embarrassing moment in Gospel Music. One by one they told a story. I was watching this particular telecast from my bedroom in Mechanicsburg, Pennsylvania. The show was live at nine A.M. What came to my mind was that, although their stories were funny and embarrassing, they just could not compare with my toilet paper episode.

The program was winding down when suddenly, Jim Bakker said. "You have all told your stories, but I think there is one about someone in the Couriers having toilet paper on him." I sat straight up in bed when I heard that. I knew that all the participants in this program had heard my story. In fact, the Couriers had just been at PTL, and during the lunch hour, after the morning program, I had told Uncle Henry, Jim's sidekick, the whole thing. Uncle Henry almost wrecked the dinner table laughing, and now they were about to tell it on national television to literally millions of people.

Finally, Jim Bakker began to tell the story as he'd heard it. He had it mostly correct, and by the time he was done everyone was laughing. Someone began to sing, "When The Roll Is Called Up Yonder," and then, to the amazement of the television audience, someone threw a roll of toilet paper across the set in front of Jim Bakker. At that point the program was winding down, so Jim told Doug Oldham to go to the singing set and do another song to close it out. The cameras zoomed in on Doug and his soundtrack started. All of a sudden there were fresh roars of laughter that took Doug by surprise. The camera then panned back to the interview set, and there was Uncle Henry lying on the floor with his feet straight up in the air. He had laughed so hard and tilted back in his chair so far that he'd fallen over backwards.

Doug never did sing. My story absolutely *ended* that hour of PTL, and I was sitting there in my bed laughing uncontrollably. Then the telephone rang. It was my dear mother and she was livid. Shame on them for revealing my name and telling the story. She was going to get a letter campaign going to protest what they had done to her son. She finally settled down when I told her I had seen the program and that if I could laugh along with them, so could she.

Jim Bakker later told me they got the most unfavorable letters they had ever received up to that time because of how the toilet paper was rolled onto the set. He told me that the person who did that was reprimanded and almost fired. He never did try to apologize to me for what happened, and if he had I would have told him it was the funniest and most interesting program I had ever seen on PTL. I have never been embarrassed over this incident, partly because I knew it was a complete accident. I have always taken what I do in ministry very seriously, but I have never taken myself too seriously because we are all very human.

ULTIMATE AFFIRMATION

After this disastrous week we were making our way home to Pennsylvania when Don Baldwin suddenly broke the silence. We had barely broken even for that week, and he did not see how we could continue our ministry any longer. The two wives had again been helped by our church, with food for the table. We had all been aware of our situation but had tried to ignore the facts. It had not been as critical for the three single men, but it was becoming too much for the two married men.

I was driving again, and the tears made it difficult to see in the darkness of that awful night. The only sound was the hum of the engine. Literally, it was panic time for me. What would I do? No license to preach and no other profession to lean on. Waves of despair swept over me. I am sure that the other men were feeling the same way. It had been such a wonderful move for us. Now it sounded like it was over.

In those quiet moments God spoke to someone in that car. When I have questioned each member about that evening, each one denies starting to sing. Even today I wonder, as I write this story, if an angel might have done it. But the song was "I Know the Lord Will Make a Way for Me," and one at a time we all began to sing. Then the quartet harmony took over and we sang softly the entire song: "I know the Lord will make a way for me, I know the Lord will make a way for me. If I live a holy life, shun the wrong and do the right, I know the Lord will make a way for me."

In a few minutes a quiet peace came over that car, and each guy took a few moments to talk. We determined that night, regardless of the circumstances, that we knew the Lord would make a way for us.

Looking back over the record books I have kept for years, I know the year, the date, and the approximate time that this episode happened. After that night our offerings picked up, our record sales began to rise, our crowds got bigger, and lives were changed—especially our own. As I look back I can see that God was testing us to see if we would stay loyal to Him, because He had greater things in store for us.

- 7 -

Growing Pains

After that crisis things improved steadily. We were not getting rich by any means, but God was providing. In May of
1959 we started what would eventually be one of the biggest
events in the entire Gospel Music field, for many years. In the
South, promoters had been promoting Gospel concerts for
years. So we decided to start one of our own. We rented the
Penbrook Community Building in Harrisburg and advertised
it on our weekly radio program.

Our first effort, on May 22, 1959, drew about a hundred people. We sang everything we knew. The people enjoyed it so
much that we scheduled another concert for July. One of the
attendees at the July concert was a little girl named Jill Black-
ner. Her mother had brought her to see us. I remember Jill
because, after listening to one of our radio programs, she had
mailed us a nickel for our ministry. Today Jill is a grown lady
who has traveled with Courier Tours to Europe. Her mother,
Jean, supported our ministry for years.

Our concert series began to grow. We brought in a popular trio called The White Sisters. Ira Stanphill came and did a concert. Cliff Hoage and the Christ Ambassadors from Chambersburg, Pennsylvania was the first local group to join us. We soon outgrew the Penbrook Community Building and moved to a junior high school in Harrisburg. We brought in the popular Sons of Song from Nashville; then came Bill Hefner and the Harvesters Quartet from Charlotte, North Carolina.

Each time the audience grew. Bus loads began coming from all over Pennsylvania, New York, New Jersey, and Maryland as the news spread about the great concerts in Harrisburg. As time went on we rented the Zembo Temple and filled it to capacity with twenty-five hundred people. We then split our concerts between two buildings in Harrisburg, the Forum and the Zembo Temple. Each singing group would travel from one auditorium to the other during an evening of music. We also used the Scottish Rite building in tandem with the Zembo Temple.

Then we set our sights on what seemed impossible. We walked into the Farm Show Arena that held at least eight thousand people and began to wonder if we could fill it. At this juncture we met a young man, Dave Kline, who was in the banking business. I always knew when Dave was in the audience without even seeing him, because he always put a ten-dollar roll of dimes in the offering plate. As we became acquainted with Dave, he told us that he would like to help us promote Gospel concerts. In the years that followed, Dave Kline became the single most effective promoter for us. He also hosted a radio program for years, and used this as a platform to promote the concerts. In total he sold countless thousands of tickets.

Dave eventually went to work for the Hershey corporation and was able to help us obtain the famous Hershey Sports Arena for various concerts. We eventually filled up the Farm Show Arena two times a year and used the Hershey Sports Arena as well. In fact, we held the attendance record at the Sports Arena for several years, until Kenny Rogers finally broke it. In those years we booked practically every Gospel group in the nation, and most groups had record sales for many years at our concerts. All of this occurred in the first eight years of our ministry.

Because we booked major groups into Harrisburg, these same groups began to book the Couriers in their local areas, which gave us considerably more outreach at no additional cost. We ended up attending many National Quartet Conventions in Memphis, and then in Nashville, until the venue was changed to Louisville, Kentucky.

ENCOUNTER WITH ELVIS

Now let's fast forward to Memphis, where the Couriers were appearing at the National Quartet Convention at Ellis Auditorium. By this time, Elvis Presley had become well known to all the big stars of Gospel Music. One famous Gospel group had worked with Elvis in Las Vegas. From what I understand, this group had told him about an up-and-coming Gospel group called the Couriers. So Elvis came to the Quartet Convention that year and made it known that he was staying until he heard us sing.

A small riser was built for Elvis and his wife, Priscilla, so they could sit backstage and listen without being harassed by peo-

ple in the audience. This particular evening we were scheduled
to be on late. Sometime during the earlier performances, Elvis
was introduced to the audience and walked on stage. He could
not sing because of contractual matters, but even so I was
never so flabbergasted in my life at the response. When he
stepped on the stage you would have thought that God himself
had appeared. The auditorium exploded, and people by the
hundreds rushed forward with flashing cameras. For ten minutes I stood thunderstruck as the darkened auditorium was lit
by flashbulbs like it was daylight. Being very naive, I never
thought that anyone from a background of Las Vegas gambling
casinos, womanizing, and rumors of drug addiction would
elicit such a response from Gospel people. It disappointed
me deeply.

Elvis did stay for our stand, and when Dave Kyllonen as
always put a little challenging message between songs, Elvis
shouted from the edge of the stage, "Quit preaching and sing!"
I guess he did not want to hear anything that might convict
him. Later on, Hovie Lister took me back to the Gospel Smoke
Room (which I did not even know existed) and introduced me
to Elvis. I politely shook his hand as Hovie produced a fifty-dollar bill for Elvis to sign. I have wondered to this day what happened to that fifty-dollar bill and how much it might be worth
to some collector. Other people backstage got into the act as
well. Elvis was sipping a can of Coca-Cola, which he put on a
nearby table when he finished. There was a mad scramble to
pick up that can, as a collector's item I guess.

Later on we heard that the famous Gospel group that had
sung backup for Elvis in Las Vegas had recommended the

Couriers to replace them when they left Vegas. All I know is that several weeks after the Memphis convention we received a note saying that a Colonel Parker from Memphis had called to speak to one of the Couriers. The only Colonel Parker we knew was Elvis Presley's manager. Believe it or not, we never returned his call. We will never know what it was about, but rest assured that if we had been asked to back up Elvis the answer would have been a resounding no.

I believe we should be the salt of this earth, but given the reports I had heard by then I wanted no part of that scene. And considering what transpired later with good people I knew, I think my first reaction was further vindicated. Perhaps this sounds holier than thou but it is not intended that way. It is just good common sense to narrow the risks. I could say more, but I'm just glad that God is so merciful. Perhaps we will see Elvis in heaven someday. I hope you have made your reservations as well.

PERMANENT DEFERMENT

After the beginning of our concert series in 1959 I received another potential roadblock. In the mail one day came a letter from Uncle Sam, inviting me to join the military. Again I was in turmoil. We had just weathered a big storm and now I might have to put my ministry on hold. Fortunately, I had kept in good contact with my draft board in Logan, Iowa, where I registered when I came of age. When I explained my situation to them, they told me that if I could get recommendations from church officials I might be able to get a deferment. We were not at war at the time, so there was no big push for recruits.

I asked my former district superintendent in Iowa, Rev. T. E. Gannon, and my good friend Rev. Gene Bell in Pennsylvania, to write letters requesting deferment because of my ministry. Meanwhile, I went to the Army Depot in New Cumberland, Pennsylvania, for my physical, which I passed with flying colors. But in a few weeks I got a letter from my draft board, which I opened with much anxiety. The letter stated that since I had kept the draft board informed of my ministry and was not trying to avoid the draft, but was only trying to follow my career path in ministry, they had voted to defer me from the draft and wished me well.

Once again, God intervened and showed me that He was in charge. If I had gone into the service the Couriers would have had no choice but to replace me. I probably never would have returned to that ministry, and though I am positive that other avenues would have opened up, God clearly wanted me in the Couriers. It was the only group I ever wanted to sing with.

We also received another important boost, in 1959, that catapulted us into more churches than ever before. We were invited to be guest musicians at the great General Council Convention of the Assemblies of God in San Antonio, Texas. This meeting of thousands of Assemblies of God pastors was held biannually in various cities. One of the executives was Thomas Zimmerman, who was elected general superintendent of the Assemblies of God that year. He was a personal friend of ours, as I explained earlier. I'm not sure how much he had to do with it, but our datebook then began to fill up faster than ever, and we ventured farther and farther afield. This required us to spend many more days on the road, which had to be especially hard on the two married men.

It also made us realize that the time had come for us to buy a motor coach. Many major groups had already gone this route, and given the extensive schedule we were now keeping we had to do something to enable us to rest while we were traveling, and also to make room for our ever-increasing product line and our larger sound equipment.

Unfortunately, we lost thousands of dollars on the Chrysler Imperial. When we finally sold it with 113,000 miles on it, was worth almost nothing. However, in December of 1959 we saw an advertisement for some 1948 GM motor coaches. This was exactly what the Blackwood and Statesmen Quartets were using, so we inspected them and asked why they were for sale. We were told that Fidel Castro, who had just taken over in Cuba, wanted to upgrade that country's fleet of buses. Greyhound had contracted to put a rest room in the rear of each one while refurbishing the entire coach. But when Castro embraced a communism-style government our own government put a stop to the sale, which left several fully refurbished coaches sitting in Florida.

The price was only $5,500 but we had no money. So Don Baldwin's father-in-law, Louie Smith, lent it to us. We were busy singing at the time, so two of our best friends, Howard Landis and Jim Shambach, went to Florida and brought the coach back to Pennsylvania. Howard told us later that he inquired of the owner of the fleet of coaches about a warranty. The owner's answer was priceless. Howard said the man pointed at the gate leading from the lot to the street and said. "When the rear end of the coach clears that gate over there, the warranty is over."

The date of the coach's arrival in Pennsylvania is not recorded, but it had to be when the weather was still quite cool. The coach pulled into a local Howard Johnson restaurant late one evening. It was so late that our friends did not call us until the next morning to tell us they were back. When we got to the Howard Johnson, there in the parking lot was our new mode of transportation. I climbed into the driver's seat and pushed the starter button. The engine turned over slowly, but to our chagrin it would not start. We tried again, to no avail. We then called our local bus company and they sent over a mechanic.

Without hesitation he got a can of ether out of his truck and sprayed a shot into an entrance to a strange-looking apparatus on top of the engine. This turned out to be what the experts called "the blower." When I hit the starter button the engine roared to life, belching so much white smoke I thought it would blow up. This was my first introduction to how to run a diesel motor. Cold weather starts were hard, and in the days and years to come I would learn many more lessons about maintaining a motor coach. Even so, we recorded more than 500,000 miles on that old coach. It took us to the Far West, to the Northwest, to the East Coast, to Florida many times, and even to the far reaches of Canada.

The GM let us down only twice in the four years we owned it. The first time was in my hometown of Woodward, Okla-homa. My parents took us to our next dates in Colorado and

Wyoming until the coach was repaired. The other episode was a major breakdown that came while we were traveling in below-zero temperatures in the province of Saskatchewan, Canada. We were on our way to Regina, the provincial capital. In the middle of the night our engine began to lose oil pressure and we slowly came to a halt on the side of the road.

The highway was totally deserted. We had seen two or three trucks all night long, but no automobiles. With no heat and just a few blankets we knew we could freeze to death, but about the time I began to shake uncontrollably from the cold a truck stopped in front of us and the driver came back to see what was wrong. We were so cold that we were not thinking properly, but he insisted that we all pile into his truck. I don't know how we all managed to get in, but we did. The driver took us a few miles to a small town named Herbert, where he dropped us at an all-night truck stop. I am sure we would not have survived the night without this trucker from heaven.

The next morning we called a towing company in Regina and were towed all the way there, where we found that the engine had thrown a rod and had to be overhauled. Neil Enloe and Don Baldwin flew home to Pennsylvania, and Dave and I settled into a local hotel for the three-day wait. Dave's wife, Judy, flew in the next day to be with him and I spent most waking hours at the bus shop watching the repairs. It never got above eighteen degrees below zero even during the day.

Eventually the engine was ready and we headed straight home. We left town so quickly we did not think to check to see if we had any heat. Miles from Regina the coach's heaters were still not working. We were so anxious to get home that we wrapped our legs in blankets and kept on driving. As we traveled eastward and a bit more to the south things gradually warmed up. After we got home I took the coach to our shop to see what was wrong. The mechanic went to the rear of the coach, opened the engine compartment, reached in, and turned a valve. This was the valve that sent hot water from the radiator to the heating coils in the front of the coach. It had not been turned back on after being closed during the repairs. Another lesson learned by a very embarrassed Gospel singer who was supposed to be in charge of maintenance.

- 8 -

Moving Up

By this time we were beginning to sing with major groups in the South, including the Blackwood Brothers, the Statesmen, the Rebels, the LeFevres, the Oak Ridge Boys, the Rambos, and the Speer Family. The Couriers were grateful to men like James Blackwood, who encouraged promoters to include us in their concert schedules. The Blackwoods and the Statesmen essentially had control over several concerts across the nation. They could have kept us out of the circuit, but James Blackwood saw the need to include newer groups in the mix. Instead of thinking only of his own future, he knew that for Gospel Music to expand others would have to take their place someday.

Singing with these other professional groups introduced a whole new learning process. I remember being in St. Louis with the Statesmen Quartet. On our last song, the audience gave us a standing ovation. We were so proud. The next evening we were with the Statesmen again, in Centralia, Missouri. That evening they sang us off the stage—we didn't even beat our applause to the wings. We were like whipped pups. Then, to make matters worse, we found out that it was a tradition at the St. Louis concert for the audience to give a standing ovation to any new group on the program.

The group that helped us the most in those early days had to be the Blue Ridge Quartet. They were already popular in many parts of Pennsylvania, doing all the county fairs and other venues. They also had a program on radio station WWVA in Wheeling, West Virginia, and this got them in front of a wide audience. One of their strongholds was the towns along the Ohio River. When a promoter wanted two groups for a concert, the Blue Ridge would call us to join them. They had all the contacts for songbooks, pictures, and a host of other things to sell to enhance income. They shared all their knowledge with us so many times. Burl Streval and Freddie Daniels are gone now, but we remain good friends with Bill Crowe and Kenny Gates.

First-Class Coach

In our travels we were always picking the minds of other people in Gospel Music. J. D. Sumner from the Blackwoods was the father of the idea to travel in motor coaches. He was laughed at for suggesting it would ever work, but his idea was a winner. I saw the Blackwoods' first coach at a concert in Springfield, Missouri, while in Bible school. Today most traveling groups in many areas of music continue to use motor coaches for travel.

At a concert in 1963, the Blackwood Brothers and the Statesmen drove up in brand-new 1963 Flxible coach. (Yes, "Flxible" is the correct spelling.) We were immediately impressed.

We knew we had to upgrade someday, because our old 1948 model was now costing us many dollars for repeated repairs. We talked to J. D. and said we could not afford to upgrade, but J. D. then asked us what we were paying for repairs, at which point I checked the numbers and realized that we were throwing away more than $300 a month. It didn't take us long to change course, take the plunge, and buy our very first brand-new coach, a 1964 Flxible. This was a dream to drive compared to the old 1948. Torsion ride, power steering, and a generator underneath for extra power. We were riding high.

We had been invited to be part of one of the first syndicated Gospel Music programs on television, the Gospel Singing Jubilee. The Florida Boys, The Happy Goodman Family, and the Dixie Echoes were the southern groups headlining this hour-long program. To our total surprise, Les Beasley, the manager of the Florida Boys, invited us to be part of it too. It was excellent exposure for us. We traveled to Nashville and spent several days recording programs. And because of the program's exposure, promoters began asking all four groups to appear in more places.

Although this was fun it became very costly for us. Our fees were not very good and our sales were slim. The other three groups were seasoned singers and had many friends in the South. It was actually a relief when we were not invited back for the second year, although we missed the fellowship of the other groups and the friends we had made over that year of exposure. I do remember that, on one occasion, both the Goodman Family and the Florida Boys coaches broke down on the road. The new kids on the block had the brand-new

Flxible at the time. Can you imagine the Goodman Family and all the Florida Boys, plus all their product, piling onto our coach? All told we had at least fifteen people in our coach, plus all their clothes, instruments, and product. Our coach drove to the next concert loaded to the gills.

When our days with the Gospel Singing Jubilee were over we went back north and began more extensive work in Canada. Here we had already met with much success, and we were able to keep food on the table without having to travel such great distances between engagements.

By the time we did the Gospel Singing Jubilee program a young man by the name of David Young had taken Eddie Reece's place at the piano. He was known as "Little" David Young because of his short stature, but he was a giant in our group. Little David was a spark plug with a winning smile and a real way with people. It had to be hard on him and his wife, Colleen, to leave their roots in the South and move to much harsher winters. I was surprised that David stayed as long in our group as he did. We were burning the candle at both ends. It was nothing, even at this early stage of our ministry, to be performing more than two hundred seventy-five dates a year.

Little David had this incredibly high tenor voice, and between us we did some high tenor duets in which I was hard-pressed to keep up with him. In the four years he was with us he taught me more about being comfortable with myself on stage than anyone else. So many nights I was on the same platform with the "icon tenors" of the day—Bill Shaw, Bill Hefner, Rosie Rosell, Jim Murray, Coy Cook, Johnny Parrack, Little Willie Wynn, and Larry Ford, to name just a few. These guys had years of experience on me, but little by little I gained confidence by watching these fine men perform. Little David's encouragement from the piano was also a huge factor.

Through all those "golden years" of singing on the concert circuit, and even though it was much easier vocally to sing in large auditoriums because we could turn up the volume and depend on the microphones more, I was still more fulfilled when we went back to singing in more churches across the nation. It was exciting to sing with the other groups, but when we had a chance to really settle into a true ministry of singing and preaching the Word, I was the happiest. In our services in church, leading up to our message given by either Dave or Don, I was usually the one who took the lead on a final song that led people toward making a decision to surrender their lives to Jesus and serve God. That fulfilled my calling so much. Praying with people at the altars each night was also inspiring and fulfilling.

Dave and Don became such good preachers. I do have one humorous story, though, about one of Don Baldwin's sermons. For several weeks Don had been preaching on the dangers of Christians becoming indifferent in their walk with the Lord. Each time he pointed out that indifference was slowly creeping into our churches. He used an illustration involving people who were once on fire for God, but now had become uncaring. One night, as he came to the close of his sermon, he made a last emphatic statement, saying, "Church, I am so concerned about the lack of indifference." By this time he had the people so wrapped up that there were loud "Amens."

When Don said that I looked over at Neil with this quizzical look on my face. I really thought I had misheard. What he

meant was that he was concerned about *indifference,* not the *lack*
it. Anyway, at the end of the service there was an altar call, and
then we sold our product, fellowshipped, and forgot what Don
had said. Two nights later he said the same thing. Once again
Neil and I forgot to correct Don. Finally, one evening we
remembered to tell Don and he just would not believe that he
said the word "lack" at the wrong time. Well, when he came to
that final point he again started to say lack of indifference, but
corrected himself. Neil and I just sat there, poker-faced, not
cracking a smile. But many times, after Don left our group we
would jokingly ask him if he was still concerned about the
"lack of indifference."

TYPICAL YEARS

One of the most reliable barometers of a road ministry is:
Are you being asked to come back to the same places again and
again? If so, you must be doing something right.

In trying to give you a bird's-eye view of typical months in
typical years, let me pick out 1962 and 1963 when Don Baldwin and Little David were still with us.

I wrote in the margin of January, 1962, these simple words.
"Great Year Ahead." Later, as I looked back, I noted that this
was a record month for attendance, sales, and people coming
to know the Lord. Our schedule was almost overwhelming. In
the first sixty days we traveled to the West Coast, then up to
western Canada, then back across Canada to Pennsylvania.
I recorded low temperatures in Winnipeg of thirty-five degrees
below zero. For that solid week, crossing the provinces of

Duane & Jean Ann
Nicholson

Duane Nicholson Family

Couriers with bus driver, Tom Baker

*Cartoon from South African
newspaper*

*Artist's concept of
Christian Statue of Liberty*

Concept photo

Couriers with Little David Young —
circa 1965

Couriers with Don Baldwin
— circa 1961

Couriers with Don Baldwin & Jerry Evans—
circa 1963

With Ted Rossey and C.M. Ward

Ted Rossey and his "Mobile Sanctuary"

Couriers' Moms and Dads

*General Superintendent's
Medal of Honor*

Couriers' first residence

Dave & Judy Kyllonen at Steelers' game —
40th Anniversary

Duane with James Blackwood

Dave & Judy Kyllonen

Original Couriers with Hilton Griswold.
Couriers built the snowman

1968 GMC bus

Neil & Ruth Enloe

*1965 Flxible bus between
Giant Sequoias*

Couriers' parents

Barbados, West Indies — Those suits were HOT!

Farm Show Arena, Harrisburg, PA — Home Concert

Couriers with Phil Enloe—
circa 1968

1973 MCI bus — our best ever!

First time in Canada.
Toronto Evangelistic Center—1958

Couriers with Don Baldwin
1948 GM Silversides bus—circa 1961

Couriers' families—1976

Younger days

Original Couriers—
circa 1957

Pennsylvania Youth Convention—
event that attracted Couriers to PA

Original Couriers
Rehearsal in Canada—circa 1958

Younger days

Down Memory Lane

1953 Cadillac Limousine
like the one Couriers had in the late 1950s

Some songs bring out the animal in us!

50th Reunion Concert—
Original Couriers

Neil & Ruth Enloe

Rev. Paul Olson—
inspired Couriers to
do missions work

*Couriers with Eddie Hawks
and Phil Enloe—circa 1966*

*Couriers with Tim Enloe
Canadian TV—circa 1985*

*Couriers and families—
circa 1973*

British Columbia, Alberta, Saskatchewan, and Manitoba and then singing every evening, we never shut our motor coach down. If we had, the oil would have frozen and the motor would not have turned over.

We would travel each night, stop at a truck stop to take showers, and sleep in the coach as we drove to the next venue. It was such a welcome relief when we got to a warmer climate. I was so glad when we were finally able to shut down the engine and sleep in quiet. After returning home we immediately left for Florida. Can you imagine being in bone-freezing temperatures one week and in eighty-degree temperatures a week later? It is a wonder our vocal cords could endure such changes.

While in Florida on this particular trip, we learned through the papers that John Glenn was about to become the first American to be catapulted into space. Looking at our schedule, we realized it would be possible for us to see John ascend from a vantage point in Daytona Beach, on our way to a date in Jacksonville. So we stopped our coach on the side of the road and listened to the countdown by radio. At first the countdown was delayed so we continued northward, constantly listening to see if the countdown would start again. Sure enough, when it did we were able to watch John Glenn being shot like a cannonball into space. I can still see that rocket with the tiny capsule on the front, gaining incredible speed with smoke spewing out against the blue sky. I cannot imagine what John himself must have felt, but we had a ringside seat.

To continue the year of 1962, we spent the middle and summer months all over the eastern seaboard. We went to the Maritime Provinces of New Brunswick, Prince Edward Island,

and Nova Scotia, and in the fall we made our way back to California, up the coast to Oregon and Washington, then back across western Canada. We were breaking sales and crowd records almost every month.

Now it was 1963, which meant more of the same, beginning with a West Coast trip of twenty-five days. Then in March we made another twenty-one-day trip to western Canada. Finally, in November of 1963 we made our third western trip that year, one that would be etched forever in the minds and hearts of the Couriers.

We left Harrisburg in November in our old relic of a motor coach, the '48 GM. It was to be a twenty-three-day trip with no nights off. Our coach was loaded to the gills. We had every underneath bin loaded, with LP records under our beds and everywhere we could store them. The coach groaned out of town to our first date in Pittsburgh. Then it was on to Rice Lake, Wisconsin; Jamestown, North Dakota; Winnipeg, Manitoba; Moose Jaw, Saskatchewan; Edmonton, Alberta; Medicine Hat, Alberta; Calgary, Alberta; Vancouver, British Columbia; Seattle, Washington; and finally, San Jose, California.

Our concert in San Jose came on November 21. After the concert the Couriers and the Harvesters Quartet boarded our motor coaches and began the drive to southern California for an evening concert on the twenty-second. We drove most of the night and pulled into Bakersfield for breakfast. All the Couriers except me got out and were in the restaurant. I had driven the second shift and was still asleep when we stopped. I awoke to find everyone gone. I got dressed and made my way toward the restaurant.

Then I saw Bill Hefner coming toward me. I will never forget his words, to the effect that something tragic had happened. At first I thought it was someone back home, perhaps a family member or a friend. Then he told me the terrible news about President John Kennedy being shot in Dallas. Bill was always joking around but I could tell by his demeanor that he was entirely serious. In the restaurant I saw waitresses and customers crying, and then we were told that the president was dead. The saying that everyone knows exactly where they were when they heard that Kennedy had been shot is so very true. It sure held true for us.

We managed to finish that trip, but the sadness was evident everywhere we went. December went by slowly, and after a nice vacation we finished out the year on New Year's Eve in cold, wintry Buffalo, New York. When most Gospel groups were finishing up their year in the sunny South, we were braving the cold of the North!

In March and April of 1964 we made another marathon trip to the West Coast. We began this one in Toronto, Ontario, made our way across Canada, and then drove down the West Coast of the United States, back across the midwestern states, and home once again. Meanwhile, many of our days off were not really days off at all. We were still doing the radio program, and then in later years we would travel to Lancaster, Pennsylvania, to WGAL TV8, to tape a Sunday morning Gospel program. This would take an entire day of hard work. On and on the beat went.

AND THEN SHE APPEARED

May of 1964 was another life-changing month for me personally. It began, as usual, with traveling hundreds of miles, this time to Grand Rapids and Detroit, Akron, and then East Providence, Rhode Island, to appear at Zion Bible Institute. Doctor Leonard Hero was the president of this school and it was a Memorial Day celebration. I was still single at the time, but it seemed that everyone was looking for a wife for me except me. Since beginning full-time work with the Couriers I had gone out with a few young ladies, but it was mostly after concerts at a restaurant and then back on the road again. I was literally too busy for a steady relationship.

I can honestly say I was not worried because I had the assurance that someday the right young lady would come along, and I would know it. I was more concerned about making the wrong decision and ending up with a very unhappy wife, left alone while I was on the road. But Don Baldwin did not make matters any easier. When he introduced the group each evening he would mention that I was single. Then he would ask for a show of hands of any mothers who would like to be my mother-in-law!

Now we were at the Zion Bible Institute church auditorium, getting ready for the service. As I went back to Doctor Hero's office I peeked through some double doors at the front of the auditorium to scan the crowd. I had just a small slit to look through but I couldn't help noticing a petite little blonde angel sitting with what I assumed were her parents. She looked quite young but she certainly caught my eye. Of course, when I got on the platform I took a much longer look and my heart skipped a beat or two. I must admit that I really had to call on the Lord to help me concentrate on the business at hand.

As it happened, it was my job to man the product table after each service, to which the little blonde and her parents came after the service. I don't remember all the details, but for some reason they hung around the table after most of the others had left, and I remember taking her and her mom and dad on a tour of our motor coach. I then said good-night to them and they left. I felt at the time that she was probably way too young for me. I was twenty-eight years old and she could not have been out of her teenage years yet. I literally chalked that little lady off my list, but I must admit that I never completely got her out of my mind.

Another year went by and once again the Couriers were to appear at Zion Bible Institute on Memorial Day. As I walked along the side of the church auditorium and entered the same side door as before, I again stopped at the double doors and peeked through the slit. To my complete surprise there sat this same little blonde angel, in about the same seat as the year before. Once again my heart skipped a beat, and again I had to work very hard to concentrate once we went onstage.

Now, I didn't know this at the time but this young lady was good friends with the daughters of one of the faculty members of Zion. The Hill family lived directly behind the church auditorium, and after this evening of music the Couriers were invited to the Hills' for an evening snack before we hit the road, probably on an overnighter back to Harrisburg. When I walked into the living room, there sat this little blonde. This time I was formally introduced to Jean Ann Morton by the

Hills' daughter, Meredith, and we wound up sitting together and talking the entire evening. Before we left I got her mailing address and then began a letter-writing marathon. She got a letter almost every day for months.

MAJOR TRANSITIONS

Seven days after I met Jean Ann, Little David and Don Baldwin left the Couriers. We had known for some time that David was wanting to spend more time with his family, which was now growing. Our schedule was overwhelming to him, I believe. When our motor coach would pull into the parking lot of the Dutch Pantry Restaurant, where we had a special parking spot, Little David would be in the front well of the coach and out the door even before the wheels stopped rolling.

One night he did this in a driving rainstorm, jumping into his car and roaring out of the parking lot. Unfortunately, he came to a big dip in the roadway not a half mile from his house, and hydroplaned in deep water. Steering was impossible and the car slammed into a large tree. Little David told us that he backed off the tree and drove home with a flapping flat tire and a smashed front fender. He never even inspected the damage; he just rushed into the house and went to bed.

Don Baldwin, on the other hand, had expressed a desire to start a recording studio and a recording label in Mechanicsburg, Pennsylvania. He felt that being on the road constantly would take too much of his time. One evening as we were traveling, Don told us of his plans to leave the group. I remember how upset Little David became. He said he was unaware of what Don was thinking and was planning to tell us soon that he was leaving.

Dave, Neil, and I were certainly concerned about this traumatic turn of events. Little David had been our main spark plug at the piano, and Don was the manager, MC, and the main idea person in our group. Originally it had been his desire to go full time that convinced all of us to do so. Both Don and David said they would stay on until we found replacements, but we knew that if we were to continue we had to find new members right away. We gave them both dates by which we would replace them, not even having a clue who those two people would be or if we would even continue.

One side note is that Little David was not leaving to join another group. He told us he had fulfilled a desire to play for us and was now going home to do recording work and raise his family, never to go on the road full time again. True to his word, even though he had many great offers to return with major groups, he did exactly that—and what a family he and Colleen raised. All his children are now married and have wonderful Christian homes.

A week before Don Baldwin and Little David Young left our group we contacted Neil's younger brother, Phil, and a friend of Phil's Eddie Hawks, to see if they would join us. We did not try Phil out because we already knew he could carry the load as baritone. We did try out Eddie Hawks, after which he joined us as our piano player. Both were young and energetic, and both were excellent choices. We put them under such tremendous pressure to perform, it's a wonder they don't hate us today. But people liked both of them, and they gave a hundred and fifty percent of themselves to the job.

Even so, when Don and David left we still had some serious issues to work out. One of the most pressing was that we had signed a contract with Warner Brothers Records and had already produced and had on our racks an album that was a radical change from a traditional Gospel album. It was an exciting challenge for the Couriers because it involved more than just guitars, drums, and a piano or organ. It was a fully orchestrated album, recorded by parts of the orchestra from Bowling Green University in Kentucky. One side of the album was rather jazzy in nature and became the talk of the industry.

The biggest problem was that we had been asked to purchase five thousand of these very different albums. By today's standards the album was very tame, but back then it was thought to be too "worldly," so it was not selling well. We were stuck with all these albums and no money to pay for them. We were devastated because to us this was an incredible album, and we'd had so much fun singing with a live symphony orchestra. Today that same album, *Nothing But yhe Gospel Truth,* is the most sought-after one the Couriers ever recorded.

However, when we called Warner Brothers and explained our predicament, another miracle took place. Warner told us to send the albums to them and the debt would be canceled. Later we found whole boxes of these albums in record stores, especially in Canada, so we bought them back at discount prices and put them on our own racks for sale. God was working on our behalf.

SINGLE NO MORE

On December 17, 1966, Jean Ann and I were married in Revere, Massachusetts. It had been a whirlwind romance. The only time I got to see Jean Ann in the year that I courted her came when we traveled through the Boston area, either singing there or going through on our way to Maine or Canada. Dave Kyllonen, who did all our booking, has told me that when I started getting serious about Jean Ann the dates began to roll in from New England like never before, which I verified by checking our records.

Jean Ann worked for a dentist during her high school years. Now she was working full time. I remember meeting with her when she was dressed in work whites on her way to the office. If we were coming through the Boston area late at night or early in the morning, I would take that driving shift. I would call Jean Ann and meet her on Highway 1 at a pancake house north of Boston. We would sit in her car and talk about the future, and then I would get back in the coach and drive a few more hours, now fully awake after such a sweet time. In the meantime the guys were peacefully asleep in the coach. She did fly down to Harrisburg for a couple of our concerts and stayed with some of my good friends.

On one of these trips I finally gave her an engagement ring, in the most incredibly different place you could imagine. My mother and father had driven in that weekend, as well, to meet Jean Ann for the first time. Jean Ann's parents had also driven down from Boston. Sunday afternoon, after the big Farm Show concert, Neil and Ruth Enloe were having an open house at their newly purchased home in Mechanicsburg. I was going to give Jean Ann her engagement ring that same day. But not wanting to over-shadow Neil and Ruth's big day, I took Jean Ann for a ride. I found only one secluded spot to finally stop the car and give her the ring—a small cemetery located not a mile from the Enloes' house. If any of you readers have an album by the Couriers entitled *Down Memory Lane* you will see on the cover a picture of Dave, Neil, Phil, and me standing by an antique car. That small lane, about where the car is sitting, is where Jean Ann and I sat when I gave her the ring. I have asked Jean Ann to forgive me many times over for choosing such a morbid spot to give her a diamond engagement ring. Since then I have also had to ask her a few times to forgive me for other things too, but no apologies were ever more sincere than that one.

I never had second thoughts about marrying Jean Ann, although she must have had many second thoughts when she was alone while I was traveling the world. It was not fair then and still is not fair today. I owe her my entire life of ministry. I cannot imagine being on the road for forty-two years of marriage, almost continually, without her loyal support and prayers. In the traumatic years that came our way with the loss of my voice in 1979, and the ensuing breakup of the Couriers in 1980, I never would have made it without her prayers and her steadfast faith in God.

I did try to make up for botching the engagement ring presentation. I did not tell her where we were going on our honeymoon, but she finally got the picture when we flew to Miami and then boarded a plane for Montego Bay, Jamaica. Jean Ann was born in Jamaica and was raised in Montego Bay until she was thirteen years old, by Open Bible Missionaries Ivan and Kaye Morton. I took her back there and we had an absolutely idyllic time, basking in the sunshine and roaming the beaches of beautiful, romantic Jamaica. It is still a highlight of our lives and we have returned many times since.

Fulfillment made a big change in my personality. After marriage I began to settle into a more secure life, with something to look forward to. I have already confessed to a restlessness and a lack of confidence in my ability to sing with the major groups of the day. I was still not totally comfortable—I did not want to feel pressured into competition instead of ministry. We combated that by praying with other groups before they went onstage, and asking God to bless their singing. This set the stage for an evening of ministering together.

We had been through the age of one-upmanship with the PA system being turned up for some groups and turned down for others. Groups were jockeying to see who would go first and who would be last in the so-called "feature spot." We did not want to be part of that scene. Many times we volunteered to be the first group on the program to set the promoter at ease. It paid dividends, because I believe other groups began to really enjoy singing with us instead of viewing us as competition. I also think the audiences, who are most times smarter than the performers, began to sense the change of atmosphere among the groups.

On the other hand, I had left CBI early for ministry and that was somewhat curtailed by concert circuit work. It was more lucrative money wise with bigger flat fees for paid admission concerts, and we sold more product with larger audiences. We seldom set a fee for church work and sometimes we took a beating. Even so, more times than not we received much more from churches than what came in the offerings alone. Pastors were as generous as they could be, knowing we were providing for our families.

- 9 -

Life-Changing
Call

In January 1967, just a month after Jean Ann and I were married, we Couriers took our first major missions trip. An evangelist named Paul Olson had been our friend for many years. Whenever he had crusades in the East he would book us for an evening. He was also involved in major overseas ministry from time to time, and he began to suggest that we needed to broaden our ministry by becoming singing missionaries. He was so confident that this was God's will that he said he would book us wherever we chose to go.

It would be a major decision for us because there would be no financial rewards—only the giving of our time. We were certainly not flush with funds, but we thank God for the vision Paul Olson had for the Couriers. It changed our lives forever.

After much prayer and consultation with our wives we decided to try a missions trip. Due to limited financial resources and without big-time faith, we decided to make our first journey outside the United States to the West Indies. We chose a twenty-day visit to Jamaica, Barbados, Trinidad, and Guyana, South America, and set about to raise what we thought we needed—$4,500 for the entire trip. This would provide airfares and money to keep the ship afloat at home for twenty days.

We failed miserably in raising the funds, but by the time we got started it was too late to back out. Posters and advertisement had already been sent out. In desperation we went to our local banker, and he agreed to lend us the money.

To our shock that first missions trip was a resounding success. Every service was packed, with hundreds of people coming to hear the Gospel group from America and the preaching of God's Word. Hundreds of people were saved, and no offerings were taken for our benefit; all incoming funds were used to defray the expenses of the meetings. And once the local newspapers found out that we were not taking any money out of the county—unlike a notorious evangelist who had been there before—they began to give us great coverage.

We came home excited and ready to go again, at which point we quickly found out that God is often faithful beyond our wildest dreams. Two days earlier, a check came to our office from a church group that had disbanded. Because they were a nonprofit organization they were required by the IRS to give any remaining monies to another nonprofit group. We had known about this situation before going, but the list of possible receivers was long, ranging from the Couriers to Billy Graham. We of little faith thought that we would be left out when the final decision was made, but not so this time. The check was for the exact amount we had borrowed, $4,500. This simple answer to our prayers validated our original decision and catapulted us into major missions trips for the next thirteen years.

Other Gospel groups could not fathom how we were able to set aside time to afford our missions trips. They all wanted to do something similar, but when they questioned us about how much money they could make to support themselves they could not understand how we did it without taking a dime from any mission station in the world. The answer was simple. No other group in America had such solid support from their immediate local area. We had friends of our ministry rather than fans. People knew how we lived our lives; they knew we were not extravagant. We also had a major television ministry that reached thousands of people, and we tried in every way to be good stewards of all the money that came to us.

Here is how we managed to do so many missions trips without being a burden on any missionary: We combined trips with our friends with our missions trips. For example, when we went to the Holy Land we took people with us. They paid a certain amount as a group; their fares were not overpriced, but they knew that we made a modest profit. Meanwhile, we three Couriers got our fares paid by the travel companies. Then we almost always scheduled a missions trip after the Holy Land experience. Our wives would bring the traveling group back to America while Dave, Neil, and I would travel on to other parts of the world, with most of our airfares already paid.

On other occasions we would book services in countries such as England, Sweden, and South Africa. These were countries of means, and we would take offerings and sell our product, telling the people that we were going to other countries on the same trip that could not afford to pay us anything. So England, Sweden, and even South Africa gave us support for additional trips to poor countries in Africa, Asia, and even behind the Iron Curtain. We also hosted several boat cruises and vacation trips to the West Indies. We would take our people ashore at each stop for a one-day crusade. Many times, before we would leave an island nation we would also take an offering for special local projects. We raised thousands of dollars that way.

As our missions projects began to grow, our local friends also sent us offerings for our projects. One important part of our ministry was that we always raised the money for the project first and then trusted God to provide for our families so we could pay our own bills. Not once did we ever fail to raise the necessary amount, both for the project and our own needs. In fact, each time we made a trip our offerings got larger, even as the numbers of people getting saved also began to swell. It was phenomenal to watch it all take place. You just cannot outgive God.

Needles for Everyone

One missions trips stands out above all the others. When Phil Enloe joined Neil and me in ministry in the 1980s, we received a call to minister in England and Poland. At that time, Poland was still under Russian control. We were harassed for six hours by the Polish border patrol. We finally entered the country for a short visit to a couple of cities. Upon leaving, I got angry in my spirit at the control that Communism had over these sweet people. The guns at the border were not pointed out to keep people from entering, they were pointed in to keep Polish people from leaving. I never forgot that trip.

Not much later I returned to Poland with another ministry and got even more upset at what I saw. I came home and told Neil and Phil that we needed to do an extensive missionary trip to Poland. I had talked to my minister friend in Poland, Piotr Ceislar, about bringing a gift to the Polish people who needed everything. Piotr told me that the diabetic children of Poland were in need of insulin needles. Swedish Christian people were sending insulin, but needles were in such short supply that the children were being forced to use the same needles over and over. So I told Neil and Phil that we needed to take a supply of needles with us for an extended stay. I then began to look for ways to buy the needles at a discount.

At first I had no luck at all, and I was becoming desperate because we had already set dates for a two-week stay. Then it happened, and the miracle was incredible. I got a surprise call from Ron Hensley, who had sung in a Gospel group called The Vicounts, which Don Baldwin had started years before. Ron asked me where we were going on our next missions trip. I told him we were going to Poland and he said he wanted to go with us. I then met Ron in a local restaurant but told him I had one problem. We wanted to take insulin needles to Poland for the children but we could not find a discount price.

Ron looked at me with utter amazement. "Duane, do you know what I'm doing for a living right now?" At that point Ron just blew me away. "I am working for the largest manufacturer of insulin needles in the country! I am hauling insulin needles all over, and I can get you a good price. I am good friends with the boss."

Ron called two day later and said he had a price of seven cents per needle, one cent less than what they could make them for. On the shelf they sold in boxes for at least twenty-five cents per needle. On pure faith alone I immediately ordered two hundred fifty thousand needles, then sent out a plea for people to buy at least one box containing one hundred needles, for the unheard-of price of $15. As the money began to roll in I contacted Polish Airlines and they agreed to ship the needles free of charge on the very plane that we were taking to Poland. I then contacted the exporter in New York, at the airport. It would cost $600 just for paper work, but when I told the exporter what I was doing he said, "I have a nephew who is a diabetic and uses two needles a day. Could you bring me a couple boxes of needles for him?" I immediately agreed, and when I handed the free needles to him I got a receipt for $300, exactly half of what was usually charged.

The next miracle was that Ron offered to take the needles free of charge in his truck to JFK airport. Then, a week before we were to deliver the needles, Ron called with another miracle. He said that the insulin company had ordered a brand-new machine from Germany. It was not due for another few months but was being sent to New York early and Ron was supposed to pick it up. The company would therefore pay Ron for going to get the machine and delivering it to the factory. So, in effect, Ron was paid by the insulin company to take our needles to JFK.

Meanwhile, when the Polish government heard what we were doing they allowed us to minister in the local movie theaters.

Scores of young people were won into the kingdom and a brand-new church was started in a community in Poland, which is another huge story all by itself.

And God was blessing us at home as well. From 1964 until 1980 we had three brand-new motor coaches and put over a half-million miles on each one. Rumor had it that because we always seemed to have new coaches we must be very rich. On the contrary, I am here to tell you that our story is one of absolute faith in God's providence. Not one of us had a lot of financial wisdom. None of our fathers ever made more than $30,000 a year, and my salary in the Couriers never exceeded $400 a week for years. We owned nothing but a small office building in Mechanicsburg, Pennsylvania. If we ever figure out how we survived and did what we did, it will cease to be a miracle.

For example, the huge crowds at the Farm Show Arena and the Hershey Sports Arena did bring in nice sums of money, but guess what? In those days, each LP album that we produced cost us more than $2.50. By the time our biggest concerts rolled around each year we were deeply in debt to the record companies. I can remember being $7,000 behind, which the concerts would pay off but with little left for us. Selling albums for $5 gave us a profit margin of no more than $2.45 per album, and some cost more than that. Record companies did not sell many of our albums in stores. The bulk of our sales was generated by us. Critics might tell me that I should not divulge such things, but I think we need to be as transparent as possible to a very cynical world.

I do know that we never went anywhere by accident. God always seemed to bring us to the right place at the right time. We did not put heavy demands on missionaries; on the contrary, we often took missionaries on special side trips to give them breaks from their daily routines. On cruises we would invite the local missionary or local pastor on board for wonderful meals and a time of relaxation. On more than one occasion we really were healing balm to discouraged missionaries and pastors. We also left money, cameras, clothes, and PA systems with local churches and missionaries.

On the other hand we worked hard, sometimes singing and preaching several times a day. I remember singing seven separate times one Sunday—five times in American Samoa, then twice more in Western Samoa. In the West Indies we would sing in two schools each day, and then in a crusade each evening for two weeks at a time. Many times we came home with just the clothes on our backs, but it was infinitely rewarding to come home broke and then watch while God replenished our finances.

INTO NEEDFUL PLACES

Here is one more example. We were asked to go to the little island nation of Dominica for a week of meetings. Harold Scovmand, the man who helped us so often in the West Indies, had set up a meeting with some Canadian missionary friends. Harold flew us into Dominica in a Piper Cherokee single-engine plane that he used in his construction business all over the West Indies.

When we arrived we were immediately told that a terrible tragedy had taken place just days before. Healing services were being held at the church we were going to minister in, and great healings were taking place, for which whole busloads of people were coming down from the mountain communities. One evening a truck loaded with more than thirty people was winding its way down the mountain road when the driver became ill and pulled over to let his partner drive into town. The emergency brake was the only thing holding the truck from careening down the mountainside when the exchange of drivers occurred. The new driver then failed to put the truck in low gear before releasing the emergency brake.

Immediately, the truck began to gather speed, at which point the driver could not get the truck into any gear at all, let alone low. Very quickly the truck gathered tremendous speed, and at the next hairpin turn it plunged into a line of trees and began to fall toward the road below this turn. There was no protection for the people riding in the back. More than thirty people were thrown down the side of the mountain. When the news reached the city, Don Scheske raced to the scene but by then it was pitch-dark. Everyone was afraid to climb down to see if anyone was still alive. Don obtained a long rope and made his way down with a flashlight. Only one person survived.

Needless to say, Don and Janice were distraught. To make matters worse, some of the local Catholic Priests said, "I told you so! We warned people about going to this Pentecostal Church!"

We decided to stay with our scheduled meetings even though the church was devastated, at which point we Couriers spent the entire week singing songs of comfort. Sometimes Neil would go to the piano and play some old hymn and we would just sing along, but little by little healing began to take place. We have always felt that God sent us to Dominica for the express purpose of lifting up the peoples' spirits and bringing comfort to a very stressed-out missionary and his dear wife.

I have lost track of how many times we ministered in the West Indies. It was always nice to leave cold Pennsylvania in January or February to go to some Caribbean island, where we sang and preached to countless thousands of people over the years. However, twice we had a hard time getting there. I guess the devil knew that many people would be saved and tried to stop us from going.

The first episode involved the worst snowstorm ever to hit the New York City area, in 1969. We were taken to JFK Airport and dropped off at the Pan Am terminal just as it was beginning to snow. My wife was with me on this journey to Barbados for seventeen days of continual ministry in an open-air crusade at Queens Park. We'd had crowds of more than ten thousand each night in previous years. The People's Cathedral Church, pastored by Rev. Holmes Williams, was the host. Attendance at that church had grown into the thousands as it reached out to the unsaved.

As we waited for our plane, the storm got worse and the winds became very strong. At times we could not even see the tail section of the huge 747s sitting just outside the terminal windows. Finally they announced that all flights were delayed and many were canceled. Little did we know that, along with thousands of other people, we would be stuck at JFK Airport for the next three days. No one could leave because the roads were impassable, and no one could get in to bring food or take people to hotels and motels.

We found out later that people actually died in the parking lots when the tailpipes of their cars became blocked by snow and carbon monoxide seeped in. In the terminal, we were trying to sleep on the floor on newspapers. My wife was six months pregnant, and we finally lobbied the terminal officials to let women and children sleep on the airliners. I took my wife onboard, and as she slept on a seat I curled up on the floor and tried to stay warm.

Each day people would line up at the only open restaurant. Food soon became scarce, and the announcement was made that the only milk available would be for babies and small children. On the second day, Jean Ann and I began to exercise by walking around the Pan Am terminal. On one such occasion we came upon an ugly scene. A male passenger was at a terminal desk berating an airline agent. He had wrapped his hands around the agent's neck and was shaking him, all the while yelling that he had to get out of the terminal. Several people were standing there, doing nothing to help this poor agent, so against my wife's better judgment I walked up and tapped him on the shoulder. I demanded that he take his hands off the agent, and as I did so I pointed at my wife who was obviously very pregnant.

"Sir, you think you have been in this terminal a long time? Look at my wife. She wasn't even pregnant when we got here!" I don't know where the inspiration came from, but the man abruptly turned and walked away.

The other episode involved flying once again with Harold Scovmand. Harold came to Pennsylvania, picked up the three Couriers, and flew us to Vero Beach in that same Cherokee airplane. We were bound for Trinidad for a crusade. After spending the night in Vero Beach, we loaded up and began our nonstop flight. Now, I had been a licensed pilot myself for a good many years, so I was planning to spell Harold a little bit by flying while he got some shut-eye, which I eventually did.

We drifted by Nassau and started down the Bahama Chain. We were never out of sight of at least one island on this part of the journey—the only long, over-water portion would be from South Caicos Island to the coast of the Dominican Republic, a distance of one hundred fifty miles. This would be the most treacherous part of the trip if we had engine problems. The plane had four fuel tanks and we were flying on one of the wing pod tanks when I took over. I soon noticed that the fuel was getting low in that tank so I switched over to the other wing tank. However, after flying for another few minutes, I noticed that we were still draining fuel out of the almost, empty tank I had switched from.

I immediately woke Harold and we turned around and landed at an airport I had spotted a few minutes earlier. This isolated airport was on Long Island at a place called Stella Maris. Upon landing and taking the fuel selector valve apart we found nothing obstructing the fuel flow. So we put things back together and climbed back in the aircraft. But when we finally got the hot engine started and began our checklist, we found that it was missing badly. We then checked the two magnetos and found that the left one was the culprit. All aircrafts have redundant parts so that if one fails another can take over. But if we lost the other magneto we might be in serious trouble, so Harold decided that we should stay on Long Island while he limped back to Florida to get the magneto fixed.

By this time people had come down from the other side of the island, and we found that there was a nice tourist resort just a mile from the airport. So Dave, Neil, and I went to the resort to await Harold's return. We thought that Harold would call our wives and the pastor in Trinidad and inform them that we were okay, and we would continue in a day or so. Two days went by and no Harold. By this time the pastor from Trinidad had called our wives, wondering where we were. Our wives then called our pastor and the entire church was praying. For all they knew we might be down in the ocean. Harold finally showed up at Stella Maris and told us he was delayed an extra day because, once he got the left magneto fixed and took off, he was fifty miles off the coast of Florida when the right magneto quit completely.

That meant that if we had continued on from Stella Maris with only the right magneto, somewhere along the trip that magneto would have quit and we would have had to ditch in not very friendly waters, one hundred fifty miles or more from shore. God had put us on Stella Maris, via a false reading of the fuel tanks, for the express purpose of revealing the real problem. We continued on to Trinidad and had a fantastic meeting.

Other missions trips come to mind that profoundly affected our ministry in so many ways. One even affected a song that we loved to sing. We were in Rustinburg, South Africa, at a Bible school. One of our favorite songs was the anthem "I Sing the Mighty Power of God." We had an incredible soundtrack that literally lifted everyone, including the Couriers, into heavenly places. We were in the middle of this song when the electric power went off, shutting down our PA system completely. We could have quit singing, but instead we completed the song *a cappella*. When we got to the end the students jumped to their feet and began to praise God. The place was in an uproar of praise. I think we even sang the song again. It made such a profound impact that we never sang the song again with the sound track. It became our signature song, and it has blessed people again and again. It was a testimony that our power sources may be shut down, but God's power is never shut off.

GOD'S IN CHARGE

Sometimes what we thought were our most feeble efforts turned out to be the most successful. One example happened in Jakarta, Indonesia. We were singing in a dark, dingy church auditorium. Either the electricity was not very strong or the bulbs were of small wattage, because we could barely see the several hundred people sitting in the pews. We also had no PA system with us, and the church's own system was very small. A busy street ran just outside the church and the noise of vehicles passing by was deafening. The temperature had to be around a hundred degrees, and to make matters worse, lighted kerosene lanterns were placed around the platform so people could see us. Those fumes were incredible.

We arrived late and Neil had no chance to check out the dilapidated piano on the platform. When we stepped forward to sing and Neil hit the first key, it was the last time that piano was played. We stopped the service and Neil took the front off the piano. Termites had hollowed out the sticks connected to the keys, so when a key was struck the sticks disintegrated into dust.

Then Neil saw a small portable pump organ. He sat down and began to pump the bellows. We began an up-tempo version of "Since Jesus Came Into My Heart." Neil was huffing and puffing and sweating as he pumped that ancient organ. When the song was over, Neil informed us that the bellows on the organ were leaking and he could not play it any longer. He did not want a heat stroke. We finally decided to sing some old hymns of the church, *a capella,* and when that was finished Dave gave a mini sermon and an altar call. To our amazement more than one hundred people literally ran to the altar for salvation. Clearly, it is not by our might nor our power, but by the power of the Holy Spirit that things happen.

We had some very strange encounters on the mission field as well. One particular day comes to mind. We were with Missionary Jerry Falley in Liberia. The day before we left for home, Jerry asked us if we wanted to visit a real jungle village. He warned us that it would be a somewhat rigorous trip. And we said yes.

We put on our hiking boots and carried plenty of water, because Jerry told us that we would have to walk a considerable distance. We were really excited—in other travels we had been to native tribes in mud hut villages, but we were always able to drive to them. We left Monrovia, the capital city, and motored thirty-five miles inland on some fairly good roads. On the way we passed the home of the president of Liberia. He was a local Methodist pastor as well.

The road became increasingly rougher until it finally ended at some river's edge. At that point, hidden in tall weeds, was a small raft made of fifty-gallon barrels and planks, but with no oars in sight. All we saw was a small cable stretched across the rather wide river. We boarded the raft and literally pulled ourselves across, hand over hand. On the other side we secured the raft for the return trip and struck out into dense foliage.

Soon we were met by someone from the village. He explained that men from the village had hacked out this trail for at least three miles. It was quite hot but we were still excited. Finally we smelled smoke and heard voices. Suddenly we burst into a large clearing. Out of the mud huts came all kinds of people—women, children, and men clothed only in loincloths. The children were stark naked. Someone was ringing a bell and the missionary told us that was the call to the little church because we would be singing and ministering to this village.

We were taken to a large, open-sided building. Inside were crude benches. As we waited for the people to show up, we were wondering how we would be able to sing to mostly naked men and women? To our surprise the people began to arrive all dressed up in their native garb, including the children.

The service began with the people singing. There were no instruments to speak of. Most of the people were carrying what looked like old pork and bean cans on sticks. Inside the cans must have been stones or dried beans. They shook the cans in rhythm to the singing. No one was singing on key, but let me tell you it was an emotional moment for all of us. These primitive people had been won into the kingdom of God and they were making a joyful noise unto the Lord. All I could do was sit there and weep. They had none of the earthly goods that I had experienced but they had Jesus in their hearts!

We sang a few songs, Rev. Falley gave a short message, and the meeting was over. We made our way back through the dense jungle with joyful hearts. A few weeks later, after returning to the United States, we heard the horrifying news that the president of Liberia had been assassinated. Since that visit Liberia has gone through terrible times of disorder and killings. I have wondered many times what happened to that little village in the jungle. I suspect that life goes on unchanged, as it had for hundreds of years.

Another hilarious episode occurred on the island nation of St. Lucia. To promote our week of revival services we contacted the manager of the primitive television station on the island. It was located in Castries, the capital city. We were going to sing just one song, but the station had no microphones, so we were going to play one of our songs and lip-sync. The station played videos most of the time, and some international news programs.

To run advertisements the station used a Rolodex-type cylinder that revolved. A television camera was aimed at this cylinder, and as it turned you could read the advertisement in large, bold letters on each page. Our announcement that we would be singing on television and holding revival services was on two cards. When we got to the studio, the operator put the announcement that we would be singing on the Rolodex. He also had a phonograph player hooked into the sound system. We told him which song to play, and after the announcement was made via the card the operator turned the small Sony camera on us.

The camera did not have much of a wide angle, so the three of us had to stand almost cheek to cheek to be in the same frame. When the operator started the song we began to lip sync as well as we could. Then a dog began to scratch on the metal door of the studio, and then to bark. All of a sudden Neil started laughing. Then he began to sing off key! Not to be undone, I did the same thing, and Dave started laughing as well. To cover up our laughter, which the people could not hear, we really started getting into the song. Soon we were having a ball, flailing our arms and gesturing wildly. You could see the man running the phonograph getting excited as well.

Finally the song began winding down. The last sentence was, "Come, my yoke is easy and my burden is light." When we came to that part of the song the needle stuck on the words "Come, my yoke is easy," and kept sticking so that we had to repeat "Come, my yoke is easy" at least four times. The operator thought that was part of the song, so he was enjoying our antics, while we kept trying to make him understand what was happening. Finally after the fourth repetition he caught on so that this is what went out over the airwaves: "Come, my yoke is easy . . . *ZZIPPPP!*"

With that, the song was over and the camera swung back to the Rolodex for our announcement about the revival. At that point we all fell apart. The television operator must have thought we were crazy. Dave Kyllonen's wife, Judy, had joined us in St. Lucia and was watching the program. She said that she had never seen us so animated. Certainly it was a day to remember.

-10-

The Days of Dave, Duane, and Neil

After a year or so, Eddie Hawks left our group to further his education. Later on, after our first missions trip to the West Indies, Phil Enloe decided to leave as well. We did not take their decisions lightly, but we also knew that when someone had decided to leave, it was best to set a firm date instead of waiting for replacements. Both Eddie and Phil had been tremendous assets, but now it was time to move on again.

When Eddie left we still had no one else, so Neil took his place at the piano and we started singing with our soundtracks. That was working well. One benefit of staying as a trio was a financial one. We were now into full-time missions work and it was easier to do missions with just three people.

Perhaps more to the point, we were not thrilled about starting over again with two new personalities. Dave and Neil and I had been there from the beginning and knew what struggles and sacrifices we and our wives had made. New people could never understand that fully. Plus, people overseas did not care how many people we came with—they were just glad to see us at all. A contrary consideration was that promoters might not be so eager to book a trio. Male quartets were a bigger draw. But even so, after much soul-searching and prayer we decided to remain a trio.

At this point, Neil would sometimes go to the piano but we began to utilize soundtracks more and more. At first we were roundly criticized by those who preferred live background music, and to be honest, I would agree that it's more fun to sing with live backup.

But apparently we started something, because most groups in America today use soundtracks quite frequently. Overseas it was a huge blessing because of the lack of good pianos to play. I remember one concert when an irate man came up to me and said we should be singing with live music. I told him that the next time we came we certainly would do so if he would come up with the extra $2,000 for live musicians, at which point he became very quiet.

One incredible blessing that I believe was a huge help came about when Channel 8 in Lancaster invited us to do a Sunday morning television show from 8–8:30. Channel 8 is still the number one TV station in all of central Pennsylvania. The exposure was phenomenal. As people began to tune in and listen to our announcements about our concerts, church dates, bus tours, boat cruises, Holy Land tours, and missions, every facet of our ministry prospered.

The statement that you cannot outgive God was also proven true all over again. We were tithing 10% and more of our time to missions without seeing any money coming in, and now God repaid us in a big way. The television program continued for eighteen solid years. Even today, when we sing as Dave, Duane, and Neil and minister in the Channel 8 area, scores of people come up and tell us what a blessing the television ministry was to them.

As I have said, 1966–69 were momentous years. Among other things we had our worst highway accident, which easily could have ended our ministry. It happened like this.

We three were asked to minister at Braeside Camp, a meeting ground located just outside Paris, Ontario. On this occasion Jean Ann accompanied me. She had come along because of a very strict rule we had with regard to people traveling in our motor coach. No women except our wives were allowed to travel in our coach, even to a restaurant after a service, unless accompanied by a husband, father, mother, or one of our own wives. Our secretary, June Graham, came from Ontario and had flown home for a week. To save money, she asked if she could ride back to Pennsylvania with us after the Braeside event, which is why Jean Ann was with me.

As we were driving back to Harrisburg, at around 5:30 on Monday morning, I was awakened by our driver and asked to take my shift. It was a rather cool morning in July and there had been patches of ground fog, but that was not what caused our problem. As I was about to make a turn I looked up to see a huge 18-wheeler bearing down on me on the wrong side of the road! I immediately took evasive action by turning the coach away from the truck and hoping it would miss me. It still hit on the driver's side right in the middle, but if I had not swerved we would have collided head on, and I am sure both the truck driver and I would have died.

After the sideswipe I guided the wounded coach to the side of the road. I was afraid to open the door to the sleeping compartment. When I did I saw such a mess! I called out each name and was relieved that everyone answered. Once I knew they were all okay I hurried to the truck. The driver was still in his seat, in shock. He thought he had hit a commercial bus filled with passengers, and he was apologizing profusely for falling asleep at the wheel. I helped him down; his only injury was a broken kneecap.

State troopers agreed later that my action in swerving away saved both of our lives. The trooper also commented that if the truck had not hit me the driver would have crashed into a cement abutment just ahead, and he would not have survived. There were absolutely no skid marks from the truck. He hit me while fast asleep. The only injury in our coach was a head injury to June Graham, but the coach itself was totaled. Our lawyers wanted us to sue the trucking company, but we found out that the owner had only three trucks and only two of those were being used. We could have put him out of business but we decided not to.

Instead, we took our insurance money, went to Detroit, and bought a brand, new 1969 GM coach. This was our only major accident in all the years we have traveled to date. That includes more than three million miles, and only the grace and protection of God have kept us safe.

The Long Journey

As I have related, the journey of the Couriers had been a slow, steady stream of tests, challenges, changes, and victories. Now it seemed that Dave, Neil, and I were reaping the rewards. The telephone rang constantly, many calls coming from missionaries all over the world, wanting us to come. My records show that from the early years of our ministry until the first breakup of Dave, Duane, and Neil we sang no less than two hundred eighty-five dates a year. Couple that with fifty-two recordings of our television program, plus countless days and nights in trains, airplanes, cars, and coaches, and you have a schedule that even today would be mind-boggling.

How in the world did our wives put up with this coming and going? Each trip on the highways of America was dangerous, let alone our trips in foreign countries on even more treacherous roads. In America, the interstate highway system was such a blessing. We watched from the windows of our motor coaches as this momentous building task was accomplished. We breathed a sigh of relief every time we came to a finished portion of the system, because they made our journeys much less tedious. That system has saved us countless hours, not to mention the lives of multiplied thousands of people.

Meanwhile, our motor coach's odometer rang up over a hundred thousand miles a year, year after year. We completely wore out two brand-new motor coaches, and when we sold our final coach, a 1973 MCI, it had more than a half-million miles on it. In seven years of use we had averaged more than seventy-one thousand miles a year on that coach alone.

Along the way we did full concert schedules with the Imperials, Andrae Crouch and the Disciples, and the Oak Ridge Boys, and West Coast trips with the Rebels and the Harvesters. We were with the Oak Ridge Boys on their final swing across Canada and the West Coast before they made the switch to country music. Indeed, we still have a close relationship with the Oak Ridge Boys. Richard Sturben, bass, and Joe Bonsall, tenor, both say that the first Gospel group they ever heard was the Couriers.

The Oak Ridge Boys put tremendous energy into their presentation of the Gospel, but sad to say it was misunderstood by many a Gospel crowd. In particular, one song upset many people. They were singing a song about Jesus being the Great Physician and they referred to Him as "Doctor God." People thought this was disrespectful, but I thought it was a clever way to get the attention of the unsaved. I think the frustration really got to the Oak Ridge Boys, and they decided to reach out to a new audience. I have never discussed this with them at length, but these are my own thoughts. They were also being criticized by their peers, and that was just simply wrong, in my opinion—and I think I am entitled to that!

Now, after a rocky start in country music the Oak Ridge Boys have had a very successful career. Their country hits are too numerous to mention. But even better, in a recent periodical Joe Bonsall proclaimed boldly that each of the Oak Ridge Boys has a personal relationship with God and is a born-again Christian. In the end that is all that matters. In fact, when I had a serious heart attack in 2003, Duane Allen called to tell me that he and the other Oaks had been praying for me. Every time I see that they are in our area, if possible, I am there to cheer them on.

Let me close this section by making it clear that, in my attempt to portray my feelings about becoming a more ministry-oriented group, I in no way mean to imply that the various members who left our group were not interested in ministry. Eddie Reece started his own singing group and later on pioneered a church in California. Eddie Hawks became a much sought-after minister of music and still presents the Gospel through his music ministry at Victory Church in Lakeland, Florida. Phil Enloe and his beautiful wife, Jan, are still involved in a full-time road ministry and reach out to thousands each year. Little David Young has blessed hundreds of singers by recording them and has also mentored his own children in his own family group all these years. Don Baldwin blessed many a Gospel group with his recording studio, and then later became the promoter and provider of children's Gospel stories by the famous Louie puppet of Rev. Dan Betzer. I sincerely believe that if each member I have mentioned had stayed in our group, we still would have moved in the same direction, toward more missions and church work.

- 11 -

Trouble Ahead

In January of 1978 I had an experience that almost ended my ministry with the Couriers. Our huge concerts at the Farm Show Arena and the Hershey Sports Arena were now becoming a thing of the past. Local promoters and churches were booking major groups into their own venues, and prices had gone up so much that, where we'd once had twelve groups on each program, we could now bring in no more than three.

We decided to downsize our concerts to the smaller arenas of the Forum and the Zembo Temple. We were still drawing good crowds, but nothing like the eight thousand or more of years gone by. We did these concerts once a month, and at the end of the first one we decided to record a new album to help our finances and give us fresh music. Record sales were important, and we also needed to constantly bring new songs into our ministry.

At this time I was experiencing voice fatigue from the constant singing of more than 280 dates a year, mostly in churches in which we didn't dare turn up the PA system too loud. Many nights we would sing for long periods on a system that was hardly on at all. As I have stated before, the concert work was easier because we could depend on the PA system more. Churches were a different story, and the increased physical effort had begun wearing on my voice. Beyond all that, the Couriers were also known as power singers. And because we were a trio we had to make an even bigger sound when we sang against groups that had five people, as the Kingsmen did for some time. Plus, our arrangements were high and our endings were long, so it was really telling on me.

When we went into the studio to record, it was fun but also very taxing on my voice. We would spend the first few hours just trying to correct bad habits that had crept in since our last recording. We were also trying to get in the groove with new songs that we did not know very well yet.

The usual order for recording songs was to make sure that Dave Kyllonen's solo parts were recorded early in the session. Since he sang bass it was imperative that he be fresh so he could hit the low notes clearly. Early morning was the best time for him. Then we would do the songs that Neil had solos on. I was always last. We followed that same pattern for years.

UNDER THE KNIFE

During the later part of one of our sessions I was doing a solo part and my voice would not clear up. Something was wrong with my vocal cords. I tried resting for a while and even gargled warm salt water. It was getting late and I was getting frustrated. After several takes that were ruined by the same frog I remember clearing my voice harshly and loudly. I felt a sudden sting in my throat, but I put it out of my mind and somehow finished my solo part. As I look back, I believe that this was the beginning of my voice problems. Little did I know at the time how devastating it would turn out to be. My impatience got me into deep trouble, and there was no time to recover.

As we continued our grueling schedule I began to struggle with high notes. When a service or concert was over I then had to go back and sell the product. When I would finally get on the motor coach I could hardly talk. I would refrain from talking very much until the next service to save my voice. Those who know me well will understand that this was a monumental task. I have never been known as a quiet thinker.

Finally I went to a throat specialist. After examining my vocal cords he told me that I had a small nodule on one of them, which brought up two options. Take six months off from singing and perhaps the nodule would go away, or have it removed surgically and possibly be back singing in three weeks or so.

Now, you have to understand the loyalty to ministry that I had. Plus, we did not have the luxury of enough singers to cover for someone who was not able to perform. I had sung many times when I could hardly stand up. I missed my only sister's wedding and all my grandparents' funerals. Finances were a part of this in the early years, but later on it was my belief that the ministry must go on no matter what.

Now this same mentality took over. So I opted for the surgery and that proved to be the wrong decision. The rest of the

Couriers went to Estes Park, Colorado, for a big music festival and I went under the knife in late July, 1978.

I was then ordered to take at least three weeks off and not talk, let alone sing. I was to write everything down. That was the hardest thing to do, and I have been told that I was not a very good patient.

Meanwhile, sometime before 1978, the Couriers had hired a bus driver, Tom Baker, and also a ministry coordinator, Rev. Paul Wislocky. By this time we also had two full-time secretaries, Dolores Lehman and Hilda Bernard. So the pressure was on to keep the ministry viable. Paul Wislocky filled in for me during this time, and August was also a fairly slow month. We were having great success with our youth camp ministries, but the Couriers did not sing at the camp. We were heavily involved in daily activities with the campers, and I probably should have stayed home away from the long days and nights, but I did not. Those three weeks of recuperation stretched into four and five without any improvement in my voice. I was believing God for complete healing and nothing seemed to be happening.

Somewhere along the line I was told about one of the best throat specialists in the country. He treated all the Metropolitan Opera stars in New York. When I visited his office I found out that he was the inventor of the medical tool that is inserted down the nose with an attached optical light and a tiny camera. This tool was then put in place and I was asked to sing while the doctor observed. When the procedure was over he told me exactly what the problem was. The previous surgery, done with a knife, had taken more than the nodule off one of my cords and had left a slight bend right where the nodule had been. When the cords are functioning properly they produce a clear sound. Any deformation or bump on a cord will disrupt the flow of air and the offended cord will not function correctly. I was getting hoarse because the air was not passing though properly.

I was given voice exercises to practice. I then went to a voice therapist in New York, who discovered that even the pitch of my voice had changed. I was talking lower than I used to in an effort to save it. That alone was tiring out my voice, because the cords were not taut and were literally "flapping together." I had to tell myself to keep my voice in the higher register. Jean Ann began constantly reminding me to raise my voice pitch.

In the meantime I was fighting depression and despair, and the same feelings that assaulted me when the Couriers almost broke up on that fateful night in West Virginia came flooding back. If I had to retire from singing, how would I provide for my wife and two daughters? The devil sat on my shoulder many a day and mocked me. *Where is your God now? You have given everything to this ministry and now look at you. You are a sorry mess!*

In those lonely, desperate days, the hours I had spent on my knees in Bible college, the scriptures that I had memorized, the experiences we had already had in our ministry, and the strong, silent faith and support of my wife brought me through. In my own strength I would have given up completely.

Even so, one of the worst feelings came after I had gone back to singing a couple songs a night. Each evening when my voice would again fail me, I could feel the sympathy of the audience and I did not want them to pity me. After each service I would escape back to our motor coach and sometimes lie on my bed, weeping uncontrollably. It was excruciating. My heart felt like it would literally burst out of my chest.

Finally, September and October of 1978 went by and a twenty-seven-day West Coast trip came up. Dave and Neil told me that I should stay home and use these days for complete rest. We also knew that in December we were taking eighteen days off. I would have a total of forty-six days to rest and heal my cords. Paul Wislocky would take the entire West Coast trip as my replacement by singing lead, while Neil switched to tenor.

It was one of the most painful days of my life when I went to the motor coach and said good-bye to the others as they embarked. I have never felt so abandoned and alone even though the other families, who would stay home, were standing and waving with me. It is a feeling I will never forget as long as I live.

The Lord was good and the guys had a great trip. Each day I would look at the itinerary and sit in my living room, envisioning what they were doing on that particular day. Having been on this journey scores of times, I could literally tell you where they were, where they were eating, and who they were with.

Sales were also good. The guys told me later that they believed it was sympathy sales. People felt sorry for them and bought all they had. I think they told me this to cheer me up, but I had a different theory. Canadians have always been loyal and have always enjoyed the Couriers, no matter the circumstances.

After the guys came home they finished a few dates in December and prepared for Christmas at home with their families while I buried myself in our record books. When I prepared a summary for Dave and Neil, I realized that nothing had changed. We sang two hundred ninety-two times, taped fifty-two Sunday TV broadcasts, and had given more than ten percent of our time to our missions program. We'd had a record year financially. I guess God was showing us—especially me—that He could still bless us through whatever difficulties came along.

AWARDS! AWARDS!

When Jesse Peterson started a recording label, Tempo Records, he asked the Couriers to be on that label and gave us national exposure. While we were on the Tempo label we had a hit song written by Neil Enloe called, "Statue of Liberty." Neil got the idea on a youth boat cruise in New York Harbor, and the song was awarded prestigious Dove Award at the 1976 Gospel Music Awards in Nashville. Dave, Neil, and I were selected to sing it at the awards ceremony. The song also garnered another Dove Award at the same time. Later, our live album, *Ovation*, won a Dove Award for the Inspirational Album of the Year.

In the year that "Statue of Liberty" won the Dove Award we had a record year in total dates performed. We did more than three hundred. Two dates on most Sundays accounted for approximately one hundred four of the total dates. When you understand that we had to tape our television programs many days a year, you can understand that there were few days that we were totally free. On many of those off days we spent time in our home office taking care of business. This busy schedule was another reason why my voice began to fail, I believe. We just could not say no. Singing while dead tired does not bode well for any singer. Rest is an important consideration for a healthy singing voice. We were also sleeping on a bouncing, noisy motor coach and had to take our turns driving.

STILL NOT BACK TO NORMAL

When we resumed our singing engagements in January of 1979, my voice was better but I was still not capable of singing an entire program at full voice. Some people told me that I had a legitimate reason to sue the doctor who had taken too much off my vocal cord. The idea was that I should be compensated for loss of income because of malpractice, but this was not an option for me. By this time the Couriers were well known; if I sued, it would be in all the major newspapers and on radio and television. What kind of testimony would that be? I probably would have destroyed this doctor's practice, but in the light of eternity what would that accomplish?

The singing engagements continued. January faded into February, and we again left for a western Canada tour. Our crowds were fantastic and our sales were incredible, but I still could not sing up to par, especially on our "power" songs of "I Sing the Mighty Power of God" and "Statue of Liberty." Nonetheless I labored on, expecting that some evening the miracle would happen.

In May we had a major engine failure. I was expecting something to happen because I knew we were running on borrowed time. The engine had more than five hundred thousand miles on it and was losing compression. It finally breathed its last outside of Washington, D.C. I was driving along early in the morning when all of a sudden the engine lost power. Looking at the oil gauge I knew it was over. The needle was not registering any oil pressure. I guided the coach to the side of the interstate. I walked back though the coach, saying of all things, "Well, praise the Lord the engine is shot." The guys looked at me like I was crazy.

In retrospect this was a defining moment for me. I was forty-three years old and had been a Christian for thirty. I had been through the end of WWII. I had grown up being ridiculed for being a Pentecostal preacher's kid, and I had been a bashful, backward teenager not knowing even in Bible school what God had for me. I suffered from homesickness, had meager money at school, and had launched out into full-time ministry even though I sometimes had to share a hot dog with one of the other Couriers to survive. I had gone through a possible breakup of our group, I had been in charge of our motor coach through many breakdowns, and I had spent many nights away from my family. I had been also asked to sing the hardest part in a Gospel group, and night after night I had literally "gutted out" songs even if my part was not there, such that people asked, "What was wrong with the guys tonight?" I had been told by Southern Gospel people that I did pretty well for a "Yankee Tenor." And now I was singing with half my voice and the bus had broken down again while I was driving.

On other occasions I had almost developed ulcers, knowing that it was my responsibility to make sure our equipment was functioning properly. I cannot count the times I came off a trip and, instead of going home to my family, let everyone out of the coach and headed for the repair shop in Harrisburg. It would be quite a bit later that Jean Ann would drive to Harrisburg to pick me up.

When I was able to praise God despite my voice trouble—with an expensive motor overhaul suddenly looming over me—I knew I was on my way to complete victory. Not necessarily complete victory over voice problems but complete victory in my inner spirit that had been torn away over the past year or so.

Another incredible event happened over the engine failure. The total cost of the engine was going to be more than $7,000. We did not have that kind of money. When the job was finished we had just enough money in our account to get the coach out of the shop with a promise to pay the rest monthly. Then a miracle happened. The very day I got the coach out of the repair shop we headed for Illinois and other parts of the Midwest. Our first stop was with our good friend Glenn Pyles. Glenn and Margaret Pyles run a small trucking company. They are among the most generous people I know. Glen and Margaret have poured thousands of dollars into ministry in Panama, and from time to time they have also supported our ministry. When we came to Illinois Glenn always insisted that we fill up our coach from his diesel fuel tanks, free of charge.

Glenn's elderly father was also a truck driver. Even at an advanced age he was still employed locally, driving a big tanker truck. He happened to be in that very first service after the overhauled engine. During the service we mentioned that we had just had our engine overhauled and were fortunate to have the coach because we could not pay the entire bill. I think the entire conversation with the audience over this lasted not more than two minutes. After the service Glenn's dad came to me and with tears in his eyes and told me that during the service God had spoken to him about paying off the rest of our engine bill. Into my hand he handed a check for the balance of the engine overhaul. I really believe that our attitude of praise even through tests and trials was heard from heaven, and God supplied the needed funds by speaking to our friend.

Meanwhile, my voice "overhaul" was also needed but was not happening. It was hard to understand that at the peak of our ministry, with Dove Awards, a major record label, great album sales, large crowds, and more bookings coming in daily, I was still struggling vocally.

One very bright spot in all of this was the recording of a new Christmas album. I call it my miracle album. I was very apprehensive about recording, given how taxing it can be on the voice. But now recording the album with a broken voice seemed almost unthinkable, so what happened could only have been God's will. Neil has often said that this album was one of our best recordings of all time. And we have the record to prove that a miracle did take place—my voice was as clear as it had ever been.

After recording the album, we left for an extended vacation with several friends to Mexico. Puerto Valarta provided a welcome relief from the rigors of traveling. At the time it would have been hard to believe that storm clouds lay ahead that would disrupt my life for many more months.

When we returned home, it was back to the same old fast-paced life. But I came back to reality quickly when the same old problem voice problem was still evident. We left once again for the long journey westward through Canada and down the West Coast of the United States. It was frustrating to be a perfectly healthy person, except that when I opened my mouth to sing I soon became exhausted.

BROUGHT BACK BY GOD

The amazing thing was that every time I got to my lowest ebb, God would bring something to me that would buoy my spirits. Even the engine failure had turned out to be a blessing. Now I was back on the road again, and here came the depression and despair. It did not help that we were thousands of miles from home, traveling most nights and most days to get to the next service.

On one such occasion, on our way to Edmonton, Alberta, we made a stop in the little border town of Lloydminster, Alberta. We had no commitment on that particular day because it was a holiday in Canada. We stopped at a small shopping center for food. I was the first to get off of the coach, not wanting to talk to anyone but just to satisfy my hunger. The restaurant was at the far end of mall. I was about halfway there when I heard footsteps behind me. The place was almost vacant so I could hear the clicking of high heels quite plainly. I knew that my guys did not wear high heels, and suddenly alongside me came this well-dressed lady. She stopped me in my tracks by asking if I was one of the Couriers.

When I said that I was she informed me that she had seen our coach pull into the center. She then told me a story I will never forget. About a year before, she was feeling quite sick and went to her doctor. After extensive tests the doctor told her she had cancer and gave her about six months to live. Devastated, she went home and told one of her friends, who then gave her an album by our group. The album was entitled *Comfort, Strength and Happiness.* This friend wanted her to listen to a song called, "I'll Keep Holding on to Jesus." She liked the song so much that she played it twice a day for weeks. In the mornings when she arose she would play the song, and she would tell the Lord that she would serve Him no matter what. In the evening she prayed the same prayer.

In a short time she began to feel better. However, when she told her doctor how she was feeling he explained that sometimes the body rallies for a while before finally succumbing. But the doctor told her to come back in about a month. When she came back again, the doctor did the tests all over again and discovered that somehow the cancer was completely gone. All she had to do was keep coming back once a year to make sure.

Then she said these words to me: "If you never sang that song for anyone else, you sang it for me. I had never heard of the Couriers, but that song gave me faith to believe that God could heal me. Thank you for your ministry." With that I bowed my head with tears running down my face, and when I looked up to thank her, she was gone. Now, you can believe what you want, but I am not sure whether she was a real person or an angel that God sent to minister to me. Either way, it was another great boost to my wounded soul. By the way, the other members of our group never saw the lady who talked to me that day.

We ended 1979 in one of our favorite churches with one of our favorite pastors and his wife, Ron and June Stevens. We first went to Ron's church in Brampton, Ontario, when he had only fifty people. Year by year, as we returned for building program after building program, the church grew. Ron traveled around the world with the Couriers and on many occasions would join us on tours of Canada and the United States. Now the new sanctuary that seated seventeen hundred people was completed and it would be packed to the roof for New Year's Eve, 1978.

THE FINAL YEAR

In the margin of my record book for 1980 I wrote: "25th Year of Ministry." Little did I know that fifteen days later I would return to this same page and add these shocking words—"And the Last."

In reality, when I think back I recall that we had always said that our ministry was temporary. We thought that from day one, or at least some of the guys did. Dave Kyllonen has often said that he thought we would sing for a year or two and then settle down into individual ministries. I did not view it that way because it was and always will be my passion to sing with the Couriers until Jesus comes or I go to be with Him. I really believe that Dave, who had a direct call to preach, would not have stayed as long as he did without our missions, camp meeting services, and the opportunity to preach the Word on so many occasions. That is another reason why I never balked at our preaching ministry. It was the glue that kept us together.

Now we were a wounded singing group. Dave confided that without the strong singing before he preached, he was losing heart. Down deep I felt the same way but was hoping against hope that my voice would return. If the shoe had been on the other foot I would have been up against the same dilemma that Dave and Neil were facing. None of us wanted to sing with anyone else. It's the same today—God put the three of us together, and it was all three or nothing. That is what I felt at the time, and still do.

I was not privy to who brought up the subject of quitting before it was discussed on the coach, but it does not make any difference. That conversation had to come at some point. But when I look back I still see the hand of God in every move. As a direct result, Dave was able to nurture his three daughters and allow them to mature and become parts of vital ministries today. Kristie, Robin, and Connie have all married ministers of the Gospel. Likewise, Neil's children are all serving the Lord. Beth is involved in music in Philadelphia, Heidi is married to an ordained minister, and they are part of a vital church in Camp Hill, Pennsylvania. Tim Enloe and his wife are traveling evangelists much in demand across the nation.

Closer to home, my oldest daughter, Shannon, went to Bible school at my alma mater, as did other Courier children. She met a young man there, and now she and Kristian are in full-time evangelistic ministry with emphasis on worship music and missions. Aria, my oldest granddaughter, is an avid reader, an excellent student, is studying piano, and can already sing a harmony part. She has accepted Jesus as her Savior. My other granddaughter, Elise, is a real charmer. She is also studying piano and is singing as well. She and my wife share a love for decorating and shopping. At six years old she is way ahead— look out, world!

My other daughter, Meredith, is married to Fred, a preacher's son. She has been involved in the nursing home business, meeting the needs of the elderly. Fred is a good provider and has worked in several terminals in several positions with Conway Central, one of Americas premier trucking companies. They attend a thriving church in Reading, Pennsylvania. Meredith is my quiet waters that run deep, and she has a strong singing voice as well.

In the natural, breaking up was the most foolish thing we could have done. Scores of people in Gospel Music told us that we were making a big mistake. Even James Blackwood, who had became a very close and dear friend, told us that we should not break up.

"I have had a great career in Gospel Music," he said, "but if I had it to do all over again, after seeing what you men have done I would have followed your example. You literally built your own ministry. The Blackwoods are now singing in the churches that you guys stayed with from infancy to megachurches, and we are able to reap what you have sown. I would have picked two other men of like faith and done what you have done over the years." With that he urged us to carry on.

Jesse Peterson, the creator of our record label, Tempo, said that all he could figure out was that God had other things in store for us, and the nest we were in had to be shaken so we'd get out and do them. I think that is the best explanation of all. In shaking our "group" nest God caused the formation of three separate ones. In those three separate nests were eight children who started eight more nests when they moved out. In those nests now are fifteen children who will someday be shaken out and will start their own, and so it goes.

So far all nests have been built on the solid rock, Christ Jesus. I believe with all my being that this has happened because the three of us followed God with our hearts and not with our heads. I did not see it that way at the time, but God knew all along what needed to be done.

FINAL DAYS

Our sales and crowds never diminished, right up until the very end in April 1980. The final date was set for April 19 at the Forum in Harrisburg. Meanwhile we began discussing how various things should be handled. Assets would be divided up between Neil and Dave, since they were going to continue ministering in song and word. The motor coach was immediately put up for sale. It did not sell until another year had passed, to an up-and-coming Gospel group named Heaven Bound from Kinston, North Carolina. At that particular time we all were needing extra money to live on during the difficult days of transition, even a year later. The payment from Heaven Bound, which they never missed, was always split among the three Couriers, and many times it was the means of much-needed support.

It seemed, at the time, that the whole subject of keeping the Courier name was overlooked, but I am so glad I kept both the Courier name and the nonprofit intact and alive. That would pay dividends a few years later, when Neil and I joined forces with Neil's brother Phil, who returned to the Couriers after a seventeen-year ministry of his own. I was not about to let my twenty-five years in the Couriers go down the drain after all that prayer, blood, sweat, and tears.

My biggest regret to this day is that we had to put three loyal employees out of work. Hilda Bernard had started with us, volunteering her time. She became so valuable that we hired her fulltime a few years later. Tom Baker had quit a large trucking firm to drive for us. With us he had no retirement, yet faithfully served for more than four years. Rev. Paul Wislocky left Assemblies district work to join us as ministry coordinator. Under his guidance, both spiritually and financially, we grew into a more successful ministry. Now we were literally pulling the rug out from under them.

There was some discussion about keeping our office and coordinating the various ministries from there. It sounded like a good idea, but it did not involve either Hilda or Tom. We were going to continue on and leave Hilda and Tom to make their own way, and I freely admit that I was totally against this. I made the decision that if we all were going to go our separate ways, then it should be all of us taking that same chance—or none of us. If that ruffled feathers, then so be it, but I was taught to be fair to everyone no matter what. My two partners agreed with this decision and we waited to see what would transpire.

Within a short while God supplied jobs for all three employees. Paul Wislocky became the senior pastor of our church, Christian Life Assembly. He led the church in several building programs and retired in 2007 after attendance had surpassed three thousand. Hilda Bernard became

Rev. Wislocky's executive secretary and is still employed by this ever-growing church. Tom Baker worked for good friends of the Couriers for several years, then headed the maintenance team of Christian Life Assembly of God for many years more. He is now retired.

Neither Dave nor Neil seemed to want to continue the television program. As far as I was concerned the station would have to find another ministry to do the program. It was then that Dave, Neil, and I were called in to see the program director, Nelson Sears. It had been his idea to hire us years before, and it was a stroke of genius because our time slot became the highest rated on all television stations in the area. Now Nelson was concerned that they would lose that high rating. He then asked if any of us were staying in the area and would have time to continue the program.

In our discussion we told him that I was the only one who might be able to do that. No decision was made until I was called into Nelson's office by myself. He and I had formed a friendship because he had become a big fan of the Oak Ridge Boys, who were now big stars. When I told him about knowing the guys so well, and that Richard Sturben and Joe Bonsall had been friends of ours and got into music because of our influence, Nelson was all ears.

Later, when we were taping some of our final television programs as the Couriers, Nelson came to the studio and asked me to come to his office again. He told me that many church organizations wanted the spot, but the station owners did not want any single denomination to take it over. If they did, other denominations would want the same treatment. Nelson said that we were given the program because we sang in all kinds of churches and represented none of them exclusively.

On My Own

I was not afraid of doing the program; in my mind I had already outlined what I would do, including screening local Gospel talent and interspersing that with video tapes of major Gospel groups. From time to time I might sing a song or two with my family if my voice was up to it. Then I told him that my biggest obstacle to doing the program was the weekly fee that we paid to the station—$250 per program. We had never asked for this money on the program and we had depended on our mailing list for funds. Many times we took money out of our road ministry to pay the monthly bill. But now I would not be out there on the road to generate funds, and we were not allowed to ask for money on the program.

At that point Nelson leaned over and said, "I think we have that problem solved. You can have the program free of charge on one condition. You cannot tell anyone that you are not paying for it." Then with a big grin he said, "If you ever tell anyone about this and it gets back to me, I will deny it!"

I was flabbergasted and overwhelmed. Once again God was watching out for me. And eventually, the "new" program became more successful than ever before. By using local talent we got the highest ratings from the local community, and they stayed that way over the next few years. I also began to advertise Christian bus tours and Gospel concerts. Soon Jean Ann and I were filling up motor coaches and taking people all over the nation.

It was also a great time of local ministry for me. Just before going off the air one Sunday, I remember telling the people about losing my voice, and for the first time I really knew what it meant for people to hurt. I said that if anyone watching the program had a special need or was in the hospital I was willing to come and pray for them. I then went even further out on the same limb when I said that people could stop by my house for prayer if they had a need. Now, that was really taking a chance!

Almost immediately after the airing of that program, a knock came at my door. A couple was standing there, distraught over the news that their son had crashed his motorcycle and was in the hospital in serious condition. They were on their way and had stopped for me to pray for him. We prayed, and then I followed them to Camp Hill, about fifteen miles away. I stayed and prayed again as he fought to live, and when the doctors had him stabilized I went home.

A week later I learned that the young man had had a relapse and was once more on the edge. Again I went to the hospital and stayed until the crisis passed. Eventually, the young man recovered to a normal life. That took place in the early 80s. Just about a year ago I was visiting a local church to hear some friends in concert. At the close of the service a lady came up to me. She told me that she was the mother of that young man for whom I had prayed years before. He was now in his early thirties, married, and living a normal life, but she had never forgotten that terrible night.

I have said all that to note that even in my own troubles I felt compelled to reach out to others much worse off than I was.

Little by little, God was working on me in so many ways. Compassion for other people actually helped me learn to rest in Jesus through my own troubles. Little by little God was healing my spirit and my voice.

I did change the name of the program to *Sunday Gospel Music.* My good friend Cam Shillington from Kingston, Ontario, made wonderful new opening and closing segments for the program, free of charge. The golden voice of Cam intoning the words, "Welcome to Sunday Gospel Music. And now, here is the host of Sunday Gospel Music, Duane Nicholson!" are words I will never forget.

FINAL CONCERTS

Before our last concert at the Forum in April we still had many dates to fulfill. It was very difficult, night after night to answer questions and say final farewells to those we might never see again. We had built such friendships with people all over the nation. It was excruciating. We had more than fans; we had friends who stuck to us closer than family.

In February we had a welcome break from the constant "final tour" experience. We went on a Holy Land Tour and another missions trip to our beloved Africa. Both were like therapy. We immersed ourselves in ministering to people who did not know us, and we did not have to explain each evening why we were quitting and hear the groans of people who had not heard we were breaking up.

Our missionary field on this trip was Kenya. We were guests of Canadian missionaries and sang in Nairobi at the great

Kenyatta Convention Center to several thousand people. One of my personal highlights came in the port city of Mombassa. The missionary took me out to a reef off the coast, where we took in the wonderful underwater beauty for hours. I was an avid scuba diver and we just snorkeled to our heart's content.

When we arrived home we were soon on the road again to honor our commitments. We traveled to Toledo, Ohio, the site of the recording of our Dove Award album. We sang one more time at the Assembly of God church in Binghamton, New York. Pastor Piedmont had us in his church once a year for years. For the last time we sang at the great Youth Convention, this time at the Hershey Sports Arena. Along the way we said good-bye to thousands who had supported us over the long years. We sold out of everything we had in stock, and the altars were filled with young people seeking God.

I stood by Rev. Ron Bailey on Friday morning at the candlelit communion service. I had asked Ron to take my place singing "The Lord's Prayer." This had been my signature song at the convention for many years. I knew I could not depend on my voice holding up for the high ending, and Ron was a little hoarse himself that Friday morning, but I stood with him and prayed that God would clear his voice. He did a marvelous job.

We visited our home church, Christian Life, one more time as the Couriers. The Courier families were among thirty-some people who started that church in the Dutch Pantry Restaurant in Camp Hill, and in Dave and Judy Kyllonen's garage. Then in true Courier fashion we left on a journey to Davenport, Kansas City, and Denver, which was always exciting. The largest Nazarene church in the nation was there. This church sponsored a Saturday evening concert once a month. It was called SNID, for Saturday Night in Denver. It had grown so popular that Friday night concerts were added to accommodate the crowds. We were to sing to four thousand people in two evenings.

A very sad event occurred while we were in Denver this time. We had heard that the Cathedral Quartet was in town as well. We had traveled with and promoted the Cathedrals many times over the years, and Glenn Payne and George Younce were two of our best friends. I found out where they were staying and called their hotel on Saturday morning. I tried both Glenn's and George's rooms but got no answer. I thought that was strange because Gospel singers have late evenings and do not get up early, especially on Saturday mornings. Not until we arrived back home several days later did we find out that George Younce had suffered his first heart attack early Saturday morning, and the entire group was at a local hospital.

This was the beginning of health problems for George, who passed away several years later. It has been especially hard to see so many of our peers in Gospel Music pass from this life. We have lost James Blackwood, J. D. Sumner, Hovie Lister, Jake Hess, Doy Ott, Big Chief, Rosie Rosell, Rex Nelon, Howard, Vestal, Rusty, and Sam Goodman, Jim Hamill, Danny Gaither, George Younce, Glenn Payne, and a host of other Gospel artists of our day. The Couriers had been privileged to meet and sing with so many of these Gospel icons over the years. How could three Bible school students have been so blessed?

Finally, I must mention traveling to Longmont, Colorado, for Sunday services after the SNID concerts. We had been in

Bible school with Rev. James Miller. He had played for the King's Ambassadors, the group that interested Neil in going to Central Bible Institute. The church was packed with people, the altars were filled, and our sales were incredible.

Despite what was going on in our hearts, our sense of humor never failed us during this difficult time. We told crowds that things were going so well that we might have discovered something. Stay together one more year and announce each evening that we were quitting, then retire on the extra money that was coming in. Of course, God always has ways of bringing us back to reality very quickly, and through the years He did just that. On the Monday night after an incredible few days of successes, we were in Colorado Springs and our offering was $190, with record sales of $200.50. I don't know where the 50 cents came from—perhaps it was a tip.

Actually, no service was ever a failure because we always felt that God directed us every time we ever performed. We left Colorado Springs after that service and drove home to Pennsylvania, nonstop. I did not sleep much on that trip.

The Saturday of our final concert together was a blur of activity. We had not only to set up at the Forum, but because of an overflow crowd we had rented Christ Community Church in Camp Hill. I believe that one of our featured groups set up sound at the Forum, but to be honest, we were so busy we had no time to even think about what was happening. It did not fully register until we sang that final song at the end of our stand. Our loyal friends stood to their feet and applauded one more time, while we walked offstage to whatever God had in store for each of us.

I hoped God had plans for me because I certainly did not see things very clearly. Dave and his family had already been practicing and booking dates to continue, and I assume that Neil was doing the same. I was somewhere in limbo, because I just could not carry a full singing program at that time. It would have been disaster and I would have run out of dates rather quickly.

The next day was Sunday, and Jean Ann and I sat in a pew in our newly formed church in Camp Hill. My singing days were over—or so I thought. At that point the withdrawal pains were excruciating.

VICTORY FROM THE ASHES

As I close my portion of this book I need to say that through all the years, until I rejoined Dave and Neil, God has blessed my family beyond comprehension. I listened to a great evangelist make a statement years ago that I can absolutely verify. "God never takes anything away from you that He does not replace with something better." I can truthfully say that the first twenty-five years were great, but the next years have been even greater.

From January 1959 until April 19, 1980, when the original Couriers discontinued our ministry, these are fairly accurate figures:

> We recorded 520 radio programs and performed 5,651 dates.

> The number of television programs, not counting a short stint on a Harrisburg station, was 572. I continued the program by myself for another eleven years to add to that.

The number of dates spent recording our television program was 286. Thus the total of days singing and recording was 5,937.

However, these figures cover only our first twenty-two years of ministry. From 1980 to 2000, here is the rest of the story:

2,803 singing dates either with Neil's son, Tim, my daughter Meredith, Ron Hensley, or Phil Enloe. The bulk were with Phil.

I personally taped 561 more television programs at WGAL TV.

In all those figures I have not included multiple bus tours, cruises, 15 Holy Land journeys, and 13 years of traveling to more than 75 nations in missions work.

We have ministered more than 10,000 times since April 1958. Add at least three years of weekly ministry in Bible school and you could easily add another 100 dates.

Not included are days spent recording 54 albums. Each took a minimum of three days, which adds another 162.

There are not enough pages to describe the situations we found ourselves in. There is no way to describe the loneliness, the sick days, the treacherous highways, the breakdowns of equipment, the restaurant meals, and the hours on aircraft. We met hundreds of missionaries, preachers, evangelists, singers, promoters, youth leaders, and thousands more laypeople. We sang to tens of thousands in open-air services in the West Indies. We sang for dying friends in hospital beds many times, wishing we were God and could raise them up. We sang in countless nursing homes, private homes, and for kings, prisoners, and parades.

Add in all the missed birthdays, anniversaries, major holidays, and even births of children and perhaps you can get somewhat of a feel for what we went though, carrying the greatest message in all the world. That message is the simple statement that "Jesus saves," and it's the only hope of this world.

In the years following our breakup I was able to take my family on the road and give them a taste of ministry. When I began to get calls about getting the Couriers back together for some church dates, I called Neil and we put together a group for special occasions. As I have previously stated, Ron Hensley, formerly of the Vicounts, sang with us several times. We enlisted Neil's son, Tim, to sing with us as well. He traveled with us on one overseas journey and it was amazing to see him begin to mature and feel the calling of God upon his young heart. We even had my youngest daughter, Meredith, sing with us for a short time. She is famous for being the only female to ever sing full time with the Couriers. My favorite song with Meredith was "John the Baptist," and no one did it better than she did.

Phil Enloe then joined with Neil and me and we sang together until 2000. Phil brought great energy and joy; he also brought some incredible songs. He wrote one of my favorites that I wish we were singing today, "I Am the Word!" During Phil's second time with us we returned to the West Indies, and also ministered in England and Poland. I returned to Poland two more times as well. My voice continued to improve as I learned to trust God for each note.

Meanwhile, Dave and Judy Kyllonen were investing in the children in their own family ministry, Homefires. Neil and

Ruth Enloe, as well, were on the road weekly with their family. My family joined me in song for a few years and I was able to travel with both of my daughters on occasion. We recorded two albums, and I especially treasure the one that features my family singing with me.

FINAL THANKS

I must add at this point my gratitude to Dave and Neil for leaving me with the television program, and with that the ability to maintain contact with friends for bus tours and the concert series. These were lifesavers for me. Dave and Neil could have successfully continued on with another singer, but they did not do that.

Over the years we have not sought the rewards of this world. Some have come to us by way of the Gospel Music Association Dove Awards, and by receiving on August 10, 2007, the General Superintendent's Medal of Honor of the Assemblies of God. This award is supposed to be given to a layperson or laypersons, so this was the first time it was ever given to ministers. We are grateful for the Executive Presbytery of the General Council of the Assemblies of God for bestowing this honor on us at the 52nd General Council in Indianapolis, but our ministry was only as strong as those who allowed us to minister in their church, auditorium, or mission field.

The real unsung heroes of the church are the pastors who reach out every day to their communities, and our precious missionaries who labor far from home. Not one of these pastors or missionaries needed us to have successful ministries, so we are eternally grateful to them for allowing us to follow God's plan by sharing their labors.

Finally, I must mention my good friend Doug Boyer. Doug Boyer came to our office one Monday morning many years ago to tell us that the day before, during our television program, he had given his heart to the Lord. Since that day Doug has been a wonderful friend. When the Couriers disbanded he took me under his wing and let me help him in his funeral business. He did not need to do this, but I think he wanted to encourage me. Doug started his own singing group, The Brotherhood, and from time to time during those emotional years of change he would ask me to sing with them or help them with their singing. Later Doug received a strong burden for Native Americans and began building churches on American Indian reservations across America, especially in the Southwest. As I write these words I am still engaged in helping Doug fulfill his ministry to some of the most forgotten people in our nation. Thank you, Doug, and your wonderful wife, Marna, for being my friend so many years.

All three of us, when asked to write this book, agreed to write about how each one came to be in the Couriers, plus our own private feelings about the long journey together. As my part of the story began to unfold in my mind, I tried hard to keep out the words "I" and "me," for it was far more than I or me . . . so very much more. There were no superstars in the Couriers, just some men who wanted to use their talents for The Lord. I am deeply grateful for the men and women God used to light my path. God gave me a voice and brought the right people along so it could be used for His glory.

We have been asked many times what our favorite song of all time would be. I cannot speak for Dave or Neil, but that question is almost impossible to answer. Over the years my favorites have changed, based on what I was personally going through at the time. But now, as I enter that "final quarter" of my life, I believe that my favorite song is "Until Then!" The words echo my sentiments at this point in my life, when I do not know when the final notes and words will flow from my lips.

> But until then my heart will go on singing,
> Until then with joy I'll carry on.
> Until the day my eyes behold that city,
> Until the day God calls me home.

We started out to be an arm of evangelism for the church of Jesus Christ. No more and no less. If we have accomplished that I can rest in peace.

How It REALLY Happened

by Neil Enloe

INTRODUCTION

Cause me to know the way wherein I should walk.

(Psalm 143:8)

Life is a school classroom that includes daily lessons, tests at various intervals, and a final exam by the Great Teacher. After almost a lifetime of school days I'm convinced of a few things about the Teacher. His need is not for possessions; He owns it all anyway. His need is not for power; He said, "All power is given unto me in heaven and in earth" (Matthew 28:18).

In fact, He is all-powerful, all-knowing, and everywhere at once. For Him to design and carry out His great plan of redemption strongly suggests—rather shouts—that His *real* need is fellowship. And like us, the crown of His creation, He wants to be wanted. So He created us to be needy people, reliant upon His provision to keep us in fellowship with Him.

If God himself would drive up to my home with a truckload of $1,000 bills, and would dump it on my front lawn, I would fall all over myself in gratitude. The next day I would again thank Him, but with perhaps a little less enthusiasm than on the first day. The third day I would also praise Him, but I would start to feel the pressure of getting a few things done in my life. Ever after that my keen sense of gratitude would continue to diminish from day to day.

As the realization that I now had no financial worries settled in, I probably would still express my gratitude but it wouldn't ever again carry the passion with which I thanked Him on the first day of His blessing. The reason? My needs were met for the moment.

But He, knowing our nature, gives us enough for today in the knowledge that we'll be back soon to ask for more. Therein He brings about fellowship. What a wonderful scheme! Even Jesus taught us in His prayer model, "Give us this day our daily bread." He was teaching us how to maintain daily fellowship with His Father.

An essential ingredient that motivates us in this earthly life is having something to look forward to. If we stop looking forward we stagnate and die. But often our earthly existence is painfully played out from one struggle to the next. So one of the vital lessons that our struggles teach us is that of trust. Our Great Provider wants us to know that He's totally and abundantly reliable, dependable, and able to meet every challenge.

Fellowship begets trust. Through examining His record of my past experience I find that He has never failed to come through when I've called on Him. So why shouldn't I lean on Him when a new challenge presents itself? When I know that I'm in fellowship with Him and that He is trustworthy, I have cause to breathe a lot easier. This is certainly a stress reliever.

Thus I lean on my relationship with my God to bring about the surety of my future. Whatever it may bring will be under the total control of the God who lives in my heart.

We may not know the process but we certainly can know the outcome because the One who gave His very life for us controls our destiny. Our future security is not in the deceptive hands of a careless fortune teller, but in the loving and strong hands of Him who not only made us but who has our best interests at heart.

I therefore live each day not knowing where His hand will lead but confident in His divine direction and goals. And while I'm in His watchful care I know that His ultimate plan for me is to be forever in His presence. With that in mind it does not matter what the daily particulars are. He holds the reins; He takes me where He will. There's a real sense of adventure in a life of submissive abandon to the will of a providing God. I love it and I trust Him completely.

—Neil Enloe

- 1 -

Humble
Beginnings

"Thou shalt be saved and thy house."
(Acts 16:31)

Come on over, Sally. You can make it! You'll be okay—just pay attention, now! Move a little to your right, sweetheart. Slow! Slow! Now—grab that sapling and don't let go of the reins. You can make it! God is with you!"

This was the voice of a very short, slight-of-frame man calling to his even smaller wife across the Wabash River as she attempted to lead a team of jittery horses that were pulling his only wagon. It just happened to be carrying his two small children as well, and all their household provisions—mostly homemade. Macfarland "Mac" Johnson was probably more scared than Sally, but he had to keep up a confident front so she wouldn't panic.

The young Johnson family had been living on meager sustenance in southeastern Indiana, and the Wabash River was the last obstacle that stood between them and their hopes for a better life. Sally was making the treacherous springtime crossing of the angry waterway that lay between herself and her beloved, who had crossed the river earlier to explore the homestead land being offered by the federal government to those who would go in and improve it. The land had only recently been made arable by dredge ditches that drained off the standing water of the lowlands and marshes of southern Illinois. Now, in the late 1880s, the offer of free farmland provided a ray of hope to the young Johnson family.

Somehow Sally got the horses, the rickety wagon, and their two small children across, to be reunited with Mac. Finally it looked like they would be able to make a new life for themselves, and indeed they did. As they rolled up their sleeves the Lord blessed them, and before long they had a vibrant hundred and twenty acres of corn.

Several other children were added to the brood in time, but it was the second-oldest son, Grover Franklin Johnson, who remained on the land to work the family farm. At the same time he furthered his education and became a schoolteacher for two one-room schoolhouses named *Number Nine* and *Center Twig*. Known simply as Frank, he married Sarah Webb and built his marriage around his farm and his church. Two sons and two daughters soon came along, and the eldest son he named Joyce Clyde Johnson. And no, that's not a typographical error! The second child he named Dorothy—but then, she was a girl! Next came Mabel and Junior Franklin.

When Dorothy grew up she moved away to be near the big city of St. Louis, Missouri. She was blessed with head-turning good looks and the common sense of a farm girl, and all the guys wanted her attention. She took employment at "the Tannery," formally known as the International Shoe Company and located on the east side of the Mississippi River in Illinois. On the job Dorothy met Clifton Enloe, a dashing and fascinating young man who swept her off her feet and conducted her to the altar in marriage.

Clifton was an irrepressibly happy soul who lived every moment to the fullest. Ever the entertainer, he kept Dorothy in stitches and made life exciting for her as they settled in nearby Wood River, Illinois, a small town known for its smelly oil refineries.

Soon children started to come . . . and come . . . and come. There were six in all—one girl and five boys, with the girl first. Their home was a madhouse of activity, for sure. While they did not have much in the way of earthly goods, with Clifton now becoming a barber by trade, they had the affection and fellowship of each other. Their great love as a family was built upon faith. Their church was the absolute center of their joy. The most anticipated activities of the week were the three or more times when they found themselves attending the house of God.

Dorothy Enloe gave birth to her third child on June 5, 1938. In the Enloe household the custom was for the father and mother to take turns naming the children. Clifton had named Charlotte, born first, and Dorothy had named David, born second. So when the third child was born the honor fell to Clifton, who named the boy Marvin after a minister whose preaching he especially appreciated. However, women have a way of figuring into decisions of this kind, so Dorothy added Neil as the middle name of the newly born young man. As the years passed three more boys joined the family, all boys—Bob, Phil, and Danny.

Marvin Neil Enloe. That's my name. Most households have a father and a mother. Not the least among the several roles of the man of the house is that of *authority*. The woman of the household often exercises her unique role of *influence*. So *Authority* boldly said, "His name shall be Marvin," while *Influence*, very quietly beneath her breath, said, "But the middle name I gave him is Neil and that's what we'll call him." Ever since that gentle struggle to identify me, I've been known as Neil.

Being the third in a line of six siblings perhaps makes it harder to achieve distinction and identity. I wasn't the oldest, the youngest, or the only one of my gender, but my parents made sure that all their children knew love, value, and self-esteem. Yet through innovation and natural inclination I was able to set myself apart from the crowd in our home.

I became by default the hearty eater among the kids. Okay, truthfully, it was *my* fault rather than a *de*fault. Mom canned peaches every August—one hundred fifty quarts of the sweet nectar. That should have been plenty for our family, right? Only if you fail to consider that I was born in the distinct likeness of an eight-pound appetite. So every day after school when I was in high school, I would come home with a ravenous hunger specifically aimed at the golden peaches stowed away in the cellar beneath the house. Often it seemed like I was hallucinating with anticipation about "heaven in a jar."

So the peaches became my appetizer before supper. And you guessed it; the whole jar was my domain to have and to hold. When Mom called out to Dad and the six children that supper was on the table, I could stroll and not run because the edge had been taken off. But I was taught to never leave anything on my plate. Honestly, it was probably not a good rule to live by because it's not really good to eat more after we're full.

I remember a dear friend of the Couriers who loved to eat too. Ted Rossey would sit down to a gourmet meal with all the trimmings in a fine restaurant and eat to his heart's content. Then he would order a fancy dessert. When the waitress would set the fabulous dessert dish before Ted he would look sheepishly around the table and say, "You've got to neutralize the acid in your stomach."

In my time I've neutralized a lot of acid.

-2-

Parent Trap

Honor thy father and thy mother.
(Exodus 20:12)

My dad was a special guy. His devout pursuit of an intimate relationship with his Lord was the drumbeat of his very life. He loved his wife and children deeply and wanted all that the Lord had for them. He loved to laugh and entertain, but when it came to the things of God he was very serious.

Dad's barbershop was situated on the lot next to our house. He bought a prefabricated garage and had it modified to function as a barbershop, with a small back room and an even smaller bathroom. The shop had two matching barber chairs; one for his customers and one for the kids to play on. The chairs not only swiveled but also reclined. It was like having a carnival ride in the shop.

For a long time, my job was to sweep the hair off the floor, which Dad had skillfully harvested. To this day I don't know how Dad held his hands up all day long for sixty years.

Early in his life he played a saxophone, a harmonica, and could find a melody in just about any musical instrument he could get his hands on. Mom also played some saxophone, although not as well as Dad. Somewhere along the way he picked up a six-string guitar and fell head-over-heels in love. It was akin to a marriage as he strummed and picked away his downtime in the barbershop. I've seen him with a customer in the chair whose haircut was only half finished, and he would say to the customer, "Have I played my latest song for you?"

No customer in his right mind would excuse himself with half a haircut, so Dad would take a break, play his guitar, and sing. Many of his original songs sounded similar; about some obscure character from the Old Testament, to the tune of "Way Down Yonder in the Indian Nation." He loved that tune.

Among his other unique gifts, my dad was not given to interior decorating. His shop was designed after Early American Homemade. He would make up signs for his prices or whatever he wanted to remind his customers of, using a torn-off flap from a cardboard box and a child's black crayon. Oh yes, and he attached the signs to the wall with a thumbtack. But he got the information right even though he didn't have much of an artistic touch.

The Art of the Shave

I also recall occasions when customers would request a shave, and Dad would turn the gearshift-like lever on the side of the barber chair and make it recline so he could better access the grubby beard of his customer. Then he would put hot towels on the customer's face, which looked like a turban, and let it steam for a couple of minutes. When the beard was softened by the hot towels Dad would remove them, turn around to the lather machine, dispense a handful of white creamy-looking stuff, and paint the guy's beard like Santa Claus.

Then it was time to take out a very dangerous straightedge razor, pull the bottom of the leather razor strop away from the wall, and begin to run the edge of the blade up and down the strop. When he knew he had a delicate edge on the razor he would fine-check it with the face of his thumb, being careful not to cut himself. By the time he had prepared the razor's edge, the hot towels and the whipped cream goop had further softened the beard of his reclining guinea pig. With delicate finesse Dad would then begin, starting with gentle, short strokes in the area of the upper lip against the nose. Come to think of it, I never really asked why he started in that location. One slip of the hand could remove a stranger's nose. But Dad was a professional, and fortunately he never had such an incident.

During many such events, conversation would ensue between the professional and the victim. However, in the course of small talk about anything from sports to hunting, to music or whatever, if the customer would happen to swear Dad would stop his razor mid-stroke. He would then step back and wipe the lather off the blade so it glistened. Never growing taller than five feet, six inches and never weighing more than one hundred fifty-eight pounds soaking wet, Dad became a giant of authority with a straight-edged razor in his hand. He would walk around to the front of the chair and look into the eyes of the defenseless blasphemer and say something like this:

"Sir, next door in my humble house is my wife and six children. The earnings from this barbershop put food on our table and clothes on our backs. We really need and appreciate your business in this shop. But you have just misused the name of my Lord and Savior, Jesus Christ. Do you see that sign on the wall to your left? It says, 'No Profane Language, Please.' See the one on the wall straight ahead? It says, 'No Swearing, Please.' See the one on the wall to your right? I made that one up myself with a crayon and the flap off a cardboard box. It says, 'A feller's tougher who's not a cusser.' We don't talk like that in our shop." And with one last flash of the razor he would say, "Understand?"

Thus a holy boldness came over an otherwise meek and mild man who took his salvation seriously, and he would take a strong stand for righteousness whether at home or on the job. As a little boy looking on I would think, "If Dad's God is that important he must be some God!" In all my growing-up years I never saw Dad compromise his faith in any way.

Dad passed away at the age of eighty-six and a half, after living a healthy life. He went to the hospital for the first time in his entire life at age eighty-six. And in six months he just simply shut down. He died in his sleep. What a way to go!

True Humility

Sometime during the last year of his life he did a noble yet unusual thing that spoke volumes about his sincerity toward

God. He went up and down our street where he had lived for almost sixty years, knocked on the doors of our well-known, longtime neighbors, and said to them, "I just came by to say that I've tried to be a good neighbor, but if I have ever offended you in any way, I'm asking you to forgive me."

The truth is that he had never done anything to hurt anyone, especially his own neighbors. But who knows, he might have had a premonition of his own passing and he didn't want to stand before the Lord with any unsettled offenses against his fellowman. What a guy!

My mother took on the impossible task of raising six children on a barber's earnings, and did it with dignity and honor. Often she made my shirts out of feedbag cloth, and they might not have been in keeping with the latest designer fashions, but they were always clean. She was a hardworking farm girl to whom her own father once said, "Dorothy, you have kept me from having to hire a man to help me with the farm work this summer."

Mom told me of an incident that took place when she was a teenager and was plowing with a team of mules. One of the two mules would only turn to his left and would refuse to make a right turn. So she had to bear in mind how she was going to navigate the turn at the end of the row. All went well until she ended up in the last row and headed for the corner of the field. Beyond the boundary at the end of the row was a dredge ditch that was about twenty feet across and six feet deep. A right turn was an absolute must, but the stubborn mule wouldn't do it.

After a seemingly endless struggle, the mule had finally

inched his way to the top of the steep slope that slanted down to the dredge ditch, endangering not only both mules but also the plow and the young girl driving the team. In fact, the mule's front feet were dangling over the precipice above the dredge ditch. Finally Mom got verbal with the mule and said, "Okay, buster, you got yourself into this predicament and I've tried to get you out of it. Now you're on your own."

She then threw down the reins and walked away toward the house. When I asked her how the incident turned out she told me that on her way home the mules caught up with her, heading toward the barn. Somehow they had managed to rescue themselves.

Mom succeeded Dad by thirteen years. Unfortunately, she never really accepted his death, and with the passage of time, as she grew more physically frail, she held to her deep love for her soul mate and missed him immeasurably. She spent her last year living near me. It was a marvelous time to get in on my mother's life on a daily basis after having been on the road singing for forty-five years and not having the luxury of an easy trip from my home in Pennsylvania to the old homeplace in Illinois. She never lost her kind, sweet personality. What a delightful lady, who endeared herself to all who knew her.

When the day of her home-going arrived, her room was filled with her children and grandchildren, who gathered at her bedside for one final time to do what we knew best, singing songs of gratitude and praise to the Lord whom Mom had lovingly served from her youth. What a heritage.

My sister, Charlotte, married Fred Ingram, who practiced chiropractic until his retirement. Charlotte and Fred raised two daughters and a son and are now living in retirement in the hometown of their chiropractic business, Chanute, Kansas.

My older brother David and his wife, Karen, raised two daughters and a son and are living in Tennessee in retirement.

My brother born next after me, Bob, is living in Florida in retirement with his wife, Estell, having raised two sons and a daughter.

Phil, after Bob, lives in Florida with his wife, Jan. They have four grown children, all daughters.

The last Enloe child, Danny, lives near our old home in Illinois with his wife, Suzie. They have two grown daughters. Danny is an excellent tenor.

So from the union of two devoted young people, a barber and a farmer who quoted Joshua of old who said, "As for me and my household, we will serve the Lord" (Joshua 24:15), came six children, three of whom are in the full-time ministry. Phil, Danny, and yours truly have spent a lifetime in music evangelism. The other three siblings are also serving the Lord and benefiting from their godly upbringing.

Many years ago, during the Christmas holidays, all six Enloe children, now married and each with families of their own, gathered around the kitchen table of the old homeplace with both of our parents. Having been raised in a family tradition of relentless teasing, I seized the moment and put forth the following.

"The Lord spoke to me in my slumber last night and revealed something profound about our family. He showed me that Mom and Dad had six children, and each of those six kids grew up, married, and had three children—or two children, in Danny's case—and stopped. The Lord revealed to me that we all quit after three because we realized, from watching Mom and Dad raise their six children, that after the third one we would start getting ugly ones."

Charlotte and David thought it was funny and deemed it to be eternal truth for sure, but my three younger brothers failed to see any substantive humor. Me? Being the third child, I just made it under the wire. Even now, when the Enloe siblings get together, such good-natured ribbing is the order of the occasion. Both Mom and Dad were given to teasing and I suppose it's hereditary among their children. But far more important, in spite of our relentless teasing I remain deeply in love with my sister and my four brothers. We're still a strong family unit even after the passing of our beloved parents.

- 3 -

Young and Restless

Let no man despise thy youth;
but be thou an example of the believers.
(1 Timothy 4:12)

Let's go back to about 1953, to the little First Assembly of God Church in Wood River, Illinois, where my parents made sure that we children experienced the fellowship of the church congregation as our primary social outlet. The importance of this was so deeply ingrained in our very being that it superseded almost everything else, including five days a week in school.

That's not to say that school was given little importance; quite the contrary. But we were given the strong message by our loving parents that the Great Teacher would someday give us a final exam that would determine whether we would ultimately "pass." And as important as good grades in school were, we certainly didn't want to fail the test that had eternal consequences.

So with this as a backdrop, I often found myself in the midst of a series of revival meetings in my local home church. These were meetings that were put on nightly for at least two weeks. Going to church every night, and getting to bed late with the alarm poised to wake me up early the next morning, I found the revival services fatiguing. So they took on a slightly different meaning for me than that of a "two-week revival." I privately thought of them as a "too-weak revival." Given my young age and my lack of any real interest in the meetings, I often took a cynical attitude.

Certain patterns were predictable. On the last night of the meeting, after the final love offering had been taken for the guest evangelist, the pastor would stroll to the pulpit and say something like this: "Have you enjoyed Brother and Sister So-and-So's ministry these past two weeks?" The congregation would respond with a hearty, or sometimes with a merely gracious, "Amen!" The pastor would then go on to say, "I've been checking the schedule of these dear evangelists and have found that they have next week open, so they could continue for another week." Here I am, a tired church brat who had all he could take of short nights, and I'm privately shaking my fist and saying under my breath, "Pastor, don't you dare invite this guy to stay on!"

At the same time, many of the guest evangelists were positively captivating by virtue of their music, their preaching, or some other redeeming factor. For the most part I really enjoyed them, especially the ones who were musical.

On one occasion we had an evangelist who held no fascination to me. He wasn't tall; I couldn't look up to him. His preaching didn't challenge my life. He had a guitar strapped onto his belly, but I really wasn't taken with his music. His wife wasn't even pretty; there was nothing for me in those meetings except the sure wrath of my parents if I didn't attend.

NEWFOUND PURPOSE

On the last night of that series of meetings, when I thought I was home free, something totally unexpected happened. At the end of the final sermon the evangelist gave a simple altar call for anyone who would like to surrender his or her life to Christ. I had heard my share of challenging altar calls where the Spirit of Conviction was heavy. But something gripped my heart in that moment, and I found myself taking that long walk to the altar in the front of the church. And to my embarrassment, I was making the trip in full view of all the people who thought Neil was a fine young man, especially my parents. I was not only letting my church and my family know that I had been a bad boy, but I was about to spill all to the One whose death and resurrection made the moment possible.

After laying my all on that altar I rose with a new worldview. My pastor, my church family, my parents, and my siblings all had a new definition in my heart. All the guilt that I had privately carried, in the depths of my being, had been gloriously lifted through simply confessing my need of Jesus as my Savior. Without bringing condemnation or shame on me He removed my iniquity and replaced it with the indwelling peace of His indescribable presence.

From that moment, everything in my life became filled with hope and promise. I recall going to school the next day with a whole new perspective. The building, the hallways, the fellow students, my locker, the teachers—they all looked different. And when I came home from school my neighborhood, my house, and my family all looked wonderfully different as well. These were changes that only a supernatural power could make in me. And the change in my life and perspective has been permanent.

This newfound life in Christ put form and purpose into a heart that theretofore had none. What would happen going forward? Did God really have a plan for my future? Would I accomplish something meaningful? Could it be that God was putting his hand on me in and selecting me to serve His higher purpose? These and other penetrating questions presented themselves in the quiet solitude of my heart. I knew that the answers to these mysteries were held in the foreknowledge of God, but they did not come instantly to me. Days, weeks, months, years, and perhaps even a lifetime of seeking and searching would pass before the picture would become clear to me.

I love the gentle voice of God speaking to the private inner sanctuary of my personal being. But honestly, most of the time He has to hit me over the head with a two-by-four to get my attention so he can impart anything profound. All too often my spiritual hearing is impaired, as is my spiritual eyesight. Only because of the awesome patience of an understanding God have I been allowed limited glimpses of truth, through His Word and the promptings of His precious Holy Spirit.

From the encounter at the time of my conversion the natural effect was growth and development. Now that I was a born-again believer in Jesus Christ, I craved to know what was expected of me. So I made a habit of revisiting that altar. I pressed into the heart of God and asked some big questions, starting with what He really wanted from me. That question wasn't answered for months.

In fact, when the answer finally presented itself to me it caught me totally off guard. He didn't want anything from me. He already had it all. The simple truth is, He wanted ME! At that point I finally realized that the prize of the great struggle in the heavens between good and evil . . . was me. The scripture says, "And whosoever will, let him take the water of life freely" (Revelation 22:17). Nothing in my self-perception made me feel like a prize. It still doesn't. But I've come to realize that I'm included in that "whosoever." What a humbling realization that is, for nothing I am or ever hope to be merits that level of favor.

In my subsequent times at the altar I began to commit my life and future to God in the same way that I had committed my past. I laid my very self on that altar and gave God my everything; nothing held back. I promised to live for Him with my whole heart; to entrust my future to His kingdom. Thoughts of being a missionary, a pastor, or an evangelist kept coming to mind while I was presenting my all to the Lord, probably because my heroes in my youth were my pastor, missionaries, evangelists, and my parents.

Meanwhile, several quartets from out of town visited local churches during this time, and when possible I attended their concerts and absorbed all I could. Dad liked it too, and he often took me to hear various groups before I was old enough to drive myself to "the singin's."

Also, in our little home church our pastor would often invite touring musical groups from the regional Bible schools for special services of Christian music. My favorite group was the King's Ambassadors, a quartet and piano player from Central Bible Institute in Springfield, Missouri, that sang and preached their way into our hearts. These were wonderful times of encouragement and inspiration.

As a little boy, I was especially intrigued by the mechanics and the moods of the great classics found in the old hymnals. The grandiose melodies and doctrine-filled lyrics caught my attention. I sat in church and studied the harmony patterns, the piano and organ parts, and the interpretations of both the song leader and the individuals who were making music a vital part of their worship exercise. I found it all positively captivating. Could music be my forte?

When no substantive answers came to my pleadings I felt a rush of panic. Could God not hear me? He was running out of time. I felt that graduation from high school would be the deadline for hearing from God on this all-important issue—but nope. Didn't happen! God remained silent. No heavenly voice. No indicator whatsoever. Hey, God, are you up there?

Off to Bible College

Reluctantly, I took matters into my own hands. Since I wasn't hearing from God I assumed that He hadn't called me into His service, because I wasn't being prepared. So when it became possible for me to register and get a dormitory room in Bible school I jumped at the chance, still feeling that God had something for me to do in His kingdom. The contrast between my innermost yearnings toward God and His absolute silence could have been interpreted as conflict, but there remained that deep sense of destiny that wouldn't go away. So in the fall of 1956 I found my way to Springfield, Missouri, and signed up at Central Bible Institute.

CBI offered me an opportunity to head my young adulthood in the right direction. It was a chance to try my wings as a free-standing adult and pursue what I hoped was a divine call. In addition, one aspect of life in the Christian college community that proved to be a lifelong blessing was that of fellowship. Because I came from a loving family it was easy for me to fall into fellowship with students who felt the same pull toward ministry. Many close, lifelong bonds were formed in those wonderful years in Bible college. Fellowship is still an immense part of my human relationships. I crave it and partake of it as often as possible.

Unfortunately, at the end of the first semester of the first year I ran out of money. I called home to my parents, who were overjoyed that I had chosen to follow the Lord, and explained my financial dilemma. Even though they had five other children to consider and little income to spread around, they said, "If you feel like the Lord would have you continue your studies we'll make a way for you somehow."

But I knew the day-to-day struggles they were having in their own household finances and I just couldn't add the cost of my college tuition as a further obligation to them. When I announced to some of my fellow students that I was going home, several of them offered to help. Again, it wasn't their problem and I was going to face it like a man.

When the semester ended I made my way back to my home and my family. The God-sent magnet that had drawn me to Bible school, however, continued tugging at me and I determined to return somehow. I just knew there was something there for me.

ANOTHER DAY, ANOTHER SKILL

In January of 1957 I found employment in nearby St. Louis, working at McDonnell Aircraft Corporation in the electrical division. My job was to solder wires into a harness holding many more, which would be used to connect all the thousands of contacts throughout the F-100 and F-101 fighter jets. These airplanes were being built through lucrative government contracts, so the salary was much better than that of many other jobs. In the seven months that I worked at McDonnell I was able to make enough money to return to CBI for the next full year.

Little did I know at the time that seven months of soldering wires every day would come in handy in the future. Since I've been the one in charge of the sound system in our group, I've had to make many solder connections and wire harnesses over the years. That's just one of a myriad of details that God was equipping me to handle in my future. Another was the constant analysis of music in church and at local concerts that I mentioned earlier.

I made my way back the following fall to CBI, and settled in for a full year of study, still not knowing my future but knowing Who held it. I immediately reestablished myself in the tenor section of the Revivaltime Radio Choir, a position that had been so fulfilling to me during the previous semester. That position was not long-lived, though, because I was soon contacted by a fellow student, Don Baldwin, who led an established singing group on campus known as the Couriers Quartet.

The King's Ambassadors from CBI had been the singing group that initially aroused my interest in going to their particular school, and I felt an immense loyalty to them. And now I was being approached by a representative of the Couriers, with an offer to audition for a position in his group instead. What to do? In the back of my mind I really wanted to sing with the King's Ambassadors. They had been my inspiration all during my formative teenage years. But there was no spot open for me there.

On the other hand, I had heard the Couriers at a youth rally near my hometown during the previous year. Quite honestly, from a strictly musical point of view I was neither favorably or unfavorably impressed. Many things came into play that would cause me to not especially notice them. Hey, I was a single teenage boy and there were girls at that youth rally, so maybe it would be unfair to judge the Couriers under those circumstances. Nor in the light of eternity does it matter what my unimportant little opinion was anyway.

- 4 -

I Sing the Mighty Power of God

The singers . . . were employed in that work day and night.
(1 Chronicles 9:33)

T he Courier Quartet's beloved tenor singer, Lem Boyles, had graduated out of the group and was pursuing a life of ministry outside of college. Lem had built a legion of adoring fans during his tenure with the group, and his position would be very difficult to fill. Moreover, I was not a true tenor; although I could sing a few high notes I couldn't sustain them for very long.

BOTH SIDES OF THE COIN

When the tryout occurred I had some minuses and pluses that immediately came into play. On the plus side . . .

Harmony singing was easy as pie for me.

Lyric memorization was equally easy.

I understood certain musical principles and was not a total newcomer to the concepts and rules of music, having had limited experience with two local singing groups during my high school days.

Interestingly, Dave Kyllonen often relates that he came into the world of singing with absolutely no background from which to draw. That could have easily become a liability, but obviously he overcame it magnificently.

On the minus side . . .

I was a green, punk kid who didn't know much about life in the adult world.

I was extremely shy. My knees literally shook for the first fifteen years of our full-time ministry on the road, when I had to stand before an audience.

Big minus—my vocal velocity was pitifully lacking. In fact, when I finally got to the audition they told me after the first song that I should sing louder because they couldn't hear me. I told them I was doing my best, and that was the truth.

Every time the Couriers tried out a prospective tenor singer they found out that their second tenor at the time, Duane Nicholson, could sing much higher and better than the poor soul being auditioned. No one came into the group with as much sheer raw ability. His tones even in the second tenor register were thick, rich, and powerful.

Finally, the inevitable made itself apparent; Duane would have to switch to the high tenor part and I was offered the job of lead singer. Of course, it was more than happenstance; it was divine design, because—as proven over five decades of association with the Couriers—I was the one God was grooming to fill that slot. That's not to say I ever deserved the opportunity; no, not for a moment! I never felt as humbled in all my life as I did on the day the Couriers announced to me that, after prayerful consideration, they were giving me the nod to be the new second tenor/lead singer.

That all happened in the fall of 1957. The newly reassembled Couriers Quartet now included:

Don Baldwin—baritone, emcee, and manager

Dave Kyllonen—bass

Duane Nicholson—first tenor

Neil Enloe (i.e., "Yours Truly")—second tenor

Eddie Reece—pianist.

Was the church world prepared to embrace and support a "not-quite-ready-for-primetime" group? We would soon find out. The decision was made to take the plunge and pursue a full-time music ministry immediately after the 1957–1958 school year. We would be full time but certainly not big time.

We somehow managed to get through the rest of the school year by traveling out to area churches to sing on weekends. It was a time of trying our wings without having to do it for a living just yet. Then came the day that we departed our beloved alma mater and set out upon what has become a long, long road.

The year was 1958 and things were quite different in that era. President Eisenhower had just announced his plan for a nationwide interstate highway network, but it hadn't materialized yet. So almost without exception, all U.S. highways were two-lane roads. Have you ever fallen behind schedule, only to find yourself traveling a two-lane highway behind pokey drivers who think it's Sunday afternoon in the springtime? Frustrating, isn't it? Yet that's the everyday situation we faced in trying to navigate the narrow highways of our nation. It took an hour to get through the traffic lights of Columbus, Ohio. The same was true for Indianapolis and Toronto, and a host of other obstacles that called themselves cities.

At that time there were no bypasses. The only way to get past any city or hamlet was through the heart of town. We have friends from the West Coast who made light of the antique design of our Pennsylvania Turnpike. But remember that it was built in the 1930s and was a revolutionary departure from the tradition of the time. Duane often invites people who make derogatory remarks about our turnpike to traverse the state of Pennsylvania from east to west (or vice versa) without using the turnpike. It will very quickly make converts out of skeptics. In other words, just getting there was a huge challenge in those days.

Then there was the perception that the Couriers was a group that sang wild music without the traditional, subdued enthusiasm of the status quo songs of the church. The typical Christian mind was ultraconservative, and we were often the objects of criticism over our music. We knew in our hearts that our motives were pure, but we were young men full of life and energy, and perhaps it was easy to misinterpret our jubilance as frivolity. Honestly, we only wanted to point men and women to Christ through what we hoped was contagious, joyful music. Even so, we have probably recorded more songs from the hymnal than most any other traveling group.

By and large our music was widely accepted if not financially supported. Here we were, five young men trying to live on offerings that sometimes totaled no more than $75, and often even less. It seemed impossible to survive when viewed from the outside, but on the inside we knew we had a distinct call on our lives by the God of all resources. We almost shut down our ministry at one discouraging low point, but we persisted with confidence that the God who put His hand on our lives was the God who would make a way where there seemed to be none.

In the first year of full-time activity we found ourselves in a recording studio in Camden, New Jersey, to make our second album, entitled, *Southern Style Singing—From the Heart of the Northland*. Upon entering the studio we were greeted by the engineer who asked us to sing something so he could figure out how to best capture our music. So we did, and when it was over the engineer came out of the control room into the studio and said, "Could you sing that again? I've never heard anything like that before." We weren't too sure how to take his remark but we sang it again. This time two men emerged from the control room, the engineer and the studio owner.

The owner said, "We're not kidding; we've never heard anything like this before. As you know, South Philadelphia is just across the Delaware River from us and many young artists, like Fabian and Bobby Rydell, are very popular now. We know what America will buy."

He named several more famous local singers of the day, then continued: "You men are young, fresh, and good-looking (I think he was blind) and you have a lifetime ahead of you. We like your sound a lot. If you could keep the same exact sound and just change a word now and then, we could make you more money in the next six months than you can make in a lifetime, just by doing what you're doing now."

We went on to prove that man to be absolutely right. We could have made more money doing ANYthing else! But we knew what he meant by "a word or two." What he was inferring was that he wanted to remove the word *Jesus*. He wanted us to put the word *love* where *Jesus* had been. That would be the equivalent of removing our hearts and asking us to live on. We were about Jesus.

The original five members were all still in the group, and we excused ourselves and went to the lobby. We huddled in a circle near the water cooler. For a moment no one said a word as we all pondered the offer. Then in unison we all wagged our heads sideways, saying, "No, no, NO!" God had given us our song and our ministry, and money would not lure us away from His divine call. We graciously thanked the man but said that we would stay the course to which God had called us.

I must say that after turning down the offer, we found ourselves in need many times. But we never looked longingly back in the hope that we might reconsider. The same God who called us always made provision for us. Years later I would pen the following song:

Not for Sale

Verse 1

Ev'rything has its price, so we are told.

You can buy anything if you have gold.

But my soul was purchased on Mount Calvary.

I am sold; sold-out for eternity.

Verse 2

Though the world seems a bargain, when you're
  young,

It cannot match the price of God's own Son.

And the temporary pleasure found in sin

Can't compare with eternal peace within.

Chorus

Not for sale; not for sale.

I'm already bought by precious blood;

I'm not for sale.

My confession closed the deal;

By the Spirit I am sealed.

'Til His glory is revealed, I'm not for sale.

© 1983 by Neil Enloe. All rights reserved.

Looking back it is quite obvious that we were under the leadership of a heavenly guide. If judged by longevity alone, it had to be a supernatural journey through fifty-plus years of keeping faith, family, friends, and fellowship together. We simply could not have made it happen on our own strength, intellect, or personal talent and charm. But God led us around the pitfalls and preserved us within the purpose of His divine call.

- 5 -

We Can't Hear You

My tongue shall sing aloud of thy righteousness.
(Psalm 51:14)

The practical side of life always brings struggle, even when we're being led of God. As I mentioned earlier, one of my personal struggles was the sheer weakness of my singing voice. I was not born with foghorn volume. To create as much volume as other members of our group was a near impossibility at first. It was like having a missing front tooth. Something was noticeably inequitable but there was the hope that time would fill the gap.

When I realized that my part was the weakest in terms of volume I knew that I just had to strengthen my voice. So I decided to either get stronger or get out. I determined this in a private meeting with myself and did not share it with the other members, who were vocally running full speed ahead. But I purposed in my heart to get louder. Now—how do you do that? I'm not sure how anyone else has found a solution, but I decided to sing my voice away every night in the hope that the extreme workout would bring about more volume and more command. In the beginning I had no reserve, and it was all I could do to get through each concert.

So every night I would sing every note as loudly as I could, not really caring about any other aspect of the group sound, like blend or interpretation. I was on a quest to get louder, period. For at least a year this went on, with me feeling that my tonsils would fly out onto the stage at any moment because of the sheer pressure I was putting on my throat. Did it hurt? You bet it hurt.

But as I came up on the end of the first year of this madness I began to hurt less at the end of each concert. Could I be gaining strength through exercise? Actually, yes, things were getting a little better; still not good, but slightly better. I continued this practice for the next several years until I did develop the needed stamina, reserve volume, and the ability to maintain my part among the others.

There were also other areas that I needed to develop in my own performance that I purposed to work on. I was not born with a golden voice. I knew it even more than those who heard me and wished me the best. I had the privilege of standing next to a truly great voice. Duane Nicholson was given from birth an extraordinary tone and range in his voice. Oh sure, it embarrasses him to hear me say so but it's so very true. His majestic, soaring sound has been noticed by all who have heard us sing throughout the years. He is judged by concert-goers, critics, and peers alike to have the perfect set of pipes. I concur. So who does this meek, soft-singing little hopeful get to stand next to for a lifetime? That's pressure.

Realizing that I didn't have equivalent tools I figured that I had better get to work on other things that I could immediately improve, or I'd be lost. I began to examine diction, enunciation, and articulation. Could I make my singing more remarkable if I flaunted each individual syllable? Maybe . . . let's try it. So I began to examine the difference between singers and public speakers who were very articulate and those who obviously didn't care about enunciation. Yes! There was a marked difference. So to my quest for more volume was added a new determination to make every lyric clearly understood.

What a change came with such a simple modification. Careful articulation brought me a heightened awareness. The lyrics were the song. A song is a story set to music, which had better be worth telling. We have the greatest story to tell, and so we simply had to maximize the impact of its telling. Indeed, the thing that got me started writing songs was the challenge of making the story better told. I don't pretend to be more intelligent or perceptive than anyone else, but I certainly do pay close attention to the message of what I write and sing. Long after the sound has trailed off into silence the impact of the lyrics lingers, now resting in the minds of those who heard. And with the memory of the sounds perhaps they'll draw forth the message as well.

Another area of improvement that I needed was in adding color to my solos. I began to notice that often the high note of the melody coincided with the highlight of the lyrics. I could use that.

There were also other "weapons" that I added to my arsenal. For example, I found that high notes would excite. My range wasn't as extensive as Duane's but I had a few high notes at my disposal, and I soon found that an occasional well-placed high note could help get that all-important message across. Even using my imagination in finding that special "added touch" for each occasion became a challenge. Every song seems to have a key to opening its meaning to the hearer. My challenge was to search for that special something to make each song "happen" properly.

So I began to emphasize these techniques and they brought about a revolution in my personal performances. I recall hearing Dave say that he realized when he was accepted into the group as the bass singer he was aware that he didn't have the tools to be a remarkable singer. So he asked the Lord to help him develop in other areas that would make him valuable to the group. An excellent emcee and preacher emerged, and a fine singer as well. I, too, looked for something that would add value to the group ministry.

But the bottom line is that God heard my desperate cry for help and began to make me aware of the tools I needed to develop on my own. Again, He was leading. What a wonderful God!

-6-

I Don't Think
I Can Handle It

The Spirit and the bride . . .
(Revelation 22:17)

A s a shy kid, growing up in Illinois among five siblings in
a family of conservative Christians, I learned that certain
things came with the family culture. They were things that
weren't necessarily taught formally but were understood in
practice. For instance, a woman was to be respected as an
innocent handmaiden of God. Dad always treated Mom as his
princess. That's not to say that they didn't sometimes have
their differences but they worked them out in love and respect,
with dignity. I never saw my parents have a knock-down, drag-
out type of encounter. They were devoted to each other in true
love. Their example set the standard for my life, for dealing
with the generation that would be mine.

When I was in Bible school as a young man, my shyness
manifested itself in not dating often. Oh yes, I found girls

very attractive but I didn't feel worthy to keep company with members of the opposite sex. Looking back, I'm grateful for that reluctance because it could have led to my ruin, had I been reckless. But in time I started to date a select few on mostly casual occasions. This would be my pattern until I reached the age of twenty-four.

Somewhere down deep in my heart was the need to finally belong to someone. But I wouldn't let that craving manifest itself until I was sure the time and the person were both right. I carefully guarded my heart and kept it for my life partner, who would someday magically appear.

The Vision Appears

In the 1960s we sang a lot of concerts in New Jersey, sponsored by promoter Paul Moore. There was a girl who was working the ticket stand for Paul as a volunteer. She was a sweet girl, and while I noticed her I didn't give her a lot of thought. But as the concerts continued I became acquainted with her and thought she was a proper and pretty girl, but at that point I never considered dating her.

One summer evening when the sun shone late, we were singing in a church in northern New Jersey, when who should show up but the cute ticket seller from the concerts. After I had set up the PA system and was ready to sing, I realized that there was quite a bit of time left before the service started. I looked at the attractive ticket taker and thought it might be an opportune time to get to know her better. So I invited her to go with me to the nearby cafe to have a Coke. That informal encounter led to another and yet another, until I found myself driving from Pennsylvania to New Jersey on my days off to see this girl, Ruth Walter.

Ruth was the youth leader at the Assembly of God Church in Rockaway, New Jersey, and was already encouraging young people in Christian living before I came along. When I finally saw her in action I knew that she wouldn't need my help to live for God. She had already made the determination to follow Him and work for His kingdom. What a head start!

In the months that followed, our dating activity escalated and I found myself falling in love with Ruth, and she with me. Within a relatively short time I proposed, knowing in my heart that she was the girl for me. I don't recommend a short courtship because of the unknown hazards that can be lurking, but it proved to be right for us.

The Couriers were singing at a concert in Succasunna, New Jersey, during the time that Ruth and I were dating, and I had recently been to the jeweler to pick out a special engagement ring, the very finest I could afford. I wanted to present my best to my beloved. So during the intermission I borrowed a car and took Ruth for a short drive. With the ring hidden in the glove compartment, I pulled the car over to the side of the road, and with fear and trembling told her that I had fallen in love with her. Then I told her that I felt a distinct and deliberate call of God on my life toward the ministry, and I knew that at the moment I was in the center of His divine will with the Couriers.

I then cautioned her to not think that she could get me to the marriage altar and hope to draw me away from my calling in the future. I said that I would only remove myself from the Couriers when I felt like God was making the move for me.

What a way to propose, huh? I continued by saying that she could expect long hours and days of sitting at home wondering what I was doing, and that she would have to trust me when I said I was being true to her. Then I reminded her that I would have to trust her loyalty, too, when I was away. This was the scenario that we would face going forward, and it would have to have its base in mutual trust. Finally, with all that as background, I asked the question. "Will you marry me?"

You have to realize that my system demands instant responses. If not, I start feeling uneasy. Ruth didn't immediately answer, so I'm thinking, "Come on, don't leave me hanging. I've got an expensive ring in the glove compartment that I don't want to have to return."

But she was contemplating her very future and didn't want to get involved in something she couldn't handle. I've come to love that about her. After what seemed like an eternity, she spoke. "I'm prepared to make any sacrifice necessary to be your wife so long as it's the will of God for our lives." Whew! That was pressure! Did she say yes? She said YES! Hallelujah!

Her answer has stood the test of time ever since. Ruth has fulfilled every dream I ever had for a soul mate. She has built a home of dignity and love, having given me three wonderful children and a happy life. And yes, I would do it all over again—a million times. As of this writing we're coming up on our forty-fourth anniversary. We were married on February 29, 1964. I was a leap-year groom. The joke about my being too cheap to buy an anniversary gift every year has arisen many times, but that was the only day that fit into the Couriers' date book. We had places to sing most every day, and to take even five days off was catastrophic to our group finances.

It'll Really Be Golden

Ruth and I began to examine the ramifications of having married on leap year. We discovered that, since we only have an anniversary every four years, on our golden wedding anniversary we will have been married 200 years. That celebration will take place on February 29, 2164. You're all invited to our place for cake and punch.

Our three children, Beth, Heidi, and Tim, have all been sources of fulfillment and joy for Ruth and me. Beth now lives in Philadelphia, after earning degrees in music composition and theory from Temple University. Heidi is married to an incredible guy, Shane Wilson, who is both preacher and businessman extraordinaire. Shane has won my heart; he's like another son. Heidi and Shane have two fabulous children who live right here in our hometown: a charming daughter, Sydney, and a robust and dazzling son, Spencer. Heidi and Shane's children refer to us grandparents as "Gigi" and "Bammah."

Tim is an itinerant evangelist who married Rochelle Hollis, a delightful pastor's daughter from Kansas. Tim and Rochelle now reside in Wichita, Kansas, and have three awesome sons who bring great joy to us grandparents, whom they call "Gigi" and "Umpaw." Braedon is a quiet thinker with drop-dead good looks. Dolan is Mr. Excitement, who abhors dull moments and is happiest when he's doing something creative. Barret is ever the handsome individual, who never spoke baby talk. Can you see that all our five grandchildren are the very finest?

God Protects and Sustains

Beth, our firstborn, was more like our granddaughter, Sydney, who is always onstage. Beth was also like our grandson Dolan, in that she kept things moving and didn't like a lull in the action. When she was only eight months old, she and Ruth were in our Volkswagen Beetle on the way to Illinois to visit my parents. They were traveling on the Pennsylvania Turnpike just west of Somerset, Pennsylvania, when without notice the steering wheel locked on the car and the driver lost control. The car rolled over several times before coming to a stop. Ruth was momentarily knocked unconscious. Upon coming to, she looked for her eight-month-old baby but she was not in the wrecked car. After a further panic-stricken search she noticed a bundle of blankets lying beneath the center guardrail of the turnpike. It was her baby who was bleeding from head injuries sustained from being hurled from the car.

The day before the accident, a missionary on furlough was visiting friends and family in Ohio. When he gathered his family together for the trip to Harrisburg, Pennsylvania, the next morning, he told them, "I had a dream last night that there was an auto accident. I'm not sure if it's us or someone else, but let's be careful and prayerful today."

As the little green Volkswagen tumbled to rest on the westbound side of the turnpike, the missionary was traveling east on the same turnpike. When he saw the commotion ahead he said, "That's the dream I had last night." He stopped and gave Ruth and Beth a ride back to the hospital, even before an ambulance could be called. In the course of conversation with the missionary's family, Ruth realized that they were all Christians, and a corporate prayer went up for Beth's well-being. God heard their prayers and Beth made a full recovery. What a faithful God!

Heidi, our second born, was the sweetest baby that a parent could ask for. She was loving in nature and quietly considerate when I would have to sleep in after a long night on the road. Heidi wrapped her daddy around her little finger, for sure. She attended my alma mater, where she met Shane, who was also a student studying for the ministry with a call of God on his life. When they were engaged, Shane came to visit Heidi and they bought a car together to be the first mutual project of their coming marriage. After a quiet dinner together in the Harrisburg area, they were headed to our house when they were hit head on by an off-duty ambulance.

Shane was not seriously injured but Heidi went headfirst through the windshield. She was wearing her seatbelt but it must have failed. Our precious Heidi was wounded in her lovely face from the broken glass of the windshield. She was rushed to the hospital and a specialist in plastic surgery put her face back together. He did a superb job and Heidi has returned to normal and is again her lovely self. One of the ambulance attendants was a Christian and joined Heidi in prayer during the trip to the hospital. God came through for our family again. What a faithful God!

When Tim was about eleven years old we Couriers planned to take two busloads of people to the Midwest to take in the sights and have a couple of services along the way in churches. Since we were going through Illinois it was a perfect opportunity for Tim to spend some needed time with my parents, and we would pick him up on the way back. My mom and dad jumped at the chance to have Tim spend several days with them.

The bus tour continued on for a couple more days. When we arrived in Colorado a telephone call came from my parents saying that Tim had been burned in a freak accident at the barbecue pit at their house. We were not told the extent of his wounds so I sent Ruth back to Illinois by airplane, feeling the responsibility of the people of whose bus I was the captain. I told her, "Go and assess his condition. If it's bad, I'll come too."

When Ruth arrived in St. Louis, where Tim had been hospitalized, she immediately called me and said, "Come now." I quickly made my way to the hospital and was soon with my beloved son, who had third-degree burns over his arms, chest, and neck.

Word of Tim's ordeal went quickly around the country and he got cards and balloons. Balloons? So many helium-filled balloons that the entire ceiling of his hospital room was hidden. An elderly woman had been burned the same day as Tim, and she was in a room down the hall. When Tim heard that she was not having many visitors he gathered up two large handfuls of his balloons and took them down the hall to her. Yes, down the hall . . . burns and all. Compassion at work.

Ruth and I both saw a seriousness about life coming over Tim through this ordeal. And what we saw was actual too, because Tim began to grow beyond his years. With that mindset, Tim's heart became a fertile field for God to plant himself in. Tim responded and pursued God with all his might, even at that early age. What a faithful God!

- 7 -

Psalmist of Sorts

He hath put a new song in my mouth.
(Psalm 40:3)

Songwriting seemed to sort of happen to me. My first composition was entitled, "Open Wide Thy Merciful Arms." The Couriers sang it on the Warner Brothers release in 1963 called, *Nothing but . . . the Gospel Truth.* It was an okay song and I felt inspired to write more. However, the next attempt was indeed a catastrophe. It was entitled, "Oh Lord!" I'm sure that when many people heard it they sympathetically thought, *Oh Lord!*

After writing a few more songs I realized that it's possible to improve only through trial and error, which meant that I would definitely write some bad songs on my road to better ones. And for sure, I have not been spared the process— I worked through a lot of feeble attempts to grow up as a songwriter. Honestly, I'm not sure I've grown up yet. That applies to many other areas of my life too.

But better things were to come. I soon learned that my first idea about a particular lyric was not always my best. One technique that I've learned about writing lyrics is that I scribble down all I know about the subject and sort that information into some kind of order. Then I use those scribblings as a work sheet and slowly piece together a story line.

Are you getting the impression that songwriting is less about inspiration and more about perspiration? It's certainly true in my case. For me, a major prerequisite of a well-written song is in an effectively presented story line. I've invented ten rules that might be appropriate for your consideration. Please bear in mind that these are not laws set in stone . . . .

If inspiration strikes, grab a pencil and write down your thoughts. Often ideas present themselves in the middle of the night when you're awakened out of a deep sleep. It's the subconscious mind working on your behalf. If you think that you'll formalize your thoughts later you'll find that the ideas will not return "later." Do it now! Some of my most promising inspirations have been swapped for a little more sleep.

Don't rule out any silly notion that crosses your mind. That notion, however ridiculous it might seem at the moment, just might open the door to an important truth or association that will contribute to your final product.

Stay on the subject. Nothing confuses the hearer more than skipping from one issue to another with no sense of logical order. How many songs have we all heard that start with some noble subject only to end "in heaven by and by"? If the song is about praise, stay with praise throughout. If it's about some area of encouragement, encourage to the end.

Design a melody and a music setting in keeping with the mood of the lyrics. A stark example of how not to join a lyric with a melody would be this: My composition entitled, "He's More Than Just a Swearword" set to a melody that made it sound like Handel's "Hallelujah Chorus." Can you imagine this being sung, "Hallelujah, no swearing; no swearing!" Since the song was intended as a message to the average blasphemer, I used a common musical genre to convey the message: country music. It not only fit the occasion, but over time it has gained its own acceptance in that style.

Take the listener on an adventuresome journey of thought in your lyrics. Assume that the listener isn't thinking what you're thinking and start him on page one in the progression of your story. Then carefully lead him by supplying supporting information and reasoning, in logical order, so that when you reach your conclusion he'll be coming to the same one via your suggested line of logic.

A rule that I learned from the late comedian Jack Benny is to always play up to your audience, never down to it. Give them the benefit of being at least as intelligent as you, if not more so. Make the logic of your lyrics as noble and lofty as the subject matter allows.

Take a step back and look at the skeleton of the story, the lyrics, and the music. Without good bones the song will not long stand. Is it readily singable, do the lyrics make sense, and do the melody and story lines complement each other?

Revise, revise, and revise some more. I have learned that the success of my songs lies in many revisions, through such considerations as shading, emotion, impact, chronology, and specific word meanings. Words are colorful and powerful, even majestic. Choose them carefully to bring about a precise development of thought so they will lead to the conclusion that you want the hearer to understand and embrace.

When you think you have crafted a winner, bounce it off a trusted friend who will tell you honestly how it strikes him. In Proverbs 27:6 the Bible says, "Faithful are the wounds of a friend." Compliments don't always serve us best. The loving perspective of someone who shoots straight with you will be more useful than your own awe at your own accomplishment.

Pray! Don't neglect to ask the Lord's guidance in the writing of the song, nor to ask Him for His special anointing as the song is performed.

These are some of the guidelines that I follow as I attempt to understand the listener and his needs. They might not be suitable for every writer but they have served me well. However, I make no claims to being an authoritative source of information—I only know what has worked for me.

In total, as of this moment I've written fifty-six songs, plus or minus one or two. That certainly doesn't qualify me as an expert, given that Fanny Crosby wrote more than nine thousand hymns. She wrote so many songs that there was a groundswell of animosity toward her from her peers. She was perceived as being too successful. So being the prolific song machine that she was, she also composed many songs under assumed names, thereby taking the attention away from herself while continuing to crank them out. I should have such a problem . . . .

I'm often asked, "How do I get a song published?" That

one is really simple. Go online to the U. S. Copyright Office website and all the helps you need will be available.

Another question I'm frequently asked is, "How do I get a song out there to be heard by the public?" The only answer I know is in the way I've done it. Get in front of an audience and sing the song in such a way that they will favorably respond, as often as you can. Somewhere along the line will be another singer or industry person who will become aware of it and will want to use the song too, and you will be on your way. However, if you sing it repeatedly and get little or no response you probably are wanting in one of three areas. Either the song lacks merit, has potential but needs further revision, or you're not capturing the imagination of your audience with your rendition.

Yet another question that I have been asked is, "What is your favorite song?" I have favorites for different reasons, but one still remains atop my all-time list. The great old hymn "Just As I Am" is my choice because I believe more people have invited Christ into their hearts as that song was being sung than they have during any other song. What a distinction!

I'm also often asked, "What is your favorite song from your own pen and heart?" At the end of the day, the people determine what is a good song. What I like and what our con-cert-goers deem my best might be two different songs. We were singing at a Christian booksellers' convention in the 1970s in Atlantic City, and I had a conversation on the board-walk with Bill Gaither. He expressed the same phenomenon about his songs when he said, "Why 'He Touched Me'? I have better songs than that one." He was feeling the frustration common to writers, that when we have put forth what we feel is our best effort the public comes along and prefers another.

Another consideration must be given some weight here. The time in my life that was most meaningful to me came immediately after I gave my life to the Lord. I spent days, weeks, months, and even a couple of years seeking God's will for my life. It was a time of intense laying of my all on the altar of submission to God, with no strings attached. I wanted His divine will and calling to be made sure in my future. So I'm strongly drawn to songs that put me on the altar. With that in mind, my personal favorite of my own compositions is the following three verses:

Potter, Vessel, Oil

Verse 1

Potter, take me, I'm the clay;

Here on Your wheel I lie;

Ready and willing to be

Molded and modeled by Thee;

Shaped by Your hands

To Your demands;

I am not mine, I am Thine.

Verse 2

Vessel that I wish to be

Draws no attention to me.

Not one of beauty, I ask;

Just one that serves Your great task.

Tested and tried; spotless inside;

Proven and faultless to Thee.

Verse 3

Oil of the Spirit, I pray

Pour into my life today.

Fill me 'til I overflow.

When I run over I'll know

That I've fulfilled Thy perfect will.

Use me, I'm ready to go.

Going hand in hand with composing is the process of arranging songs. I have had the advantage of arranging for pretty much the same voices throughout my lifetime. We've managed to keep our unique identity intact because the individual voices have remained mostly the same, and the vocal arrangements have been fairly uniform in style. With the exception of the two years that David Young was in our group and did many splendid arrangements, I've had that responsibility for most of the time.

My goal has been to fully utilize each vocal ability represented in our group. Especially when we have only three parts to work with, it becomes vital to give full expression to every voice. It has been my job to enable each part to speak most effectively. However, it does take time to get accustomed to each member's particular forte, especially during the developmental years when we were all working toward making the group jell and sing as one voice.

I learned, for instance, that Duane is at his best when he is singing those rich, majestic tones that he is famous for. Another ability that Duane brings is that of a crooner. He grew up in the era when crooners were very popular and he learned the art well.

I also found that Dave was hesitant to sing solos. For some reason he was perfectly at home doing a recitation, and he still does them superbly, but it was quite different when a lyric was set to music. I've often jokingly said to him after he's delivered an incredible recitation, "Why don't you sing like that?" But through positive reinforcement and a lot of hard work on his part, Dave has become a creative interpreter of song lyrics too. Dave is certainly not lazy and he will try anything for the betterment of the group.

Fortunately, it takes just three parts to make a simple chord, and we've stripped our parts down to the bare minimum. We emphasize the fourth part either in the music track or at the piano. In more complex chords there are notes that must be included, and there are also certain component notes of a chord that are understood yet not heard, and not necessarily vital to be sung. It's my job to determine which is which. We must always maximize every other area of our approach to avoid a noticeable dearth in the sound. That's why we "rear back" and sing our loudest. We have to make as much noise as four people, especially when we're singing on the program with a complete quartet. Then each part is both integral and crucial.

Some of my favorite secular music comes from the 1940s when the United States joined many other nations in World War II. The typical lyric of the day dealt with lovers who were separated by the tragedy and alienation of war. Many songs were written from the perspective of a soldier boy in the foxhole who was thinking about his beloved back home, or vice versa—such thoughts as "When I look at the moon I'm wondering if you can see the same moon and think of me." They were lyrics of romantic imagination that allowed the listener to think about his own situation and buy into the rationale. Today it is totally different in popular music, in that the lyrics are not only extremely direct but are often predatory in attitude and nature.

I was just a kid during those years, and the music that aired on the radio before television became part of our American home furnishings was mostly the current popular hits. I was always drawn to the romantic lyrics and the innovative melodies and harmonies of that era. The bands and orchestras were big and enjoyed a full complement of brass and stringed instruments. Today it seems that just six strings of a guitar have single-handedly replaced all of those great instruments.

My father was a guitarist of sorts, so I have a deep appreciation for that instrument, make no mistake. But I am not particularly drawn to in-your-face music. I prefer to be allowed to sit back and make up my own mind whether the music I'm hearing is worth my time. And I love to listen to music that is brisk in volume, but if someone tries to obliterate all other thoughts he loses me quickly. Another popular practice among guitarists is the use of induced distortion. In an industry that otherwise uses every advantage to eliminate distortion, why do some think that distortion complements their music? Ahhh . . . I feel much better now that I've vented my little frustrations.

I have always had a love for the imaginative and innovative sound of jazz music, with a keen interest in a mix of both jazz and blues. To me there's just something very musical about those forms that I can utilize in our sound. So if you hear hints of blues and jazz in our arrangements, it's totally intentional. However, my first love in music is unabashedly the glorious hymns of the church. Very few songs written in my lifetime have risen to the level of excellence, either musically or lyrically, of those enriching, uplifting, and inspiring favorites. Much sound doctrine can be learned from those grand classics. Will "The Old Rugged Cross," "Amazing Grace," or "How Great Thou Art" be standards in heaven? Who knows? But it's my guess that they would probably be good ones to start with.

Over the years I've learned secrets that have helped me arrange around our peculiarities, to make our songs come alive. I've examined thousands of songs to glean principles that will help us most effectively deliver the Gospel story. I've learned to choose our material while keeping in mind the importance of the message and how we can best present it.

I've also learned the value of the sheer emotion of chord progression, and how to voice those chords with just the three most important notes. I've learned the musical personality of both Dave and Duane, and thus we've come to maximize our strengths even as we've minimized our weaknesses.

- 8 -

Former Members

Now there were seven brethren.
(Mark 12:20)

A most enriching aspect of my journey through life with the Couriers has been the input of former members of the group. Here are some of the ones who have had profound impacts on my life.

Don Baldwin—What an amazing and talented gentleman Don proved to be, in his decade as the prominent and illustrious leader of our group. Always the forward-thinking mind, Don continually led us into new areas in terms of promotion and marketing. His genius left a permanent stamp on our modus operandi. Don was an excellent singer, too, giving special attention to making a song "happen."

And nobody, but nobody, was a funnier man than Don. He constantly entertained the troops. In the early days when we were traveling in a funeral home limousine (so Dave's six-foot-five frame could stretch out), Don would keep us laughing all afternoon. On one such occasion we were rounding the corner at a busy downtown intersection. There were people galore on the corner just waiting for the "walk" light to activate so they could step out into the crosswalk. As we crept around the corner Don seized the moment. There stood a lady on the curb with a perplexed look on her face as the black limousine passed by. Don rolled down the car window and said, "What's the matter, lady? Haven't you ever seen a celebrity before?" And we hurried away, laughing our fool heads off, knowing that we were all nobodies.

In the early 1960s, while we were still driving the 1948 GM Silversides coach, we were traveling through the night in west Texas. The landscape was totally flat—no trees, no ditches, not even another vehicle. Don was the driver and his two hours were coming to an end. Duane was next in line, and it was about time for Don to pull the bus over and go back to wake up Duane.

Ever the innovative soul, Don began to fantasize about dashing back to Duane's bunk to wake him without stopping the bus. After all, there was no one on the road to hit us and there was nothing in the landscape for us to hit. So as he sat in the driver's seat he released the steering wheel and the accelerator for a few seconds to see if the bus would remain on the road without anyone at the controls. Other than gradually slowing down, it ran straight down the road. His next test was to get up out of the driver's seat and stand in the aisle. Again he let the steering wheel go and again the bus ran straight down the road.

After a couple more tests to make sure, Don felt confident that the bus wouldn't go off the road onto the desert, and even if it did there was nothing to hit. One final time, while standing in the aisle, he brought the bus back up to its top speed of sixty-two miles per hour before darting back down the center aisle to Duane's bunk, directly behind mine. While still watching to make sure the bus was staying on the road, Don reached for Duane's feet and started shaking empty blankets. Duane was not there—he had gone to the back to the bathroom. While Don was still trying to find Duane's feet beneath the blankets, Duane came out of the bathroom and yelled at the top of his voice, "Baldwin—what are you doing? Who's driving this thing?"

Don sprinted back to the driver's seat and resumed control. The whole episode woke us all up and we had a good laugh in spite of its life-threatening aspect. Ya' gotta give Don an A for imagination.

Eddie Reece—Eddie was the hook we hung our success on in the early days. He could make a piano explode. Eddie played on our first two long-play recordings. He was a funny man, too, when you got him going. But in his heart he was deeply serious about God. He showed me many things about piano playing without his ever knowing it. I watched him intensely every time he played. Eddie passed away in 2006 after a heart attack in the Holy Land.

Jerry Evans—Jerry played piano for us for just two years, but he was an immensely talented musician. The two recordings he made with us stand out because of his commercial style. His accompaniments were simply superb. After losing track of Jerry for many years, I got an unexpected email from him. We have renewed acquaintance and now communicate regularly. Jerry has really grown in God over the years. I'm grateful for his friendship.

"Little David" Young—L. D. was pure genius on many fronts. He was a super high tenor singer, an awesome talent on the keyboard, a quick-witted humorist, a godly man, and in those days, given his diminutive stature, a cute little boy whom the moms and grandmas loved. He dazzled as no other piano player that I've ever seen. He was positively charming, but his music also had unbelievable depth. He could handle anything we ever called on him to play.

The only downside with L. D. was that we always feared that he would be lured away by another group. He often got offers from the big boys, and it was no wonder. He was a catch. He had the ability to make any group sound better. To his credit, he was loyal to us; as he told us at his departure, "I'm leaving to be off the road. I miss my wife and children and I want to be with them." He later reminded us that while he continued to get tempting offers from other high-profile groups, he turned them all down to stay with his family.

L. D. and I remain close friends. He and Colleen had one son and four daughters, all of whom are talented musicians, and as of this writing they have fourteen grandchildren. He's a man rich in family.

Eddie Hawks—When Eddie joined us he had just graduated from high school and was newly wed to his beautiful bride, Sharon. Eddie brought back the youth that was otherwise slipping away from us older members. We gave him his first paycheck and he celebrated his newfound freedom to make his own decisions with French fries and a milkshake.

Eddie had the most loving disposition. Never was there a

harsh word or disagreement from him. In the two years he played piano for us we had much good-natured fun. Eddie has gone on to be a successful music director at Victory Church in Lakeland, Florida. He regularly arranges full orchestrations, which makes me just plain jealous. I have the highest admiration for Eddie's accomplishments. He and Sharon remain treasured friends.

Phil Enloe—Talk about a "can-do" guy—that's my brother Phil. His gifts seem limitless. He's an incredible singer/stylist with an extremely wide range. His contribution to the Couriers, in the 1960s and the 1980s through 2000, made us a better team both times. Phil's command of the Word of God is truly astounding. His ability as a public speaker is remarkable. His love and loyalty to the Lord is the benchmark of his whole being. Everything he does is part of an effort to enhance the kingdom of God.

When he traveled as a soloist he would select a verse or two from the passage of scripture he had read in his morning devotion time. He would write the verse on a pad and put it on a clipboard on the dash. All day long he would recite the verse until it became a part of his memory bank. After many years he built up a huge reserve that he could call on in his preaching. It made him a force to be reckoned with in the pulpit.

Phil has more one-liner quickies stored in him than anyone I've ever met. One night when we were singing, Duane was the emcee for the evening. At one point between songs, when Duane was doing what Phil calls "waxing an elephant" (waxing eloquent), Phil stepped forward and, with a huge voice, barked, "I was a man trapped in a woman's body!" Both Duane and I stood in stunned disbelief, thinking, "Phil has finally freaked out this time." The audience audibly gasped and Phil just let the moment fester. Not knowing how to react, Duane didn't say anything for the longest time. Then Phil again stepped forward and said, "And then I was born!" That was yet another of many instances in which Phil went out on a limb with his humor, where he could either win big or fall hard. He was willing to take that risk to make the moment even bigger.

Tim Enloe—We're talking about my only-begotten son here. Not only is he my buddy, but he did all the things I didn't accomplish in my youth. When Tim sang baritone with us, Duane and I saw a shift in the age group that responded to us. We had more young people, especially teenage girls, coming up after the service. Young people attract young people, and we saw plenty while Tim was with us. It was also a time when the popular fashion was to wear no socks. Tim didn't. He was always impeccably dressed in a way that would be the pride of any father . . . but no socks. We had fun with him by raising his pant legs to reveal his bare ankles, and the crows would roar.

Tim opened his heart to the Lord at a very early age, and now God is using him in a powerful way as a traveling evangelist. Ruth and I are grateful that God has put his strong hand of anointing on our son. Tim is a singer, songwriter, preacher, and author with a heart of gold. Our five years of having Tim in our group were special because Duane and I could see the hand of God moving him toward the call that he is now following. Every parent should be so blessed. Check out his website at: www.enloeministries.org.

- 9 -

Like Brothers

Whosoever shall do the will of my Father which
is in heaven, the same is my brother.
(Matthew 12:50)

One of Dave Kyllonen's great qualities is that he is totally genuine. Because he's a slow, methodical thinker in no particular hurry, he's sometimes been characterized as aloof. Not so. Dave is genuinely friendly and approachable. However, if you approach Dave to make conversation and he doesn't immediately respond, just know that he's pondering what is appropriate to say.

Dave and I have come to take advantage of his slow style of emceeing. He will say part of a sentence and then pause to ponder. That's my cue to insert some humor related—or even not related—to what he's just said. We've used Dave's pace of speech as a springboard for the "little guy versus big guy" shtick. Another wonderful quality is Dave's believability. When he says something people take it to the bank. And rightly so, for he believes what he says.

Duane doesn't say a whole lot in our services and concerts, but when his humor strikes, it's hilarious. Duane brought the perspective of the parsonage to our group culture. His father was a pastor and Duane knows the ins and outs of the local church more than Dave and I. Duane has a gazillion stories from growing up in the parsonage, and he has told them so many times that I could sub for him if I had to. One of Duane's outstanding personal characteristics is his compassion. He's the guy in our group who goes to the altar to pray with people.

When we were in Bible school a virtual plague of influenza swept over almost the entire student body. Those affected were quarantined in another building away from the dormitories. Guess who worked long hours in the quarantine building. Yep, Duane was there to help in any way he could. He saw scores of students who were deathly sick and he reached out to aid and comfort them. And in other areas of compassion I happen to know that he is quietly considerate and generous to people in need.

Bottom line, I have had the privilege of being yoked in ministry with two godly men of impeccable integrity. I've learned a lot from them because of their shining and consistent daily examples. They've patiently served as guinea pigs for my experiments in sorting out what styles of music we might best perform. My burden of responsibility was greatly lightened because they gave me free rein to express musical feelings toward our God. There has been no conflict whatsoever in that department, for which I'm grateful.

Other singers who have graced the Couriers in the past have left their marks too. Don Baldwin was key to launching the group and certainly carried us with his keen abilities until he left in 1966. My brother Phil, during two stints as baritone singer, lent us his huge talents for about nineteen years. Don was like a brother to me, and Phil—of course—is my natural blood brother. Phil remains an immensely gifted singer, preacher, composer, emcee, graphics artist, author, and a long list of other things. His contagious personality is irrepressible and his positive attitude springs from the very core of his being.

Both Don and Phil were joys to work with, and their senses of humor were therapeutic, to say the least. Don passed away in 2007 after a series of lengthy illnesses. Phil continues to travel and sing with his wonderful wife, Jan. I'm really proud of Phil and his ministry and accomplishments. He's a beloved brother and I loved singing with him.

GOOD SHEPHERDS — *I will set up shepherds over them which shall feed them. (Jeremiah 23:4)*

Having sung in more than ten thousand churches and concerts, and having traveled to eighty foreign countries in missionary evangelism, we've come to realize that we'll have bosses for today but yet another one tomorrow. Each pastor, each promoter, and each missionary who serves as host to us is our boss for that day. That might at first seem to be a difficult set of circumstances under which to work, but we've come to love and appreciate those whom God has appointed to lead the local congregations. These wonderful people tend to love and protect their flocks like the Good Shepherd who put them in each pasture. They are hospitable and generous, with deep compassion. And they're on call 24/7 and must bear and share earthshaking dilemmas. The pressure on a parsonage is immense, but most pastors would go to the death on behalf of their people.

- 10 -

Beyond the Sunset

The hoary head is a crown of glory, if it be found
in the way of righteousness.
(Proverbs 16:31)

S oon after I agreed to join the Couriers in 1957 we began
learning songs in the hope of recording an album. Prior
to my joining the group they had made several single recordings on 78 rpm records. Yes, I said 78 rpm records. You know,
the kind that sound scratchy and are so brittle they break
readily?

Most young people of today will only remotely remember
having heard of such a medium. But when I came along, "High
Fidelity" had just been developed and the switch was being
made from 78s to the cool new 33 1/3 rpm Long Play records,
called LPs. At that point, with the advent of improved fidelity
at a slower rotation speed it became possible to put six songs
on one side, so instead of just two songs per record it was now

possible to include twelve. And I was a major benefactor. All the nuances of my less-than-sterling voice would now be captured. I often say that we have done some bad singing in our time . . . and we have proof!.

In a short while we found ourselves in an on-campus recording studio that was usually reserved for the weekly national radio broadcast, *Revivaltime*. Our session cast consisted of four singers, our pianist, and an organist who donated her talents. No bass, no guitar, no drummer—truly a bare-bones venture. We had decided to make our best song the title of our new album. *Beyond the Sunset*, in our opinion, represented the Couriers at our very finest.

How we ever came up with the notion that a standard funeral song would open any doors remains a mystery. Likewise, little did we think at the time that someday we would face the "sunset" of our very ministry as a group. Now turn the calendar forward for about forty-two years.

In 1997, I made a startling suggestion to Duane and Phil that we consider bringing in Larry More to sing tenor for us. Larry had been a dependable volunteer at the youth camps we had operated for nineteen years and had proved the mettle of his heart. He was also a singer we had heard only in the realm of Contemporary Christian Music. He was the most shy and bashful guy we had ever met, but he had quietly learned all of our singing parts and could play all of our songs on the piano. He had done his homework in preparing for what was to come. Larry also had a trio called "Heirborn" in which he sang the tenor part. *High* tenor!

When I mentioned bringing Larry into the group, I told Duane that he would never have to sing a high note again. I proposed that Duane would drop down to the lead, or second tenor part. I would then drop down to the baritone part, and Phil would go down to bass, where he was completely comfortable. But Duane and Phil both looked at me as if to say, "Have you lost your mind? How can you even suggest that we tamper with this holy arrangement?"

Soon after on one Sunday morning we were scheduled to sing in a church about two hours from home. The night before I had felt ill but hoped I would feel better the next day, but when the alarm went off I felt worse. In a groggy stupor I rolled over to shut it off, picked up the phone, and called Duane. In a flash he knew that I was not feeling well and told me to stay in bed and recover, and that he and Phil would somehow get through the meeting. With a great sense of relief I rolled over and stayed there all day.

Duane quickly called his son-in-law, Kris Walker, who is a very accomplished musician in his own right and quickly learns singing parts. Kris agreed to fill in and got ready to leave. During the trip to the church, Duane, Phil, and Kris rehearsed in the vehicle and brushed up on enough songs to get through the service. At that time Kris's job allowed him to take on other responsibilities on the side. He was the perfect substitute for me and he handled my part well.

The next day I received a strange phone call from Phil. He told me that he and Duane had been discussing the likelihood that, given our advancing years, there would be more days when one of us would not be able to travel because of health issues. We had dragged our bodies over the road and around the world for nearly fifty years, and we were feeling the effects. Then he said that my initial proposal to bring Larry More into the group was perhaps a step in the right direction, but we needed to address the probabilities of the future. Phil suggested that we consider not only bringing in Larry but also any of our male family members who would choose to be directly involved in the road ministry of the Couriers.

The possible candidates were:

Kris Walker, Duane's son-in-law, had attended the same Bible school where the Couriers had their start. His musical skills were more than adequate.

Tim Enloe, my son, not only attended the same Bible school where we began but had sung baritone with the Couriers for five years between the ages of thirteen and eighteen, and he was loved by our audiences. But by that time Tim was involved in his own evangelistic ministry and felt like he was in the will of God where he was serving.

Shane Wilson, my son-in-law, had also attended our alma mater and was blessed with a good singing voice and a high range, and he could have made the grade too. But God had him serving as a chaplain in an Annapolis, Maryland nursing home and he felt constrained to stay by his post.

Scot Womble, Phil's son-in-law, was a singer and a trumpet player who knew his way around the music scene. Scot had a high-pitched voice and knew how to use it. And he was an excellent preacher. And he had also graduated from our alma mater.

In view of all this we determined to get Larry, Kris, and Scot to join us to form a double trio, at which point we emerged as "something old and something new"—the Couriers as they had never been seen before.

For the next two years we would remain a six-man team. But the master plan was to phase out the old members and hand the reins to the young men who would carry on after us. It was a time of bonding with the hearts and personalities of the young guys, and it gave the old guys some long-departed insights into youthful thinking. At the stroke of midnight at the beginning of the new millennium (2000), we handed the mantle of the Couriers over to three deserving young men who are now carrying out the original vision that set us in motion in 1955. While there have been a couple of personnel changes since that first new Couriers grouping, we remain proud and supportive of their efforts. You can visit their website at: www.thecouriers. com

STRANGE DEVELOPMENTS

A strange turn of events, hidden in the above, then made me realize that my deep desire to be a member of the King's Ambassadors from CBI has been somewhat realized! The tenor singer for the King's Ambassadors was an unassuming Texan named Carl Walker. At CBI, Carl met and fell in love with Eunice Duncombe, a foreign student from England. This strange pairing of a Texan and a Brit produced three sons.

Meanwhile, Central Bible Institute was upgraded to a college and renamed Central Bible College. The youngest son,

Kristian, then grew up and went to CBC, where he met Duane's daughter Shannon. Kris and Shannon married and settled in the Harrisburg area that the Couriers call home. When we made the change from a trio to a double trio, Kris was one of the new members. So I didn't go to the King's Ambassadors but the King's Ambassadors came to me in the next generation. Is God innovative or what?

Upon what we thought was our departure from the music ministry in 2000, Duane and I retired to our homes in Pennsylvania and the companionship of our dear wives. Duane had married children nearby, as did Ruth and I, but all of Phil's children were grown and out of state by this time. So he made the decision to move to Florida.

My dad had often spoken of wanting to someday reside in the Sunshine State, but it was a dream that had never been realized. He even bought a vacant lot in Port Charlotte, hoping to build a home there someday, but he spent the rest of his life in Wood River. So in time he sold the lot to my brother Bob, who traded it in on a home in Venice, Florida, where he now resides. Then Phil bought the property across the street from Bob, so they are now not only brothers but neighbors.

For almost three years both Duane and I enjoyed our free time, making ourselves busy building lives off the road. The fellowship with our spouses was sweet and we both were enjoying our newly found freedom to the fullest. Then the phone rang one day, and our lives changed profoundly. On the other end of the line was a longtime friend, Harold Terry, whose father hosted the Couriers in his church in

Williamsport, Pennsylvania, in 1957. By now Harold was attending a Christian and Missionary Alliance church in Lewisburg. The church for the moment was in search of a permanent pastor, and in the interim the church board of directors invited various guest ministers to fill the pulpit.

Meanwhile, Dave Kyllonen had retired from his family group, "Homefire," and was scheduled to preach for Harold's CMA church on a Sunday morning. Harold asked if Duane and I would be open to coming up to Lewisburg to sing a "couple of songs" with Dave. When we consented he went to Dave and said that there were a couple of guys who wanted to sing with him next Sunday in the service. Dave's response was that it would be okay with him if he had some time to rehearse with them. Harold told Dave that the two guys could probably do just fine without rehearsal, never telling him that "they" were Duane and Neil. When we showed up just before the service, Dave was stunned to see his old buddies.

The service and the singing went as well as could be expected, considering that we hadn't sung a note together in twenty-three years. We all assumed that it was a one-time occasion and would not happen again. But somehow, word got out that the three of us were out there again, and soon the calls began to come in requesting that we make appearances in churches and concerts. At first the calls trickled in, but soon they began coming at a pace we couldn't maintain. So we decided that God was reopening a door that had been closed and giving us an opportunity to revisit our original calling. Few people have a second chance at something so dear to them. Often the door closes permanently, but God in His infinite mercy has given us another run at this and we don't want to miss the opportunity to do what we still dearly love.

Problem: Now that we're doing this singing thing again, what do we call ourselves? Who are we? Sure, we've been the Couriers since the 1950s, but to call ourselves the Couriers now would be a disservice to the younger men who had taken over for us, and it could compromise their identity. So after contemplating several new group names we settled on "Dave, Duane, and Neil," which also removed the possibility of a change in personnel.

Now if Dave and Duane desire to replace me they'll have to find a lead singer named Neil who also plays the piano. I call it job security. Seriously, we decided that if one of the originals has to quit for any reason, we would all take that as an indicator that it was time for us to hang it up for good. So we're now "Dave, Duane, and Neil" formally, but many of our longtime friends still call us the Couriers. Old habits are hard to break and the Couriers of this new generation have been most gracious toward us.

- 11 -

It's Not My Job

This is the work of God.
(John 6:29)

It has always been my responsibility to build, set up, operate, repair, and do whatever needs to be done to the PA system. When I think of the tons of equipment that we've gone through over the years, it's overwhelming. This includes every gadget imaginable, holding promise for the moment that we might sound better. Starting with the very first system we purchased in Bible school, because I had taken two years of electric and electronic classes in high school, I was chosen to make sure it always worked. Many times I felt like I had a target painted on my back when the sound was not up to what the other guys expected. That's not to say that I have a persecution complex—it just goes with the territory. But there have really been very few times when the PA system quit totally.

One such failure happened during a very important appearance. We were guests of the Pennsylvania District Assemblies of God Youth Convention that drew about 8,000 teenagers to the Farm Show Arena in Harrisburg. At their very best the Farm Show Arena acoustics are atrocious. The name of the venue pretty much gives an accurate idea of the surroundings. The arena seats about 9,000 people and has a dirt floor. The dirt floor adds realism to the annual Farm Show for the cattle and other farm animals that are displayed and judged before a massive audience. But since the arena is enclosed and under roof, there is no rainfall. About the only moisture that falls on the dirt floor is from the . . . ummm, "discard" of the animals. Thus the floor of the arena becomes a potent brew of dirt and processed food and water. And of course the resulting dust circulates throughout the building so you also get to breathe it.

This is the venue where the dreaded shutdown happened. We were standing before all those excited teens and we were singing our most poplar song, "Statue of Liberty." The intro started and at the proper time we began singing, "In New York Harbor . . . stands a lady . . . with a torch raised to the sky . . ." At that precise moment the entire sound system shut down. It didn't just momentarily go off and then on again. It was a complete shutdown.

"Hey! Dave and Duane! See the target on my back?" We had gone into the arena with a fully functioning sound system and it picked this moment to embarrass me. There was just no way to be heard by the large crowd. So as the crowd grew more restless, the target grew larger. Dave and Duane have never really been unkind to me on such rare occasions, but they do want an explanation on the spot. Hey, I didn't KNOW what had happened. Even so, after several minutes spent tracing wires and letting the amplifier cool down, we got up and running again. Thankfully, the crowd cheered when we got the problem worked out.

Dave has often said that when the sound system acts up, he and Duane go for coffee. It's not their problem. Duane is in charge of transportation and product. When the vehicle breaks down Dave and I just relax, knowing it's Duane's burden. Dave does the booking and is in charge of closing the service every night. When Duane and I finish the last song we relax, knowing it's Dave's burden. Strangely though, I've never seen a target on their backs. I must be paranoid, huh?

We've always known that what has made this operation work is the clear demarcation of our jobs within the group. If someone requests information or action in any given area, the only level of expertise necessary for me is to know who handles that area. I'm the go-to guy for the music and the sound. If the people like our songs, I've either selected them or written and arranged them. If they *don't* like our songs, I'm still the one—sometimes good; sometimes not so good. If the vehicle is in good running order, thank Duane. If it breaks down, blame Duane. If the date book is full, thank Dave. If it has gaping holes, blame Dave.

Fortunately, there is an understanding among us that allows a margin of error. We have mutual confidence that each man is doing his best. We can't ask for more than that. There are tasks that we share equally too. We're all drivers and we're all carriers. And we have a rule that no one does any heroics at the wheel. Call the next driver. Our safety is at stake. Likewise, when we arrive at the church or concert hall, everyone is expected to carry the equipment and products both in and out of the building. I often get hassled by the other guys about being unable to talk and wind up wires at the same time. Honestly, I feel like I'm being inattentive to people who are trying to talk to me if I'm all over the place, setting up or tearing down equipment. It takes me a little longer to get the job done when I'm trying to hold a conversation, but I try to be considerate.

PIANO MAN—*Praise him with stringed instruments.* *(Psalm 150:4)*

Especially in the early years we would encounter many relic pianos in critical states of disrepair. Did I say that kindly enough? Truthfully, they had been candidates for the trash heap for many years. They sported beat-up cases, missing ivories, inoperative pedals and keys, cracked soundboards, an overwhelming majority of out-of-tune strings, and a long list of other maladies—too many to mention here. Oh yeah, and non-responsive actions; I literally had to beat the tar out of most of them to get them to make noise. Yes, and noise it was, because I was in no better shape as a pianist than were the many awful pianos I had to play. I was fully aware of that, and the lack of good pianos only deepened my sense of inadequacy.

In most cases the piano was too small for the room. It was never designed to produce enough sound to fill a room that would seat hundreds of people. Often there would be an auditorium that had only a small spinet piano, more appropriate for a home. One thing is certain—if you have to pound a piano with both fists to get it to make more sound you won't be doing any delicate or complicated playing. I had to keep it simple while smiling without ceasing. But I greatly admire those serious artists who have given themselves to the discipline of doing it well and right. The eighty-eight black-and-whites provide an inexhaustible palette for creating truly fine art. Every time I sit on a piano bench I'm reminded of my formidable limitations.

All the above was in addition to my being thrust into the job without warning when our excellent pianist, Eddie Reece, announced his departure. We simply could not afford to hire another member at that point, when we were so close to going under. When the other members knew that I was somewhat of a "hunt and peck" pianist, and given our flatlined finances, they approached me about taking up the slack as both singer and pianist. What a compliment, balanced against the chilling reality that I was just not prepared. But we were desperate. I asked for six months to try to hone my skills before I would consider their generous proposal—generous not in dollars because doing both jobs did not mean an increase in pay, but thoughtful on their part.

Within two weeks after Eddie's departure I was seated at the piano and scared to death, serving as both lead singer and accompanist. I quickly realized that after the piano intro to every song the job of pianist became less complicated. If I could just get past the intro while looking like a legitimate pianist, all I would have to do is play up-and-down inversions of the current musical chord. After that point the singers would start and someone would surely sing the melody. So I didn't have to learn how to play melodies. This has become my albatross as a pianist over the years, because I never really learned how to attach the melody of a song to the chords. That doesn't mean that I don't understand melody, but rather that I don't concentrate on the melody as I play. Fortunately, the singers do that.

One of my inherited traits from both sides of my parentage is the need to tease. It manifests itself many times a day and I just can't help it. Often I would find that a piano would have one note that was particularly sour, so I would dwell on that note throughout the evening. Any time the chord called for that note I would strongly emphasize it to call attention to the bad instrument. Inevitably the pastor or music director would get the hint and call me aside after the service to apologize profusely about the awful condition of their piano.

I would reply, "I would love to have that piano." "You would?" Then came my zinger: "Yes, and an axe, for about twenty minutes!" I've had more fun with that scenario. Both pastors and music directors realize that things are not always optimal when it comes to having church. Often it's a matter of make-do. As of this writing it is possible to pay more than $50,000 for a decent grand piano and most churches can't justify that expenditure.

Nowadays there is also a noticeable shift away from real pianos to electronic keyboards. While they offer such benefits as lower cost, increased portability, more varied sounds, and no need to tune them, there remains the fact that nothing, but nothing, plays like a real piano in good repair. I often say that when you stroke a real piano, it strokes back. But when you stroke an electronic keyboard . . . good luck. Some of the later, more expensive models are much better, but still must bow to the incredible response of a real piano that has been carefully regulated and tuned. Since we haven't yet started to carry our own keyboard, and the many keyboards are so varied in their operation, voices, and lengths, I still strongly prefer a good conventional piano to having to try to adapt to the local electronic keyboard. If I had the time to become familiar with the keyboard in each church, I could get comfortable, but I don't have that luxury.

-12-

When You Least Expect It

How unsearchable are his judgments,
and his ways past finding out!
(Romans 11:33)

In 1978, Duane began to labor to hit the high notes that had come so easily for his entire career. We could always count on Duane to deliver the message with his brilliant tenor voice. But for some reason the high notes weren't what they once were, and the difficulty could be seen on Duane's countenance. He knew something was wrong, and so did Dave and I. The contrast was too pronounced.

A few years before, I too had experienced some issues with my voice, whereupon an able specialist determined that I had a "singer's nodule" on my vocal cord. After having it surgically removed and going through the prescribed month of complete vocal rest, I was again singing normally.

So I encouraged Duane to visit my doctor and get some answers. When he went to his appointment the doctor told him the same story he had told me: "You have a nodule." So Duane set up a time to have it removed as I had done, hoping for the same outcome. But Duane's recovery was not easy, as mine had been. When Duane came back, his voice didn't come with him—it was only a ghost of what it had been in the past.

So we all had a decision to make, knowing that we couldn't continue to brutalize Duane's voice in concert after concert. He could have been ruined permanently, and none of us wanted that to happen. Dave and I talked and concluded that we had two options; replace Duane with another tenor or believe that the Lord was leading us all in another direction. But we *couldn't* replace our beloved Duane. He was our brother.

So after discussing the issue with Duane, we decided that the honorable response was to accept the fact that the Lord was leading us into unknown territory. So we disbanded the Couriers and each went our separate ways, still close friends and having a sense of being partners forever in ministry.

Dave organized his family into a group known as The Dave Kyllonen Family Affair and hit the road running. Duane did concert promotions and our weekly TV program, allowing him to continue his ministry until his singing voice recovered, which it indeed did. At that juncture I went solo—in fear and trembling—knowing that I wouldn't have the instant support of Dave and Duane at my side.

In all three ventures God gave us favor, and we went along for several years in that pattern. No one had any grievances against another. It was the direction in which the Lord seemed to be leading us for the time. We accepted it and kept on doing the things that we had done corporately for so many years, singing and preaching the Gospel.

After a couple of years our longtime friends and promoters began to call, wanting us to bring the Couriers back together to do a concert or church service. Dave was not available, having launched his family ministry, but Duane and I were still in town, albeit working in separate endeavors. As the calls came in we began to explore who was available to sing Dave's part in a reorganized, part-time Couriers. It was not always the same person who substituted. Duane's daughter Meredith sang with us a few times, Ron Hensley did many dates with us, and my son, Tim, sang with us for five years before my brother Phil finally stepped in.

On one occasion, when Ron Hensley was with us, we were singing for about a thousand senior citizens in Florida in a Baptist church where the seniors were having a retreat. Duane had not been back for very long and his voice wasn't responding well, and Ron was still a bit shaky as far as being comfortable with singing his specific part. It was my night to be the emcee and when I saw our singing reaching the critical stage of deterioration I knew something had to give or we would have to call it an evening. So I quietly whispered to Ron and Duane, "Have a seat, I'm going to sing a solo to give you guys a break." So I proceeded to sing a song I had written sometime earlier that was addressed to people going through the break-up of a marriage, or who had already been through it. In an attempt to reach out with hope to hurting people, here's what I sang:

Love Smashed upon the Rocks

Verse 1

The honeymoon is history; the love songs play
no more.

The lover who once held you tight, has walked out
through the door.

The endless days and lonely nights have brought
you to your knees

For broken vows and promises make painful
memories.

The children play reluctantly, they seem to sense
the change;

The happy home that they once knew they've had
to rearrange.

With thoughts of being second-hand, and no one
seems to understand,

You're left with love that's smashed upon the
rocks.

Verse 2

Then comes the voice of Him who bore the shame
of your mistake.

"I'll never leave thee," He has said, "And never will
  forsake."

He feels your hurt and knows your grief; He's been
  forsaken too.

And He can meet the deepest need that aches
  inside of you.

The "happy ever after" that once filled your hopes
  and dreams

Can turn into reality, though all is lost, it seems.

Your love forever He'll restore, no one could ever
  love you more.

He'll never smash your love upon the rocks.

© 1981 by Neil Enloe. All rights reserved.

It might seem inappropriate to sing such a song to a crowd
of seniors, but I just felt like it was the thing to do, given the circumstances of the moment. When the song was over we took a
break while the sponsor received an offering, a few minutes that
rested Ron and Duane even further. Meanwhile, I made my way
toward the lobby of the church to help Duane at the product
table. As I walked I was confronted by a gentleman in his for-
ties, who wasn't of the age group of the rest of the audience. He
asked to speak to me and this is what he said.

"I live in Michigan with my wife and children. Only recently
I learned that my wife has not only been carrying on a long
affair, but she is planning to leave me and get a divorce and
break up our family. My heart is breaking inside my chest. My
parents live here in Florida in retirement and I made my way

down here to see them one last time before returning home to take my life in suicide. I don't even want to live without the love of my wife. But tonight that song reached my heart and I have abandoned my plans for suicide. I've been reminded that Someone still loves me and gave His life so that I don't have to perish. If you never sing that song for anyone else, I just want you to know that you have spared a life with it tonight."

I assured him that there is love and fidelity that far exceeds what he had lost, and it's found in a personal relationship with the greatest lover the heart can know, Jesus Christ. He thanked me and left as abruptly as he had presented himself. I was brought to the strong realization in that moment that we don't always minister by feeling, but by sowing the seed of truth and allowing it to fall wherever the Spirit designates. He often prepares hearts in the midst of what to our rationale might be an inappropriate setting, knowing that someone needs help and hope that He alone can provide. What a loving and caring Lord we serve.

Often we have remembered the wise words of evangelist Paul Olson, who initially urged us toward missionary evangelism and told us privately, "You men will never really minister to the needs of the people until you realize that ninety percent of those who come through the doors are hurting and in crisis in some area of their lives." Those have proved to be true and timely words for sure. We've often wondered why the Lord abruptly rearranges the order of the service that we had planned, only to later discover that it served His higher purpose.

On another occasion I received newspaper clippings from about three different sources from around the country, and from friends who thought I would be interested in the story contained therein. There was a family pictured with mother, father, daughter, and some other fellow travelers. The story pointed out that Hugh and Mary Daley, from Ridgeland, South Carolina, and their ailing daughter, Donna, had been given a trip to New York City. Further down in the copy we learned that Donna was suffering from Retinitis Pigmentosa, a disease that usually causes blindness and finally even death.

Little Donna, at about age five, did not have a promising prognosis. So some friends at their little church in Ridgeland decided to grant her a final wish before she would probably lose her sight. Contacts with influential people at the nearby Gulfstream Aerospace Corporation were made, and a free trip was extended to Mom, Dad, and Donna. Soon they found their way to the Big Apple. One of the things that Donna had wished for was to see the Statue of Liberty, because she had heard her mother sing about it in her church.

Needless to say that got my attention quickly. It never ceases to amaze me that, after having dragged my weary body to all fifty states and eighty foreign countries over the span of fifty years, a song that came from my pen has made its way into a place that my voice has failed to reach. So I read on with keen interest.

Donna got her wish and made it safely home. When I finished the story of the Daley family I wondered how I could ever meet them. I certainly didn't know anyone who had even heard of them. So I read again the story and decided to make an effort to contact the Daleys. My first approach was to drag out my atlas and find Ridgeland, South Carolina. Sure enough, there it was in the southeast corner of the state, just a few miles north of Savannah. On the map Ridgeland didn't seem too imposing, so I called directory assistance and got the phone numbers of all the Daleys in the Ridgeland phone book. There were not that many listings, so I knew I had hope of finding the proper party if only after dialing a couple of wrong numbers. On my second attempt the voice of a very sweet lady came on the phone, and as the conversation progressed I knew I had found the right Daley household.

As we both exchanged points of reference, Mary Daley unfolded the details of Donna's story. I told her that I was a Gospel singer and had been for many years with the Couriers Quartet. She told me that her family attended the Great Swamp Baptist Church in their community and invited me to schedule a service in their church at my convenience when my family could meet theirs. At that time, in the early 1980s, the Couriers had disbanded and I was traveling as a soloist, and my family came along with me on many occasions. In due time we made our way to Ridgeland and met the incredible Daley family. They proved to be people of faith in my Lord too. We really connected to them, and they to us. It was our joy to make annual visits to the warm and wonderful Great Swamp Baptist Church. The Daleys and the other members of the church won our hearts and we cherish their love and friendship to this day.

As Donna's ailment progressed over a few short years, her eyesight did indeed fail and her body became increasingly frail.

During that time she struck up a friendship, even more a crush, on my son, Tim. Tim was not old enough to notice girls yet, but he still considered Donna a dear friend. By the time Donna passed away Tim was in his first year of Bible school. He got a call from Mary Daley asking that he fly from Springfield, Missouri, to Ridgeland, South Carolina, to sing at the dedication of a special memorial at the local hospital where Donna had been treated during her illness. Tim considered it an honor and made his way to South Carolina to celebrate Donna's graduation to Glory.

In the years that followed we have returned to Great Swamp Baptist Church and remembered Donna and the events that brought us all together. Hugh Daley has now joined his beloved daughter Donna in heaven.

The song that started that whole story was one I had composed in 1974, "Statue of Liberty." The occasion for writing the song came when we Couriers were invited to sing for a one-evening boat cruise sponsored by the Assemblies of God youth departments of the New York and New Jersey districts. The cruise was to start at eventide and go south into the harbor, then back along the shore of Manhattan for a spectacular view of the lights of New York City. When we arrived we found that the cruise boat would hold twenty-four hundred people and was filled to capacity. Of the four decks on the boat, the small auditorium was on the third deck and seated about four hundred people. That meant that we would have to sing six mini-concerts throughout the evening to accommodate all the people. So we would sing for about twenty minutes and dismiss the crowd. Over the next ten minutes the previous crowd would leave the auditorium and the next crowd would assemble.

During one of those breaks, Dave and I made our way to the outside part of the deck to catch some fresh air. We were leaning against the retaining rail at the edge of the boat and watching the young people enjoying themselves. By that time night had fallen and the air was refreshing. Then, without warning, there came a unanimous chorus of "Ooohs" and "Aaahs" from the young people on the boat. We knew it wasn't our charm, so we looked around to see what they were reacting to. And there she stood, the glorious green lady that we all call our own, the Statue of Liberty.

Everything patriotic in me rose up at that moment. I turned to Dave and bumped his elbow to get his attention. I said, "Dave, I just got an idea for a song." He looked at me as if to say, "Don't disturb this awesome moment with some lesser notion." He was fully proper to think that. But I had an inspiration. I told him I was going to write a song about that lady. He reminded me that we were Gospel singers, not secular singers. "Where is the Gospel in the Statue of Liberty?" he asked. Good question, Dave. I told him that I needed some time to develop the song, but it would be forthcoming.

And "some time" it took. After three months of intense poring over the lyrics, I had what seemed to be a logical presentation, relating the Statue of Liberty to a Gospel message. As mentioned earlier in the chapter about songwriting, I revised the lyrics many times before the song was presentable. Finally it was done. Somehow the initial inspiration that had come upon me in the boat never lessened, and I knew I had something powerful in this song. Its ongoing popularity, even after thirty-four years, seems to bear out what I believed. I'm told that we all have a defining moment in our lifetime, and this must have been mine.

Here is the song that continues to define me, and one that brought sweet little Donna Daley into my life.

Statue of Liberty

Verse 1

In New York harbor stands a lady

With a torch raised to the sky.

And all who see her know she stands for

Liberty for you and me.

I'm so proud to be called an American;

To be named with the brave and the free.

I will honor our flag and our trust in God,

And the Statue of Liberty.

Verse 2

On lonely Golgotha stood a cross

With my Lord raised to the sky.

And all who kneel there live forever,

As all the saved can testify.

I'm so glad to be called a Christian;

To be named with the ransomed and whole.

As the Statue liberates the citizen
So the Cross liberates the soul.

Coda

O the Cross is my Statue of Liberty;
It was there that my soul was set free.
Unashamed, I'll proclaim that a rugged cross
Is my Statue of Liberty.
My liberty!

- 13 -

But if I Fail

If any man sin, we have an advocate with the Father,
Jesus Christ the righteous.
(I John 2:1)

One of the most difficult things is to admit our failures. Even "I'm sorry" is often excruciatingly painful to say. But forgiveness is always welcome and brings awesome relief.

Far be it from me to ever pretend to be immune to failure. I've had my share of shameful moments that, with all of my heart, I hope are not put on display at the Great Judgment. I almost wrote a song one time entitled "Shame On Jesus," but decided it was a bit too bold and might be misunderstood. But at Calvary He took on *all of my sin* and *all the accompanying shame, guilt, and embarrassment.* And He has promised to not remember my sins anymore.

If I were to bare my motivation for compassion I would have to honestly say it's rooted in my need for understanding and forgiveness for my own failures. If I hope to have my friends and family stand with me in my worst moments of life I must set the example by loving them through their downsides.

Being proactive is not only a good idea, it's also scriptural. There's a wonderful passage that says: "Brethren, if a man be overtaken in a fault, ye which are spiritual, restore such an one in the spirit of meekness; considering thyself, lest thou also be tempted" (Galatians 6:1). This puts the onus of our own forgiveness on ourselves, by making it a prerequisite to forgive the failure of others first. Hmmm . . .

I set the preceding passage to music as follows:

Restore a Fallen Brother

Restore a fallen brother

With spirit meek and true.

Forgive his many failures

And bear his burden too.

Pray for God to keep him

In His loving hand.

Forgive him in his testing;

Compassion touches man.

Though he is wrong, he's family;

He feels the distance too.

Show him you really need him

And pour healing balm on his wounds.

Remember, you may someday stumble

Even though you try.

The Father waits in mercy

To hear His children cry.

Each member of the family

Is precious in His sight.

Restore a fallen brother

And hold his kinship high.

© 1983 by Neil Enloe. All rights reserved.

Another of my songs deals with my lack of inherent goodness:

Filthy Rags

Verse 1

If you could take all the good that I've ever done;

And all the compliments; there've been some
wonderful ones;

And all the kindness I've shown to ev'ryone

Dating back to the date of my birth.

Then you would see that in spite of the way I've tried,

Isaiah 64:6 puts all my rightness aside.

And my good works won't take me to the other side,

So you see what my deeds are worth. They're only

Chorus

Filthy rags, (That's all my righteousness.)

Filthy rags. (That's all they're worth, I guess.)

But I'm gonna trade these filthy rags for a robe of
white someday.

Filthy rags, (I gave to Jesus Christ)

Filthy rags. (He changed my very life.)

I'll wear a garment of His righteousness

Instead of these filthy rags.

Verse 2

When Jesus comes in a cloud with a trumpet sound

To take His bride away, I'll leave these rags on the
ground,

And I'll be dressed in a robe and a righteous crown

As the fashion of Heaven will be.

Then He'll present me before the Father's throne;

Without a blemish or spot. I'll hear Him tell me
"Well done."

And when I look at the garments that I'll have on,

I'll remember what they used to be, when they were

Chorus

Filthy rags, (That's all my righteousness.)

Filthy rags. (That's all they're worth, I guess.)

But I'm gonna trade these filthy rags for a robe of
white someday.

Filthy rags, (I gave to Jesus Christ)
Filthy rags. (He changed my very life.)
I'll wear a garment of His righteousness
Instead of these filthy, filthy rags.

© *1981 by Neil Enloe. All rights reserved.*

- 14 -

A Final Word

Finally, brethren...
(Philippians 4:8)

Webster defines *courier* as "a messenger sent in haste with an important message." Today a government courier is sent on a mission to deliver classified information often vital to national security. He is qualified, trusted, and certified to be dependable.

The name *Couriers* was selected before I ever joined the group, but I have always embraced its meaning. The mission to which we have been assigned and divinely empowered is to proclaim the message of the atoning blood of the crucified Christ. In many cases the vehicle we use to carry that message is music. My personal philosophy, shared by Dave and Duane and all other members of our group, is that the message has absolute priority in our singing. That's why we carefully select our songs on the value of their message first. After that we try to arrange the songs so that the message stays out front. Then we try to interpret that message when we sing, and finally we exaggerate the articulation of each syllable so the message is abundantly clear. We then hope that the final product will drive home that message to the hearts of the hearers.

The real difference in our presentation and that of secular singers is this: Secular singers perceive themselves to be successful if the roar of the crowd indicates a certain level of acceptance. Essentially, the secular singer makes sure that the sound system is cranked up to a brisk or even deafening volume so the audience cannot easily entertain another thought. They stand in the only light in the room, an intense spotlight that keeps the audience from seeing anything else. Then they sing in such a way that they seem to be saying, "Look at me, Me, ME!"

All of the above techniques make sense if the message is not important. But in our Christian music concerts and church services we try to be sensitive to the desires of the people with reference to audio volume. And we much prefer to sing with the house lights fully aglow so we can look into the eyes of the people sitting in the audience. When the song starts we limit our own animation so as not to be a distraction. Then we sing with all our might and say in our hearts, "Look at Him, HIM, HIM!

There is certainly an honorable place for secular singers, many of whose music I greatly appreciate, and I would not for one moment suggest that the above-mentioned tactics are wrong for their application. It's just good business. But we have been given a call to sing eternal truth, and our job is to shout it from the proverbial housetop while positioning ourselves in the shadows, so the full attention and all the glory goes to the One who called us and gave us our song.

Another noticeable difference in our method is that many singers stay hidden away from the audience before going onstage in a practice I call "maintaining the mystique." Again, this is not necessarily wrong but we have always tried to be accessible to and approachable by the people who attend our concerts and services. Long ago we realized that there are some unbelievably fascinating and exciting people who walk into the auditoriums where we sing. We have made a vast number of great friends throughout the years, by endearing ourselves to the wonderful people to whom we sing.

Yet another philosophical perspective we hold is to sing our very best without regard to how many people show up. We have never cut short the number of songs we sing, or slacked off while singing, before only a handful of people. Actually, I have done some of my personal best work before a small crowd. If we make a championship attempt before the small crowd, we are building our vocal conditioning and preparing our hearts for the time when the masses will be in attendance.

Then there is the business side of the ministry. Remember, even Jesus had a treasurer whose name was Judas. Regardless of how Judas turned out, he was deemed trustworthy by Jesus, who put him in charge of the money. The business side of the Couriers has never been my responsibility. Thank goodness, because if I had been running the business we would have bankrupted early on. But I've never been one to worry about money. I've seldom had more than a few dollars in excess, but I've never had sustained want either. God owes me nothing.

He has been abundantly generous as a Provider and has proved himself faithful to supply my daily bread. He never promised to make me rich and famous . . . and sure enough, it never happened!

During my growing-up years at home my parents always reinforced the principle that when we give to God out of our want, he gives to us out of His abundance. In those times when we seem to be running low on funds, Ruth and I always examine our giving records. When we know we have remembered God with the firstfruits of our income, we can be sure that He will come through for us in our time of need. I've learned a truth that, if I were writing scripture, I would put in these terms: "You scratch God's back and He'll scratch yours." That portion of "scripture" would appear in Enloe's Epistle.

Upon the basis of my knowing the nature of God's generosity, I penned these words:

It Keeps on Coming Back

Verse 1

Bless the Lord, O my soul forgetting not all His
   benefits free.

It's His special way of taking care of me.

When I learned to give, I began to live in His luxury.

Though I don't understand, I've placed it in His
   hands.

Chorus

And it keeps on coming back, keeps on coming back.

Ev'rything I give to Him, or give in His name

Just keeps coming back.

And when I hand it out the front door,

Don't you know He hauls it in the back door.

And I can't get ahead of Him; it keeps on coming
   back.

Verse 2

Are there special needs, even special deeds

You're desiring of Him?

Have you waited long? Are your chances slim?

Give and it shall be given unto you in a greater way.

And you'll see just what I mean; it works like a
   beautiful dream.

Chorus

And it keeps on coming back, keeps on coming back.

Ev'rything I give to Him, or give in His name

Just keeps coming back.

And when I hand it out the front door,

Don't you know He hauls it in the back door.

And I can't get ahead of Him; it keeps on coming
   back.

LIFE PERSPECTIVE — *The Lord is the strength of my life. (Psalms 27:1)*

I've lived long enough now to have observed some principles in this earthly walk. I've come to believe that the stages of life can be portrayed by rocks. Four rocks.

Rock 'n Chair

Rock 'n Roll

Rock 'n Remember

Rock 'n Can't Remember

In 1980, when the Couriers temporarily disbanded, I was thrust into the frightening world of solo singing. While it was a time of uncertainty it proved also to be a wonderful time of personal growth. I couldn't paint myself into a corner, so to speak, in my services and then, out of frustration, turn it back to Dave or Duane. No, it was my problem and I had to work my way out of it. I had never represented myself as an emcee. What a jolting reality that was. But with the loving understanding and merciful help of my wonderful Lord I was able to stay afloat. The Lord knew I was really trying to relate to the audiences and share His love with the people.

When I launched my solo ministry, the first thing I did was make a recording. The natural inclination was to do an album of all my original compositions. This would not only set me apart from all others in my choice of songs, but it would challenge me to write substantive songs. So I set out to do the recording project, and entitled it, *Neil Enloe . . . Personal.* I even wrote my own album backliner notes. Here's what I said:

I'm thankful that God has given me a ministry of songwriting. As honorable and God-ordained as the preaching ministry is, great sermons are too often and too soon forgotten. Songs, however, have a way of recurring in our memory. A melody with lyrics can restate precisely on command a verse of scripture, a message, or an inspirational thought. What a marvelous tool a song is to bring eternal truth to our awareness.

While songwriting is a beautiful open door of opportunity it is also an awesome responsibility. And I pray that God will help me move people toward Him with the songs He has given to me.

Some of my innermost feelings and convictions have been set to music in the songs on this album. Quite often songs become a window on the heart of the composer so the whole world can parade past and see what's inside.

That's personal!

As you take your moment to gaze into my window, I hope you'll see, among other things, an abiding love for my loving Savior.

My personal Savior.

P. S. - Besides, there will be no preaching in heaven . . . only singing!

Among the collection of songs on that album is one that expresses my life perspective:

I Will Live for Jesus

Though the world may turn aside

I will live for Jesus.

Even when my faith is tried

I will live for Jesus

He is living in my heart;

From His love I'll ne'er depart.

Naught of this world can take the place

Of my Lord's redeeming grace.

He is ev'rything to me;

I will live for Jesus.

© 1970 by Neil Enloe. All rights reserved.

- 15 -

I'm Outa' Here!

Let us go into the next towns, that I may preach there also.
(Mark 1:38)

Now you know my story. It's one that illustrates the leading of my wonderful Lord throughout my life. He's always been the designer of the master plan, yet He's been quietly present in the details. He determined my family culture before I was born. He has led me in a path of continuous fellowship with Him.

If I could go back and make changes, the only ones I would make are of those times when I've failed Him. Otherwise, I'd do it all over again. I bear no regrets of the times I've followed His gentle, profound leading. To think that a shy kid from Wood River, Illinois, could be privileged to minister through music to all fifty United States and eighty nations of the world, in missionary evangelism, just boggles the mind. In that regard, special recognition and gratitude must go to the dear

Canadian people who have embraced our group beyond meas-
ure. We love you, Canada!

Most of the kids who have come out of our youth camps
have gone on to follow the Lord, and many of them are in the
ministry today. We always prayed to that end. The souls who
have come to Christ in our meetings are the true reward of our
labor. All the glory and honor goes to Him.

To start naming our dearest friends would not only result in
a voluminous book, but given our waning memories we would
unknowingly leave someone out. But you know who you are
and you have our deepest gratitude for all you mean to us.

I certainly would be a Courier again if I had another lifetime
to live. When I finally lay the microphone down for the last
time, I will be grateful for the life that my precious Lord has
given to me through the years of shared ministry with Dave and
Duane, and all the other beloved members of our group.

To my dear wife and soul mate, Ruth: I'm deeply indebted
to you for your unwavering support of the ministry to which
God called me even before I met you. I know it hasn't been
easy. You've had to be both Mom and Dad while I was away at
some far-off place. The burden of the household has rested
largely on you. I don't know how you did it. You have been loving and faithful through it all. You have been my very heart,
and I'll love you forever.

My spiritual journey began with the still, small voice of the
Holy Spirit of God, that brought to my heart this message:
"God wants to communicate and fellowship with you."
I responded by inviting Jesus Christ to sit upon the throne of
my life. I further gave him my future, my dreams, and my

ambitions. When I took Him at his word, He took me at my word. That still, small voice continues to speak to the private, inner reaches of my heart. He sustains me, gives me hope, and even His very presence. How can I be so blessed?